The Dynamics of University
PROTEST

The Dynamics of University

PROTEST

Donald Light, Jr.
and John Spiegel

with C. J. Lammers,
R. S. Laufer, M. Levin,
and J. L. Norr

𝑛𝒽

Nelson-Hall Publishers
Chicago

LA
229
D9

Library of Congress Cataloging in Publication Data

Main entry under title:

The Dynamics of university protest.

    Bibliography: p.
    Includes index.
    1. Student movements—United States. 2. Student
movements—Europe. I. Light, Donald, 1942–
II. Spiegel, John Paul, 1911–
LA229.D9   378.1'98'10973   77-2364
ISBN 0-88229-164-5

Contents

Preface

The era of student protest is dead in the minds of most people, but the social and cultural forces underlying it are not. To some, this will be considered the last book of that era, but it may be the first book of the next. The pinch of economic conditions today makes students look like those of the fifties, but close observers of campus life note the qualities of the sixties bottled up. A minority of students are still concerned about local issues, such as student power in selecting college deans or faculty and in shaping the curriculum. Another minority are concerned about various abuses of power in the nation and abroad. A much larger group carry on much of the life-style that developed in the counterculture, all the while worrying about recommendations for a professional school.

The first chapter attempts to answer the large questions: Why did protests arise in the sixties? Why did they end? What will happen from here on? It draws upon cultural history, the institutional development of universities, the history of American radicalism, and changes in the family to make its argument. In concluding that basic strains remain between these structural and cultural institutions, it argues that Erik Erikson's theory of the identity crisis needs significant revision.

This book was undertaken for a second reason: the structural dynamics of university protest went largely unexamined in the spate of publications about the protest era. The second chapter reviews this literature and finds that research on campus protest went through three phases. This chapter not only provides a useful summary but indicates the need for more understanding of how protests as evolving social events work. This is the subject of the next five essays, beginning in the third chapter with a discussion of the organizational context of protest.

Chapter four is an analysis of "directed resistance," which characterizes relatively nonviolent protests. Gandhi's distinction between *satyagraha* and *duragraha* becomes the starting point for an analysis of protest strategies and their interrelations. The chapter discusses several possible outcomes and gives particular attention to the "stand-off" and to the "law of passive advantage" that makes it effective. A detailed case study of what was probably the first stand-off illustrates a number of the analytic points made in the essay.

The fifth chapter considers how faculty responded to protests on American campuses by examining many of the studies made of faculty during that time. It is one of the few critical reviews of this research. While most of this work is descriptive, this chapter goes beyond description to integrate most of the findings in the literature in a model which identifies the proximal and distal forces that influence faculty response. Its application, then, extends beyond the response of faculty to just protest.

Chapter six offers a subtle and complex analysis of how the different parties in a protest respond to each other and how these responses in turn alter the behavior of the groups involved. It thus brings order to the extraordinarily elusive core of protests, which appear to most as impulse mixed with chaos.

The last chapter, written by a distinguished sociologist, is on the tactics used by administrators in protests. Ironically, the tactics of administrators have not been the subject of much serious investigation, though their role is far from minor. This rigorous essay, which uses comparative materials from Europe and America, compensates for this vacuum.

1 / The origins and future of university protest

Robert S. Laufer and
Donald Light, Jr.

To consider the nature of protests at American universities when the campuses are now so quiet may at first seem odd. The stillness, of course, allows time to examine student protest as a social phenomenon in itself, and this volume is devoted to that task. But more important is the continuing existence—even broadening—of the social and historical trends which generated the protest of the 1960s. These trends suggest that the larger conflicts behind protest have not passed. Bound together in the present is the past and the future.

In order to understand the student protests of the sixties, one must begin with the generation of parents in the fifties, themselves children of the Depression, and describe the new world of affluence and permissive values they crafted for their children. Some of these children, particularly those with more radical parents, felt an acute discrepancy between their clean, humane values and the dirty stains of Birmingham and Saigon.[1] They came to judge their parents' values as false and to see their parents as hollow.[2]

The strains the young experienced when they came of age and confronted the world which their parents had crafted, strongly suggest that the two age groups had rather different experiences. These experiences can be fruitfully explained through what has come to be known as the psychohistorical approach.

Psychohistory has been largely utilized to explore the relationship between the personal and the social history of great men: Leonardo da Vinci, Woodrow Wilson, Luther, Gandhi, and Hitler, to name a few. There is room, however, for treating psychological and historical forces in a more general fashion to analyze the world view of a generation. There are events and experiences relevant to specific social groups, strata, or classes which make certain images salient and certain needs dominant. Without discussing the specific psychological experiences of any given person, one can identify psychological and historical experiences with which each generation must cope. In this sense we can talk of the psychosocial experience of a generation and the consequences of this experience as a generation travels from birth to death.

This psychosocial history, with its cultural and political consequences, parallels another history, the rise of the research university as a central institution of innovation for the economy and for social engineering. Ironically, these same institutions (America's major universities) and their stepchildren (good colleges and lesser universities) were also havens for the youth who were fashioning a "new culture." They served both as base camps for protest against injustices in the larger society and as objects of protest. Students first decried *in loco parentis* rules. Later they protested against the university's complicity with the evils of the military-industrial complex. Recently they have protested much less. Yet the waning of overt, mass protest does not signal a return to the society we knew two decades ago. Rather, the cultural and institutional changes of the sixties have developed still further.

We would err to assume that the confrontation on the campus was coincidental irony. The advanced industrial university and the students were polar expressions of the central goals which the parental generation pursued after the Depression and World War II. The challenge to these goals developed out of a set of questions which evoked critical images of apparently settled issues. Do we live to work or is work an expression of ourselves? Do we live to make money? Do we live to enjoy good food, or do we eat to live? Behind these questions is a basic issue: Is there ever enough? Is it un-American to stop getting bigger, stronger, wealthier, to have larger cars, houses, missiles, guns, or body counts? How shall we as a society and as individuals find peace, security, love, and a place for ourselves and our children in this complex world? The answers for the parental and protest generations were based on rather different personal experiences which sensitized each to aspects of their environment not readily perceivable to the other.

Those who would understand protest and reaction to protest must remember that the parental generation thought it had arrived at a point in history where pragmatism could replace ideology because of the unlimited capacity of technology. In the wake of protest this utopian vision was destroyed. The events of the sixties critically undermined the moral authority of established institutions and the men at the top. Small wonder that they so intensely resented the brazen attacks on their use of power.

THE PSYCHOHISTORY OF
PROTEST LEADERS AND FOLLOWERS

Scholars of the New Left generally agree that many young radicals of the sixties were raised by the more radical parents of their generation.[3] This is particular true of early protest leaders. They tended to share with their parents not only a distinct political outlook but a set of nonpolitical values which made them doers. By contrast, alienated students from conservative backgrounds often became apolitical hippies.

In trying to explain why so many activities should burst forth in the sixties, Richard Flacks has emphasized a second element, the new affluence following World War II. The economic boom allowed formerly radical parents to finally earn a good living. As an unusually educated and talented group, they fully participated in the materialism of the fifties. But this experience cut two ways. On one hand, it created a base of security and comfort which the children could take for granted. On the other hand, it undermined the parents' radicalism so that their children accused them of selling out their espoused values to a corrupt society.[4]

The generation of protest leaders did not experience the identity crisis as Erikson so delicately labeled it a decade earlier,[5] and as time passed an increasing proportion of adolescents participated in a new kind of identity crisis. In *Childhood and Society*, Erikson wrote that the task of this fifth stage of psychosocial development is a reintegration of past gains and losses into a productive, strong adult. To assist the individual, Erikson argued that society provides models of identity. These and psychosocial strengths, such as trust, autonomy, initiative, and industry, became reflected in social institutions and customs. However, for many adolescents of the sixties the mistrust of national leaders, who were continually found lying, the suppression of black autonomy, the murder of great initiative embodied in John Kennedy, Martin Luther King, and Robert Kennedy, and the false sense of industry reflected in the "organization man," undermined the promise of psychosocial integration.

At home, many of these children's parents had given loving trust, promoted autonomy, encouraged initiative, and helped the children work industriously at school. But as the children entered a society which seemed to mock these virtues which figure so prominently in Erikson's scheme, they almost felt they had grown up in a private world of false security and goodness. Working through *this* identity crisis often led to radical measures.

Protest leaders cannot exist without protesters to follow them, and their psychohistory is more elusive. First, the great body of protesters of the sixties came from that sector called the middle class, which had expanded after World War II. Second, although these young people did not have radical parents, they otherwise shared with protest leaders the discrepancies between personal values and social ills in a decade that opened with the civil rights movement and closed with American pilots dropping an average of 1,215 pounds of bombs for every individual in South Vietnam, creating 21 million craters which displaced 1,000 cubic yards of soil per minute every minute for seven years.[6] (Ninety-two percent of these bombs were not directed at military targets.) Finally, their parents had raised them according to new, middle-class ideas about childrearing that seem closely related to the culture of the sixties—a new openness of personal expression in music, clothes, dance, and politics. This history deserves a closer look.

In the hard times of the thirties, the American promise that hard work would reap rewards was not realized.

> During the Depression, my father took a great deal of psychological abuse, Oh, tremendous . . . I wonder what he had the potential to become. . . .
>
> He's like something out of Dostoevsky. My father was, I think, terribly intelligent. He learned to speak English, a couple of languages, and prided himself on not being like the rest in our neighborhood. . . . He could look at himself a little bit, and then just run like hell. Because what he saw was painful. . . .
>
> I can think of the WPA . . . my father immediately got employed in this WPA. This was a godsend. This was the greatest thing. It meant food, you know. Survival, just survival.[7]

Close to a third of the labor force remained unemployed, and idleness or irrelevant jobs injured the dignity of many workers.[8]

> Remember, too, the shock, the confusion, the hurt that many kids felt about their fathers not being able to provide for them. This reflected itself very often in bitter quarrels between father and son. I recall I had one. I was the oldest of six children. I think there was a special feeling between the father and the oldest son.[9]
>
> I remember men congregating in the store. One man bragged how he had never been on welfare and wasn't going to be on welfare. Quite a few people there resented it, because most people in Westfield were on welfare.
>
> This short temper was a characteristic of the time. Men who were willing to work couldn't find work. My father was the kind of man who had to be active. He'd invent work for himself. A child who was playing irritated him. It wasn't just my own father. They all got shook up.[10]

The advent of World War II provided escape from this misery, and it gave many their first real work in a long time. Yet World War II brought new insecurities to replace economic ones—separation and death. Small wonder, then, that after the war, people wanted financial security and a good, peaceful life.

> I remember coming back home, many years afterwards. Things were better. It was after the Depression, after the war. To me, it was hardly the same house. My father turned into an angel. They weren't wealthy, but they were making it. They didn't have the acid and the recriminations and the bitterness that I had felt as a child.
>
> I remember coming back that day. My mother had roast beef. It was very good, and there was plenty of it. There was meat left over on the table when we finished. During the Depression, one day a week, if we were lucky enough, we got round steak.[11]

No one, not even a Communist in the state department or a supposedly subversive schoolteacher, was going to disrupt this dream. From these desires, therefore, emerged both economic success and a loss of moral vision. But the latter was not generally seen until a new generation looked upon the fifties with fresh eyes. They saw a deep-seated respect for authority and social institutions in place of larger moral precepts. This reflected a great concern of 1900–1940, to make 10 million immigrants and rural migrants into loyal, productive, respecting citizens. But this uncritical respect had become a civil religion without a core.

The economy responded well. Advanced industrial capitalism emerged out of World War II and has since developed

> a whole range of new technologies and capital . . . supported by government expenditures, particularly in military investments and technological innovations. The billions of dollars of support of research and development by government and "private" industry has not only provided a new motive for innovation, but has rationalized it and made it a stable industrial institution. At the level of private business, research and development [have become] a form of capital accumulation subsidized by taxes. Thus, the economy has continued to expand at levels which would have been unimaginable.[12]

The Cold War and the devastation of the other industrial economies of Europe were essential ingredients for the continuing growth of the American economy. The rebuilding of Europe provided an outlet for heavy industry and finished products, while the Cold War provided an economic source of domestic expenditures. The important outcome of these developments for American life was the creation of new bureaucracies which necessitated trained personnel. Thus economic growth through technology produced a new, enlarged middle class.[13]

Concomitant with economic recovery, the emergence of the Cold War made the Soviet Union and Communism the national enemy.[14] This necessitated a mobilization of values, lifestyles, and thought of the American Way. The desire for stability and the growth of national bureaucracies made the task of mobility comparatively easy. In the context of affluence, the economic radicalism of the Depression became superfluous.[15] Those who were its proponents were identified as subversives and were effectively destroyed.[16] The desire to participate in the new affluence by many of the radicals or activists of the 1930s made them especially vulnerable to attack, while the general population was eager for stability.

The political inquisition mounted by conservatives also succeeded because the vast majority of former radicals essentially agreed with their accusers that liberal advanced industrial capitalism was the best of the imperfect worlds available. The accused stood morally speechless even when they attacked the constitutionality of the un-American hearings. The witnesses before HUAC seemed motivated by their desire to emphasize their Americanism and to continue to benefit from their careers within the occupational system. Some radicals repudiated their past before HUAC, while others became central figures and spokesmen in the anti-Communist drive. It was, as I. F. Stone put it, The Haunted Fifties.

The new middle class was a new *bureaucratic* middle class—neat, well-pressed gray, with careers controlled by large organizations. The institutions created a set of controls over their white-collar workers which encouraged their political passivity in return for economic security. One's career became the focal point of identity. The career supported the assertion of being Americanized and middle class. The threat of economic failure simultaneously played on the fears of incomplete Americanization and on memories of poverty, i.e., the Depression.

The organization man also expanded suburbia, a relatively new ecological form of the city that quickly covered the landscape. New small houses made of green timber enabled millions of families to avoid urban blight and crime while acquiring a thin-walled but peaceful environment for raising their children. Leisure became a problem that commissions of academics thought about.[17] In keeping with the times, leisure was largely filled by work! Some people took second jobs, but more important was the boom of the do-it-yourself industry. In the suburbs everywhere, men (both the problem and this solution pertained mostly to men) could be seen building boats, making cabinets or furniture, doing their own plumbing, or repairing the roof.

In retrospect, work–leisure was the beginning of a larger transformation. For what the generation of the fifties saw as leisure *in* work, the generation of the sixties saw as liberation *from* work. Today this is not merely an idea among radicals. Rather, the evidence from the 1972 government study showing national discontent and alienation among the new middle-class workers suggests that radicals are expressing a widespread but muted malaise.[18]

GROWING UP PLEASURABLY

According to Philip Slater and many other observers, the new suburban life isolated the wife and directed her energies toward raising her children. The breakdown of community,[19] the artificial character of suburbs, the new belief in Horatio Alger myths of success all contributed to her focusing on the children. Moreover, Dr. Spock and others presented a new idea of childhood compatible with surburban lifestyle, one which emphasized the child's own feelings, interests, and ideas.

Rigid conformity and strict scheduling were replaced by a sensitivity to each child's potential and a fear of damaging him psychologically. As grandparents today enjoy pointing out, this kind of childrearing lets the child dominate the household. Precisely. In their day, no one had time for such indulgences, but the culture of the suburban fifties almost demanded that the household center on the children. A Ford stationwagon and three children became *de rigueur*.[20] Slater describes well the neurotic consequences of this pattern for the woman, and, by demotion, for the man.[21] The children, too, of course, came to take themselves and their inner lives seriously. Moreover, while neither Dr. Spock nor his colleagues promoted new norms or social values, this new socialization process opened up current norms and values for critical evaluation.

An important change in the process of aging accompanied this new socialization. Adolescence, the creation of industrial society, was followed by youth in advanced industrial society, further extending dependence and social immaturity. Yet these overaged children grew up more independent and sensitive, more fully educated than youth in times past. This sustained limbo seemed essential for creating highly educated personnel, but inadvertently it produced a large, new age group, trained for autonomy and critical thought, yet dependent. In the affluence of the fifties, that dependence weighed easy on their shoulders.

The postwar families experienced affluence as liberating. With it they liberated their children both materially and psychologically at the same time that they supported political repression and ignored the cultural diseases of racism and imperialism. Their children, raised to be sensitive to their emotions and forced by protest leaders to confront these brutal contradictions, made good followers.

PROTEST AND THE NEW CULTURE

Out of the fifties arose both a new culture and a New Left which in ten short years proved to be a prophetic minority.[22] The Old Left died not only from material abundance but also from the tragic reign of Joseph

Stalin. To many it seemed as though political beliefs on the left and right could only lead to atrocities in the hands of powerful men.[23] The new generation of radicals agreed; their problem was to fashion their deep criticisms of society into a movement without ideology. Even more difficult, they wanted an effective movement without permanent organization. They knew too well the Iron Law of Oligarchy which Robert Michels had derived from watching socialist workers' parties become conservative and insensitive to workers' needs as the party leaders pursued their organizational goals. What emerged was *The Port Huron Statement*, a thoughtful treatise on what should be done to make American society more humane, and a New Left centering around the Students for a Democratic Society.

The New Left struck responsive chords in thousands of college students because its values seemed venerable and its style attractively unpretentious. While rejecting ideological treatises, the New Left had a loose core of values close to Judeo-Christian beliefs and the culture of American democracy—values which despised earthly oppressors and which celebrated individual autonomy and equality. Needless to say, this tone fit in with the new culture of the sixties as did the antiorganizational style of participatory democracy. From its national headquarters down to the local chapters, SDS emphasized local autonomy, full participation of members in decisions, equality, and transient organization responsive to the needs of time and place.

S. N. Eisenstadt has emphasized that protest in advanced industrial societies creates peripheral centers of power which oppose centralization in all spheres of life.[24] This characteristic at once challenges the very nature of such societies and seriously weakens the protest movement in the face of organized opposition prepared to handle dissent. The persistence of numerous, small groups trying to transform society is evidence that the radical consciousness survives. In fact, the idea of liberation has been continually refined and taken up by more and more groups. The ground which early activists broke in resisting established culture and politics has run cracks in all directions through the foundation of society.

Yet because of its intentional decentralization, the protest movement appears ineffective, though some believe the protests of the sixties moved mountains for their modest size. Organized groups such as university administrations, local police, the Department of Justice, and the National Guard—different though they may be—had the advantage of centralized power against the sporadic brushfires of protest. Yet student protests did succeed in bringing about many changes, from the end of parietals and the beginning of student-initiated courses to withdrawal from Vietnam.[25] At the same time, the protests made clear the inherent contradiction between organizing long-range opposition and opposing organizations which press down on daily life. This has been one factor leading to the demise of large demonstrations. Another has been a sense of futility; for although an historian would find that the protests had changed many patterns of life, protest leaders aimed for new institutional arrangements, and this did not happen.

It is perhaps most accurate to regard the New Left of the sixties as the first burst of a long-trend movement, a movement rooted in a cultural response against technology's imposition on personal life and against the organizational values of both government and business.[26] This means a strong belief in equality and justice which organizational values usually weaken. Being individualistic and opposing close organization or tight ideology,[27] this movement is necessarily diverse and in time has generated women's lib, gay lib, the revolt of prisoners, and a liberation movement in almost every profession. Even large parts of the black liberation movement emphasize a new black consciousness, a pride in being oneself and not what someone else wants one to be. Aside from the paramilitary minority, black groups have emphasized participatory democracy and personal expression. This spirit and action are enduring contributions of the protest movements.

THE FULFILLMENT ETHIC

The "new culture" in which this protest movement is rooted surrounds us today, but perhaps it needs brief description. It believes above all in fulfilling personal states of consciousness—feelings, beliefs, interests, talents—whatever is most meaningful for the individual.[28] Its grotesque manifestations in hard drugs and the murders by Charles Manson's commune reflect this belief as well. Whereas before, the inner self was subordinated to the demands of the group or organization, now it is celebrated. In order to let one's self bloom, a person must come to terms with external pressures and liberate himself from them—the new identity crisis. This has naturally led to greater sociological and political awareness.

If the fifties was the decade of psychology, the sixties was the decade of the sociological imagination.[29] Radicals, protesting students, newspaper and television reporters, even governmental commissions analyzed how personal problems or potentialities were affected by the organizations around them. Intellectually, none of the new culture was new, but its ideas about the good life spread more widely than they had before. The reasons for its proliferation may be found in the earlier discussion of changes in the fifties.

When self-actualization and liberation are personal goals, the question of defining the meaning of one's life becomes more difficult.[30] Consider, for example, attitudes toward work today which reflect the new culture. Some—a few—find liberation *in* work. They express themselves in their work and find it gratifying. Such people have always existed, and the new culture admires them. The change has been to make this a goal for *everyone* and therefore a new priority for managers of large organizations. This change also manifests itself in that growing minority of educated people who eschew the obvious roads to success and find work that they enjoy. The break from seeing success as continued acquisition has been an important one for the new culture. Economic hardship may crush it, though it fits restricted growth well.

Some youths—fewer than suspected—seek liberation *from* work. This group not only includes hippies, ex-students on welfare, and dealers in drugs but also union members who fight for the three-day weekend without taking a second job. Here "work" means something different than it does for the first group; it means having to do what you don't want to do in order to get by. Defined this way, Americans were liberating themselves from work in the fifties, but the new culture gives the idea much more emphasis. It is not, as conservatives fear, that the welfare ethic has replaced the work ethic; surveys continually show how much Americans—even Americans on welfare—value meaningful work.[31] Rather, the fulfillment ethic is replacing the Puritan work ethic, which makes a virtue out of any kind of work.

Since the fulfillment ethic highlights an individual's personality and since personalities have many facets, a number of college graduates have purposely moved from job to job because no one job fulfills or expresses them fully. Work for some has become an exploration of the self. In a similar fashion, the new culture has created alternative lifestyles that lend support to those who do not wish to work at a desk, get married, buy a house in a community mostly of strangers, and settle down.[32] Thus "career" means moral career as the dominant force guiding behavior.

The values of the new culture clearly reflect the values of middle-class childrearing which have spread since the fifties. Just as clearly they do not reflect the inherent demands of technology or of organizational charts. Therefore, as increasing portions of the expanded middle group in American society work in organizational settings, alienation should be growing despite affluence. Without linking the new culture to this condition, Marxist thinkers have written about alienation in the "new working class" for some time.[33] They emphasize the loss of autonomy and influence that well-paid, white-collar employees have increasingly experienced since World War II. They believe this group forms a new revolutionary force in corporate capitalism, one which is much better educated and more articulate than the illiterate workers that manned the factories of capitalism in Marx's times.

All of these thoughts about work in the new culture received empirical verification in a recent, comprehensive study of job discontent conducted by the U.S. Department of Health, Education, and Welfare.[34] Although not radical or Marxist in approach, it uncovered in detail what such writers have been saying for the past decade. People value meaningful work; they deeply resent meaningless work. Those who cannot find personal fulfillment in work seek liberation from it. High proportions of white-collar workers express discontent; middle managers feel powerless and find their jobs impersonal. The main finding which is not part of the new culture or the New Left shows that much of the discontent among blue-collar workers comes from unfulfulled expectations for upward mobility. They get more educated but their jobs stay the same. They are victims of educational inflation and in addition live by false beliefs about how to succeed in the American economy. Because of this they too remain alienated.

THE WEIGHT OF TECHNOLOGICAL SOCIETY

If this history of psychosocial forces underlying the protest movement is approximately correct, then cultural conflict will continue in the years to come. For the number of radical or liberal-radical parents has not decreased but probably increased. The economic and organizational forces creating the new middle class move apace, leaving alienated workers in their wake. Raising children for personal fulfillment has certainly not diminished, even though many parents try to couple it with being a success in society. Finally, the new culture, though quieter, seems more firmly established than ever before. Encounter groups, women's liberation, the new religious movements, clinics to teach sexual fulfillment, amateur hobby groups of all kinds, and open marriage are all doing well.[35] On the political side, the rise of George McGovern exhibited the political skills and national size of dissenters only twelve years after radical protest began. Yet presidential candidates are unlikely to reflect them again, because successful candidates lean toward the middle.

Ultimately this new culture of personal fulfillment meets its greatest challenge not in the culture of scarcity or in the older generation but in the social impact of technology. Joseph Brodsky has argued that the distinction between good and evil, between God and the Devil, has been replaced by *matter*, which has no moral categories.[36] Thus both good and evil "are in the same state as a stone." One loses even the language by which to speak morally. Absolute concepts come to seem like arbitrary categories so that finally existence itself seems arbitrary. This idea "excuses everyone and everything from any responsibility whatsoever," and it implies that the moral double talk so widely publicized during America's involvement in Vietnam ("We destroyed the city to save it.") consists of trying to cast material concerns into moral concepts when the latter no longer exist with any clarity. Utilitarianism as a basis for a modern, calculating morality is no morality at all.[37]

Brodsky, who puts this argument so beautifully, believes that material nonmorality came of age in Stalin's reign. "For precisely these two spawn of hell [Hitler and Stalin] took the first steps toward the embodiment of the new goal; moral nonexistence. It was not they, of course, who began murdering in order to build and building in order to murder; but precisely they ran this business on such a gigantic scale that they completely overshadowed their predecessors and cut off their followers' and humanity's in general paths of retreat. In a sense they burned all moral bridges."

As a response to this moral wasteland, personal fulfilment is a feeble effort. Its morality is relative, *ad hoc,* and generally irrelevant to the actions of organizations because organizational life is not relevant to it. Brodsky ends by noting that what Stalin and Hitler started by force is now continued voluntarily! Why is unclear, unless we consider the amoral force of technology. Jacques Ellul and Roderick Seidenberg convincingly argue that the very structure of technology is inherently amoral and incompatible with the values of personal fulfillment.[38] As it has expanded, it has invaded more and more of personal life and made old moral concepts irrelevant. Hitler and Stalin were only ahead of their time in their rational use of mechanical and human organization and their treatment of persons as objects to be used or eliminated. Student protest and what is called here the new culture responded directly to these consequences of technology. The rights of each individual took precedence over utilitarian goals and technological efficiency. Participatory democracy replaced administrative hierarchy. And out of the new, organizational middle class emerged permissiveness and personal fulfillment first as part of new affluence but later as a response to the dehumanizing qualities of technological organizations.

But if Ellul and Seidenberg are right, the new culture—aside from the emphasis on pleasure—is an illusion. Protests against "war machines" and "impersonal" organizations are futile and will be absorbed by technology as it follows its own laws of expansion. After all, surveillance expanded much more in the sixties than did protest. The "betrayal" of democratic ideas and individualism by large organizations and rational policy is a perspective that will pass. The new patterns of childrearing will produce people more personally flexible and adaptable to the flexible rationality of electronic technology. In light of this prophecy, one almost wishes for more protests.

THE ASCENDANT UNIVERSITY

Perhaps no other sector of American society expanded so rapidly after World War II as did higher education. While technical and professional personnel grew from 3.9 million in 1940 to 8.6 million in 1964, and while the newly expanded white-collar sector finally surpassed the number of blue-collar workers in 1956, the number of full time faculty in higher education increased from 147,000 in 1940 to 294,000 in 1960. It then increased again by over 200,000 to an estimated 509,000 in 1970.[39] The number of new positions in the sixties exceeded the total number of faculty in 1950!

In structural terms, these numbers represent the development of immense state systems of higher education. Hundreds of campuses sprang up where none had existed before, giving millions of young people the college experience for the first time in their family history. The expansion went up as well as out; every state wanted its star university to attract national attention for its research.[40] Both the expansion and the ascendency of research universities reflected a fundamental change in society itself. Daniel Bell calls it the postindustrial society, a society organized around knowledge where innovation is institutionalized.[41] At the center of this new order stands the university—the institution most completely devoted to innovation. In the eyes of critics like Ellul, this makes the modern university the most advanced agent of technological determinism. Ironically, the modern university at the same time harbors radicals and is a center of protest.

Given the families from which young radicals came, a large proportion of them attended the best colleges and universities. On these campuses, most of their classmates came from permissive, middle-class homes and were going through the extended identity crisis described before. With the civil rights movement fully matured and the war in Vietnam rapidly expanding, these young radicals found their troubled classmates eager to listen. More broadly, college provided a half-way house between high school fads and the complex business of living one's own life. In the context of the sixties, the undergraduate years on the best campuses became a time to confront the contradictions and hypocrisies in the larger society and to create new, more genuine lifestyles.[42]

Thus, the protests of the sixties crosscut a myriad of cultural experiments on American campuses. In any single protest one would find tough, aspiring lawyers who wanted to reform society, apolitical hippies who opposed the object of protest and came for the fun, experimenters in mind expansion, active radicals, and nice students from middle America who thought the university or the government had been unreasonable. Each new protest radicalized more of these marginal people because the experience itself induced commitment and because strict measures by administrators transformed participants into victims of oppression.[43] Studies indicate that radicalizing experiences do not wear off but continue to shape a person's life.[44]

Although the protest movement itself constantly shifted, the basic themes remained constant. Protest first began with the civil rights movement. Thousands of white undergraduates joined Martin Luther King and other Negro leaders in the South. John Kennedy caught the spirit of the early protest movement when he said that "the torch has been passed to a new generation of Americans . . . unwilling to witness or permit the slow undoing of those human rights to which this nation has always been committed. . . ."[45]

In the fall of 1964, as students from leading colleges returned from Mississippi Summer, they carried this same spirit and activism to their own campuses like "soldiers home from an unfinished war."[46] Mario Savio inspired nationwide response by saying:

> Last summer I went to Mississippi to join the struggle there for civil rights. This fall I am engaged in another phase of the same struggle, this time at Berkeley. . . . The same rights are at stake in both places—the right to participate as citizens in a democratic society and the right to due process of law. We are asking that our actions be judged by committees of our peers. We are asking that regulations ought to be considered as arrived at legitimately only from a consensus of the governed.[47]

This is the voice of radicalism, trying to revive classic moral concepts amidst what Brodsky called the "morality of matter." At most campuses, the issues got translated into small stuff—protest over parietals, bad food, and administrative censorship over student publications—which were nevertheless the daily realities in students' lives. These issues accounted for more of the demonstrations than many believe.[48]

The next phase of protest retained the same themes and values but catapulted them to national scope. The "assistance of the people of the United States to the people in Vietnam" (again, double talk) caused this escalation, which first became the explicit object of protest in 1966 at the University of Chicago and at Berkeley. For a number of students, the threat of being drafted activated them to protest. But for many more (including a lot of women), the issues concerned the unrelenting rationality of military escalation which lost all touch with basic human realities, which believed that more of an evil will produce good, which created millions of refugees wandering among the bomb-pocked rice fields to seek asylum finally in open tin sheds set up by the U.S. Army, and which stubbornly supported an elite, dictatorial government in the name of democracy and honor. The modern university was an important part of this protest because it housed the best of science and was organized around the principles of science. Science, in turn, had become a major productive force in war and peace as well as the foundation for the "rational society."[49]

The ensuing years made institutions and campuses more flexible and open to new forms of student activity but produced little basic change. At both Madison and Berkeley there was a five-year period of aggressive protest which achieved dramatic confrontations, recruited large numbers of students and others for protest against the Vietnam War, helped create a sizable community of the new culture, created experimental programs within the university, achieved in Madison a faculty resolution condemning the war by a five to one margin in 1970, produced changes in the grading system, yet failed to alter the relationship between the university and other institutions of the military-industrial complex. Likewise at Columbia, the demands to stop building the new gymnasium produced results, while demands for restructuring power within the university resulted in little change.

The star performers in the drama of university ascension were the faculty, and paradoxically the faculty at good schools helped large portions of students find liberal-radical solutions to their problems of conscience. Like the students, faculty were middle-class and young; almost 60 percent of all faculty today started teaching in the 1960s.[50] While American faculty are middle-class, however, their political beliefs differ from the parents of most college students. Twenty percent of the public calls itself liberal, but the figure is 50 percent for college faculty. In 1969, two-thirds of all faculty criticized American policies in Vietnam, and half agreed that white racism was the main cause of Negro riots in the cities. S. M. Lipset and Everett Ladd, Jr., conclude, "A great variety of earlier studies have agreed that the political culture in which successful, productive academics move is liberal in large measure because the probing, questioning character of their thinking makes them, like other intellectuals, critical of existing practices in society."[51] Thus, beyond American faculty being liberal about national politics, faculty at the best schools were the most liberal of all.

Already one can see the profound ambivalence of the postwar university as an institution experiencing student protest. On the one hand, it was deeply involved in the political and economic order which seemed so unjust at home and abroad. On the other hand, its faculty espoused liberal, humanitarian values similar to those of many students. Radical students called their professors hypocrites, and indeed the critical, liberal research faculty felt guilty. They sympathized with the principles of the New Left, but they were deeply implicated. In 1968, 88 percent of all faculty research funds in the university came from the federal government.

The research faculty had in turn become ambivalent. They tried to expunge "dirty" research while keeping as many research funds as possible. In a 1969 survey, over half of all faculty agreed that "big contract research has become more a source of money and prestige for researchers than an effective way of advancing knowledge." Large percentages said that specialized training has hurt undergraduate education, that the concentration of research grants has corrupted the major universities, and that most American colleges "reward conformity and crush creativity."[52] Yet they had not acted to reduce these corrupting forces.

Faculty response to student protests reflected this troubled state. It ranged from helping to plan a significant number of them to supporting strict punishments for demonstrators, and it generally contained a mixing of institutional conservatism with liberal politics.[53] The administration found itself in a still more difficult position. It was running an institution which embodied both the more advanced forms of modern technology and the most articulate proponents of the counterculture. The administration was answerable to cautious and worried parents, annoyed legislators, unhappy alumni, diverse students, and a divided faculty. The dynamics of this complex situation concern the rest of this volume. However, it should be clear that just as the cultural and psychological conditions which underlie student protest have not waned, neither has the university's position altered as both the innovating servant of a technological society and the haven from it.

NOTES

1. Dirt as a cultural phenomenon is a concept from social anthropology important for understanding the reactions of this generational unit. See Mary Douglas, *Purity and Danger* (New York: Praeger, 1966).
2. Like the title of a volume edited by David Riesman, they asked, *Abundance for What?* (Garden City, N.Y.: Doubleday, 1964).
3. Kenneth Keniston, *Young Radicals* (New York: Harcourt Brace Jovanovich, 1968); Keniston, *Youth and Dissent* (New York: Harcourt Brace Jovanovich, 1971); Richard Flacks, *Youth and Social Change* (Chicago: Markham, 1971); "The Liberated Generation: An Exploration of the Roots of Student Protest," *Journal of Social Issues* 23, no. 3 (July 1967): 52–75.

4. A sensitive portrayal of America in the 1950s is given by Luigi Barzini in "American Chronicle: Lovers in the World," *Encounter,* 40, no. 1 (January 1973): 38–53.
5. *Childhood and Society* (New York: Norton, 1950). Erikson continued to describe the stages of development this way in *Identity: Youth and Crisis* (New York: Norton, 1968).
6. Arthur H. Westing and E. W. Pfeiffer, "The Cratering of Indochina," *Scientific American* 226, no. 5 (May 1972): 21–29.
7. Studs Terkel, *Hard Times* (New York: Avon, 1970), pp. 85–86.
8. The following works contain vivid descriptions of the degradation and humiliation experienced by unemployed males in a society which defines manhood in terms of providing for one's family. Caroline Bird, *The Invisible Scar* (New York: McKay, 1966); Terkel, *Hard Times;* and John A. Williams, "Time and Tide," *The Immigrant Experience,* ed. Thomas Wheeler (New York: Dial, 1972).
9. Terkel, *Hard Times,* pp. 85–86.
10. Ibid.
11. Ibid.
12. Joseph Bensman and Arthur Vidich, *The New American Society* (Chicago: Quadrangle, 1971), p. 46.
13. An enlarged, technical, bureaucratic class necessarily accompanies the second industrial revolution to a technologically advanced economy characterized by electronics and structured around knowledge. Moreover, the rise of a new social strata is a natural source of instability. See Raymond Boudon, "Sources of Student Protest in France," in *The New Pilgrims,* ed. Philip Altbach and Robert Laufer (New York: McKay, 1972), pp. 97–310.
14. The emergence of domestic Communism as the agent of Soviet subversion preoccupied a range of "liberal" institutions, such as trade unions, universities, and New York intellectuals. See Christopher Lasch, "The Cultural Cold War: A Short History of the Congress of Cultural Freedom," in *The Agony of the American Left* (New York: Knopf, 1969); Ronald Rodash, *American Labor and United States Foreign Policy* (New York: Random House, 1969); and Paul Lazarsfeld and Wagner Thielens, Jr., *The Academic Mind* (Glencoe, Ill.: Free Press, 1958).
15. Superfluous in two senses: many party members dropped out and, perhaps more important, hardly any new recruits were joining. I.F. Stone discusses this second phenomenon in *The Haunted Fifties* (New York: Random House, 1969).
16. It is crucial to remind ourselves that the silence that pervaded the fifties acquired its bland, thoughtless quality partly because the "un-American" inquisition destroyed the radical community which sustained critical thought. The House Un-American Activities Committee brought fear, humiliation, and death to this small part of society which served it well as an astute critic of its values and policies. Those who suffered heart attacks apparently from the pressures of the inquisition include John Garfield, Harry Dexter White, Mady Christians, John Brown, and Edwin Rolfe. In *Thirty Years of Treason*

(New York: Viking, 1971), Eric Bentley also gives a long list of victims who committed suicide: Francis Young, Madelyn Dmeytryk, Philip Loeb, E. Herbert Norman, Lawrence Duggan, Abraham Teller, Raymond Kaplan, Francis O. Matthissen, Walter Marvin Smith, Morton E. Kent, Jon Winant, and William K. Sherwood.

The weight of conformity and blandness bore so heavily on the fifties that David Riesman and colleagues wrote a landmark bestseller explaining the emergence of the "other directed" man as the new archetype for America. This sensitive but weak character played out his life in a corporate society, depicted by William Whyte in his influential book, *The Organization Man* (New York: Simon & Schuster, 1956). The list goes on with Wm. J. Lederer's *A Nation of Sheep* (New York: Norton, 1961) and Vance Packard's *The Hidden Persuaders* (New York: McKay, 1957). We now know this vision to be limited; but it reflects the price paid by American democracy when it silenced radical debate.

Two excellent books on this period are Eric Bentley's *Thirty Years of Treason* (New York: Viking, 1971) and Stone's *The Haunted Fifties*. One should note that both were published long after the events. Bentley's book portrays not only the terror with which radicals faced HUAC in the 1950s but also the way in which radicals of the 1960s mocked and scorned the committee out of existence. The new radicals were more authentic, having to uphold no economic stake or social reputation which the committee could threaten.

17. Sebastian DeGrazia, *Of Time, Work, and Leisure* (New York: Doubleday, 1962); Riesman, *Abundance for What?*

18. James O'Toole et al., *Work in America* (Washington, D.C., Department of Health, Education & Welfare: MIT Press, 1973).

19. Maurice Stein, *The Eclipse of Community* (New Jersey: Princeton University Press, 1960).

20. Until 1952, Ford sold the Country Squire, a wood-paneled wagon with a name to fit the postwar image of the good life. Then Ford, whose wagons were the most fashionable, issued the Ranchwagon, a cheaper model which let those living in ranch house developments enjoy a semblance of the good life—but without panels made of wood.

21. Philip Slater, *The Pursuit of Loneliness* (Boston: Beacon Press, 1970).

22. Jack Newfield, *A Prophetic Minority* (New York: New American Library, 1966). See also Richard Flacks' important essay, "The New Left and American Politics Ten Years Later," *Journal of Social Issues* 24, no. 1 (1971): 21–34, and his earlier essay, "Liberated Generation."

23. Daniel Bell, *The End of Ideology* (New York: Collier, 1961); Chaim Waxman, ed. *The End of Ideology Debate* (New York: Funk & Wagnalls, 1969); Stone, *The Haunted Fifties*.

24. "Generational Conflict and Intellectual Antinomianism," in *New Pilgrims*.

25. The draft was used not only to press nonvolunteers into military service but also to shape a population's career choices. The deeper functions of the Selective Service are taken to task in Richard Flacks, Florence Howe, and

Paul Lauter, "On the Draft," *New York Review of Books,* April 6, 1967, pp. 3–5.

26. From its earliest stages, the New Left was concerned with the quality of personal life and the importance of one's inner world. This concern flourished and matured into the themes of "liberation" and interest in alternate forms of consciousness. See Flacks, "New Left and American Politics;" Charles Reich, *The Greening of America* (New York: Random House, 1970); and Michael Rossman, *The Wedding within the War* (New York: Doubleday, 1971).

27. Flacks, "New Left and American Politics."

28. Abraham Maslow, *Motivation and Personality* (New York: Harper, 1954); Maslow, "A Theory of Metamotivation: The Biological Rooting of the Value-Life," *Journal of Humanistic Psychology* 7, no. 2 (1967): 93–127; Reich, *Greening of America;* Theodore Rozak, *The Making of a Counter-Culture* (New York: Doubleday, 1969).

29. C. Wright Mills, *The Sociological Imagination* (New York: Oxford University Press, 1959). As a result, the nature of deviance altered fundamentally. Before the sixties, most sociologists and citizens looked at a criminal or a mental patient psychologically; they tried to figure out what was wrong with *him.* But in the sixties, proponents of the new culture and social scientists shifted the emphasis to how control agents of society label a person either as being a criminal or insane. Studies showed that "mental patient" is a social construction imposed on a person which greatly alters that person's life whether he is insane or not. In the new culture, this perspective accompanied a much greater tolerance for what the fifties called deviance, helping to allow diverse lifestyles grow. Howard Becker and Irving L. Horowitz describe that new tolerance in "The Culture of Civility," in *Culture and Civility in San Francisco,* ed. Howard Becker (Chicago: Transaction Books, 1971).

30. The relationship which Erik Erikson has urged between personal psychological experiences and social history suggests that each transformation of liberation is accompanied by a new psychohistorical experience for that generational unit.

31. The welfare ethic seems to be a political creation of President Richard M. Nixon. While skid rows have always been with us and although a small percentage of the population can seriously be said to believe in living off the dole, no significant proportion of the people has been found to hold such an ethic.

32. Increasing numbers are participating in alternate lifestyles. See Daniel Yankelovich's survey *Generations Apart* (New York, 1969), and his report, "Youth and the Establishment," done for the President's Task Force on Youth, 1971.

33. Serge Mallet, "Socialism and the New Working Class," *International Socialist Journal,* no. 8 (April 1965); Alain Touraine, *The Postindustrial Society* (New York: Random House, 1971); Herbert Gintis, "The New Working Class and Revolutionary Youth," *Socialist Revolution* 1, no. 3 (June 1970); Richard Flacks, "On the New Working Class and Strategies for Social

Change," Chapter 5, *New Pilgrims*.

34. O'Toole, *Work in America*.

35. Nina and George O'Neill, *Open Marriage* (New York: M. Evans & Co., 1972).

36. "Reflections on a Spawn of Hell," *New York Times Magazine* March 4, 1973, p. 70. The following quotations are from this page.

37. See Stuart Hampshire's fine essay, "Morality and Pessimism," *New York Review of Books* 19, (January 25, 1973): 26–33.

38. Jacques Ellul, *The Technological Society* (New York: Knopf, 1964). Roderick Seidenberg, *Past-Historic Man* (Chapel Hill: University of North Carolina Press, 1950).

39. Some of these figures and the following discussion come from an excellent article, "The Divided Professoriate," by Seymour M. Lipset and Everett C. Ladd, Jr. in *Change* 3, no. 3 (May–June 1971). Other figures come from Christopher Jencks' and David Riesman's *Digest of Educational Statistics* (Washington, D.C., 1969).

40. There are many fine books on this subject. Particularly recommended is Harold Hodkinson's *Institutions in Transition* (New York: McGraw-Hill, 1971). See also Christopher Jencks and David Riesman, *The Academic Revolution* (New York: Doubleday, 1968), particularly Chapter 3. Supplementing that book is *The Impact of "The Academic Revolution" on Faculty Careers*, by Donald W. Light, Jr., L. C. Harvey, and T. C. Corl (Washington, D.C.: American Association for Higher Education, 1973).

41. Daniel Bell, "Knowledge and Technology," in *Indicators of Social Change*, ed. E. B. Sheldon and W. E. Moore (New York: Russell Sage, 1968); and Daniel Bell, ed., *Toward the Year 2000* (Boston: Beacon Press, 1967). One would expect that a major shift in the technological and economic base of a society would generate important changes in social values, the family, lifestyle, the nature of work itself, and physical aspects of the society. Just as the Industrial Revolution produced these changes, the emergence of a postindustrial society (a poor term, because it only depicts what the new society is *not*) will produce them. Some thinkers believe that the new culture as described here is harmonious with technological changes; their arguments are persuasive. Laufer develops this theme more fully in his book, *The End of Utopia* (New York: McKay, 1974).

An extensive literature exists on the service function of science in this new kind of society. An important part of that relationship is the growth of higher education since World War II as a producer of new knowledge. See H. L. Nieburg, *In the Name of Science* (Chicago: Quadrangle, 1966); J. K. Galbraith, *The New Industrial State* (New York: Houghton Mifflin, 1971); Harold Orlons, ed., *Science, Policy, and the University* (Washington, D.C.: Brookings Co., 1968); John K. Fogler et al., *Human Resources and Higher Education* (New York: Russell Sage, 1970); R. A. Bauer and K. J. Geiger, *The Study of Policy Formation* (New York: Free Press, 1968); Clark Kerr, *The Uses of the University* (Cambridge, Mass.: Harvard University Press, 1963); James Ridgeway, *The Closed Corporation* (New York: Random

House, 1968); and Noam Chomsky, *American Power and the New Mandarins* (New York: Pantheon, 1969).

42. This theme is developed more fully in Robert S. Laufer's "Sources of Generational Conflict and Consciousness," in *The New Pilgrims;* and in Robert Laufer and Shiela McVey, "Generational Conflict," in *Supermarkets: A Critical Case Study of a Multiversity,* eds. Philip G. Altbach, Robert S. Laufer, and Shiela McVey (San Francisco: Jossey-Bass Co., 1971).

43. See Chapter 3.

44. James Fendrick et. al., "Activities Ten Years Later: A Study of Life Styles and Politics." Paper read at the 1972 annual meetings of the American Sociological Association. Also read there was a striking paper by Raymond Ademak and Jerry M. Lewis, "Social Control, Violence and Radicalization: The Kent State Case."

45. Steven Warshaw, *The Trouble in Berkeley* (Berkeley: Diablo Press, 1965), p. 1. This pictorial history is one of the most interesting, sympathetic treatments of the early protest movement and conveys the times better than more scholarly treatments.

46. Ibid., p. 9.

47. Ibid., p. 27.

48. In 1970–1971, for example, 40 percent of all protests concerned U.S. military policy, but 30 percent concerned parietals. Alan E. Bayer, "Faculty Roles in Student Unrest," *Change Magazine* 3, no. 8 (Winter 1971–72): 74.

49. Jurgen Habermas, *Toward a Rational Society* (Boston: Beacon Press, 1970). See especially "Technology and Science as 'Ideology.' "

50. Lipset and Ladd, "Divided Professoriate," *Change.* The following discussion relies on their survey.

51. Ibid.

52. Ibid.

53. See "The Dynamics of Faculty Response," Chapter 4.

2/ Point and counterpoint in the literature on student unrest

*Molly Levin and
John Spiegel*

A decade has passed since American students, traditionally oriented to vocational success and intellectual docility, surprised their elders with a revolt that gained national and tragic proportions as it played itself out over the years.

Their teachers, quick to recognize a new phenomenon worthy of journal print, soon began to measure and fit the new events into assorted theories of conflict, social change, or generational disequilibrium. What has emerged in this decade is a plethora of research and writings on student unrest. Emanating from sources covering the widest spectrum of political perspectives, the quantity itself is helpful in neutralizing any "political effect" which might be found in literature on a topic engaging the value orientations, hence politics, of even the most conscientiously objective researcher.

But more important for our purpose, the abundant fruits of a decade of observation and measurement of student activity, and the students' return, at least temporarily, to vocational goals and political quiet, offer now an opportunity for a review of the major lines of thinking and writing on the causes and the implications of the student revolt.

Some questions about student unrest which seemed *very* important in 1965 are hardly remembered in 1977. Not long after Mario Savio leaped onto the famous (or infamous) police car in Berkeley in 1964, the academic response to the threat of an epidemic of unrest broke into a dichotomy roughly made up of those charging pathology in the students on the one side and those charging pathology in the environment, to which the students were reacting, on the other side. Prescriptions were appropriate to the diagnoses: in the first case, deal harshly with the erupting students; in the second case, ameliorate the situation.

In an earlier review of the literature, a more graceful refinement of this dichotomy was made by Professor Tom Burns of the University of Edinburgh. In a pair of papers published as a result of a conference which took place at Sussex University in England in July, 1968, he grouped explanations of student unrest in the literature into three types: pathological (explanations in terms of the sociology of deviance), universalistic (explanations deriving from a view of the student movement as symptomatic of much wider structural and cultural changes in society), and particularistic (explanations based on disaffection with the social role of universities, their outmoded disciplinary and administrative procedures and their irrelevant curricula and teaching methods, plus the publicity surrounding demonstrations, sit-ins, and violence).[1]

Burns' categorization was a useful way of studying the pathology-in-students vs. pathology-in-society arguments and reflected the main questions that were asked in the early years. Changing research emphases, however, suggest that a slightly different conceptual framework may help to organize the different approaches for comparative review. Representative samples from the literature, which is simply too vast to review in total, may convey the changing interest among researchers and writers: an initial preoccupation with the question of who the student protesters were, then a predominating interest in the issues, in what the students were really protesting about; eventually, a greater and probably more sophisticated interest in questions of process and response, and finally, a search for what it meant and what it may portend. That is not to say, of course, that a sharp chronological division can be made between these research foci. Rather, one could see a new center of gravity emerging in the balance of questions that were preoccupying the researchers and writers.

THE STUDENT ACTIVIST: RIGHTIST, LEFTIST, REBEL, OR REFORMER?

The immediate interest in what types of students were protesting inspired many attempts to isolate the characteristics of the student activist.[2] Particular interest was shown in their intellectual endowment, in religious, economic, and social status, and in family background.

There was some controversy over the question of whether or not the protesters were higher academic achievers than the rest of the college population, with Flacks making such a finding, Baird contradicting it, and Lipset agreeing that left-activists were academically talented, but no more so than activists of other persuasions or moderates involved in student government—all of them drawn from the ranks of the talented.[3]

With regard to the significance of religious orientation, Lipset, on the one hand, held that family religious practices were highly predictive of activism, religious orthodoxy correlating negatively with activism—a conclusion supported by Astin's findings that activist students were more likely to have no religious preference.[4] Baird, on the basis of his study involving 5,129 students in twenty-nine colleges, concluded that the activists did not seem to be less religious than others.[5] Rather, he found the greatest difference between activists and other students in potential and accomplishment in leadership and on measures reflecting "a desire to influence events and other people." Flacks, while finding the typical activist's family quite secular, also found a significant minority with a strong religious orientation.[6] The research yielded inconsistencies which may reflect an inability to probe, by survey techniques, more basic characteristics for which religious orientation only served as proxy.

On the question of the significance of social and economic class, the Astin and Flacks studies had outlined a portrait of the activist as hailing from a relatively well-educated family, humanist in value orientation, more likely to be professional, and by implication relatively affluent. Whether the presumed affluence was a causative factor in a student's activist propensities or simply associated with the more significant factor of high education of the parents and professional employment was not entirely clear, but Lipset, for one, ventured the conclusion that economic class was not as important in affecting students' propensity for activism as their minority or majority social status.[7]

Activist students were also differentiated in a number of studies by the disciplines in which they were enrolled, conservatives being more likely to study engineering or business and liberals to study humanities, social sciences, mathematics, or pure science.[8] The disciplines themselves, Lipset suggested, have characteristic political orientations which attract students of similar outlook, an observation borne out also by the Cole and Adamsons research on faculty attitudes at Columbia University.

The student activist as a nonreligious member of a minority group, a student of the liberal arts, socialized in a well-educated and permissive family toward humanist values and self-expression became the profile that gained considerable currency, though in fact inconsistencies in the research findings on attributes of even the earlier activists (the "pioneers") have never been reconciled. By 1970 and 1971, however, with an enlarged protest population including a "second force" of followers, new studies confirmed that the later protesters were coming from family backgrounds not remarkable in any particular characteristic.[9] Perhaps this "reversion to the mean" phenomenon reflects the need for pioneers on the frontier of social change to be made of sterner stuff than the followers.

Along with these studies of selected populations of student activists differentiated by certain personality and social background characteristics, another major stream of writings appeared, generally in the historical or analytical essay mode and concerned more with motivation and behavior of students than with issues. A number of researchers, for example, analyzed student behavior and/or motivation by generating typologies differentiating between one type and another on the basis of their methods of adaptation to common problems.[10] Another kind of typology, distinguishing students in terms of dominant value commitment, was generated by Richard E. Peterson of the Educational Testing Service and arranged differing types of students in decreasing order of acceptance of American institutions: Vocationalists and Professionalists, Collegiates, Ritualists, Academics, Intellectuals, and Left-Activists and Hippies—a categorization fairly predictive of propensity to become involved in protests.[11]

Lewis Feuer's approach, as a foremost example of the psychohistorical genre, raised a storm of controversy.[12] Attributing campus rebellions to unconscious oedipal hostilities, Feuer viewed student movements as irreconcilable tragedy. While he acknowledged the "higher ethic for social reconstruction," the "altruism," and the "generous emotion" contained in student movements of the past 150 years, he took issue with their "destructive means," their suicidalism and terrorism, the nihilism which he claimed has tended to become their philosophy. Most significant was the consequence of a student movement attaching itself to a carrier movement—a nationalistic or peasant or labor movement—and transferring to it the unconscious irrational emotions that he claimed would deflect the political carrier movement in irrational directions. "Given a set of alternative paths—rational or irrational for realizing a social goal—the influence of a student movement will be toward the use of the most irrational means to achieve the end." Student movements are thus, he concluded, what one would least expect—among the most irrational in history. Further, Feuer traced back to Plato the recognition that generational struggle has constituted virtually the basic mechanism in political change. The Russian student movement of 1865–66 was cited as a prototype of the trilogy of generational politics—parricide, regicide, and suicide; and the adventures of a number of student movements in modern history were narrated to demonstrate the recurring characteristics of violence, antidemocracy, elitism, and, oddly, concurrent populism.

Feuer's bitter presentation drew ample criticism: if student rebellion was a product of unconscious and natural oedipal resentment, how would one explain the irregularity and unpredictability of rebellions through many changes of generation, the sustained participation of young women in, say, the Chinese revolutionary movement or the recent American movement, or the nonparticipation of the majority of younger-generation males?[13] In addition, Feuer's moral revulsion at the themes of generational politics—parricide, regicide, and suicide—led to some reflection on the possibly obverse themes of gerontological politics—filicide, genocide, or homicide.[14]

The factual rendering of the particulars in Feuer's account of student movements in various countries at various times led, in the end, to some controversial generalizations. The primary thesis that generational revolt is inevitably tragic and unnecessary for social change would lead one to search the Feuer narrative for evidence that social changes involving a redistribution of power were initiated by older generations without the pressure of intense social conflict and confrontation often leading to violence. Such evidence was not produced. Nor did the Feuer analysis differentiate the rightist movements of the 1920s and 1930s from the leftist movements; the differences are important to any analysis.[15] Nor were the follies and failures of student movements put into a context of similar extreme or dysfunctional behavior, no matter the generation, throughout man's long effort to find social justice. On the contrary, the theme suggested that the labor movement achieved its power without violence, that a generation of elders would be too wise to fall prey to such an organization as the Ku Klux Klan, too democratic and antielitist to join vigilante groups, and too rational to engage in such extremism as the Watergate incidents. The focus of the oedipal explanation left the impression that terrorism is a monopoly of youth, not to be found in middle-aged generals in banana republics or in Northern Ireland.

The provocation, in short, of the Feuer work lay not in the identification of generational rebellion against establishment values, which is by now widely conceded as a valid analysis, but in the use of historical antecedent viewed from the single perspective of psychopathology to denigrate particularly the morality and behavior of the young. The theme of generational rebellion, in itself, proved to be a frequent one throughout the literature on student behavior.

Another approach to the question of who protests was the inquiry into adolescent personality development and attitude formation. Many of the studies falling into this genre were concerned with the process of becoming alien or radical.[16]

Again, there was a sharp dichotomy between those who viewed the activists as socially alienated from a patently unacceptable reality (and therefore, presumably, mentally and emotionally vigorous) and those who saw them as psychologically alienated (and therefore introverted and neurotic). An influential and more benign formulation of personality development as "the search for identity," launched by Erik Erikson, made it possible to suspend summary judgment on adolescent behavior while recognizing its kaleidoscopic transformations. An example is Erikson's passage on the functional aspects of such transformations:

> If in human adolescence this field of manifestation (fidelity) is alternatively one of devoted conformism or extreme deviancy, of rededication or rebellion, we must remember the necessity for man to react (and to react most intensively in his youth) to the diversity of conditions. In the setting of psychosocial evolution, we can ascribe a long-range meaning to the idiosyncratic individualist and to the rebel as well as to the conformist, albeit under different historical conditions. For healthy individualism and devoted deviancy contain an indignation in the service of a wholeness that is to be restored, without which psychosocial evolution would be doomed. Thus human adaptation has its loyal deviants, its rebels, who refuse to adjust to what so often is called, with an apologetic and fatalistic misuse of a once good phrase, "the human condition."[17]

Theodore Roszak appeared also to ascribe the alienation of the counterculture to an attempt to work out the personality structure and lifestyle following from New Left social criticism aimed at the entire web of technocratic life, with its primacy of intellectualism and rationality.[18]

The writings of Kenneth Keniston, in a vein similar to those of Erikson, elaborated a developmental process in which adolescents are viewed as complex individuals not subject to one or another capsulated theory of activism or radicalization.[19] Specifically he took issue with what he labeled the "radical rebel" (generational revolt) and the "red diaper baby" (radical children of radical parents) theories, claiming they overlooked the complexity of human development. In a study of twelve young radicals, Keniston found that almost without exception they came from a family atmosphere in which ethical principles were primary and human affairs were automatically judged in accordance with these principles.[20] Yet he found that while the young radicals had unusually strong commitments, they had few specific plans, and he concluded that they might be suffering from a protracted adolescence, still immersed during their mid-twenties in an unresolved identity crisis. Erik Erikson recognized the same problem in a slightly different way: "One could condense all that has been said about the various types of dissent by claiming that group retrogressions originate in the incapacity or the refusal to conclude the stage of identity on the terms offered by the adult world." [21]

In retrospect, one can discern three differing approaches in the research addressed to the question of who the protesters were. There is first a group of static studies of activist vita, family background and personal history, exemplified by the Astin, Flacks, Baird, Smith, and Dunlap studies. Though there was considerable consistency between the Astin and Flacks portraits of early activists, the Baird data, based on a large sample, challenged the previous work and left unresolved the question of what static characteristics the pioneer protesters actually had. The fact that a second force of protesters emerged with characteristics indistinguishable from the rest of the college population means that it is now probably impossible to arrive at definitive conclusions about the pioneers.

A second approach, also static in nature, involved labeling of students by personality or disposition and drawing conclusions through observations of the behavior and reactions of differently labeled groups. The typologies previously mentioned exemplify this approach. Colorful and provocative, they provided their creators with an imaginative framework for ordering the phenomena observed, but without an actual data base. They remain allusive and quixotic, as probably was the intent.

A third approach, exemplified by the Keniston and Erikson writings, involved looking at the behavior of the student protester through the prism of personality development in youth. Viewing the protester through a veritable rainbow of changing attitudes and responses as he gropes to find his "true color"—his identity—the observer was encouraged to adopt a longer-range view of the outcome and was expected to accept the burden of complex interweaving of intrapsychic stage and social-historical moment to comprehend both student reaction and the stress which elicited it. Of course, Feuer was also preoccupied with student response to social-historical stress, but while the Keniston and Erikson approach was open ended and envisioned a process of change and maturation in response, Feuer appeared to emphasize the inevitability of the same dynamic which occurred previously in history, with little prospect of evolutionary change.

Through these various social-psychological studies and writings, an academic battle of sorts was waged over the question of pathology within the protesters versus pathology within the social system. In time, enough protesters joined the ranks that it became impossible to set up disparate groups for statistical study. In many cases, yesterday's nonprotester became today's activist. The inquiry then swung into a second stage—a predominant interest in the issues about which the students were protesting.[23]

LONG RANGE CAUSES AND IMMEDIATE ISSUES: UNIVERSAL, INSTITUTIONAL, SPECIFIC?

Most analysts of student protest acknowledged the interrelationship of multiple factors and issues in the disorders. Yet, several distinct lines of emphasis regarding the issues emerged. A rather specific and popular thesis, which came to be called the theory of "historical irrelevance," was that the students were responding to the discovery of finding themselves in a marginal status, unprepared by their upbringing and humanist education to take a substantial place in an increasingly technological society.

This theory was essentially an extrapolation of earlier works by Talcott Parsons and S. N. Eisenstadt which ascribed the development of youth cultures to a disjunction between the values and expectations of the traditional families in a culture and the contrasting values and expectations in the occupational sphere.[23] Although the Parsons and Eisenstadt works were addressed mainly to the situation in developing nations where a modern younger generation withdraws from the values of the traditionally old-fashioned family and forges its own culture, the substance was recast to fit advanced industrial cultures. In these societies, the humanistic value orientation of liberal families and their offspring was seen to be antagonistic to that of the occupational power structure. Using this concept of antagonism between personal and societal values as a basic area of contention, different writers took up positions on all sides.[24]

"The student radicals," said Nathan Glazer, "come from fields that have a restricted and ambiguous place in contemporary society. They remind me more of the Luddite machine smashers than the socialist trade unionists who achieved citizenship and power for workers."[25]

The problem, Bennett Berger said, was generated by the exigencies of a postindustrial society which uses institutions of higher education as warehouses for the temporary storage of a population it knows not what else to do with.[26] An extension of this opinion offered by President Kingman Brewster, Jr., of Yale University, was given wide publicity. Too many students, Brewster said, were locked into college by a combination of the draft, parental pressures, and societal insistence on diplomas and certificates to indicate competence on the job; pressed into a mold for which they were not suited, these students struggled to shape the mold to fit them.[27]

Flacks saw students become active agents of change when their numbers exceeded the opportunities for employment commensurate with their abilities, interests, and training; and when they found that the values with which they were closely connected no longer were appropriate to the developing social reality.[28]

The evolution of the university, both shaped by and shaper of societal values, came under scrutiny in an effort to understand the students' charges. Jill Conway elaborated several stages in the institutional process by which American culture came, first through the default of religious interests, to be dominated eventually by the utilitarian values of industry.

> The university as a Western European institution grew out of an established church which could claim to define and disseminate the truth . . . in colonial America because there was no clear religious establishment, there was real uncertainty about which religious groups should be authorized by society to transmit their orthodoxies. This ambiguity was resolved by allowing any religious group which could support a school to receive a charter from the state. Thus the traditional pluralism of American intellectual life developed from the acceptance of the idea that there was no single body of religious truth which must be conveyed.[29]

The secularization of learning in the late nineteenth century through the founding of state universities, and the adoption of the German notion of pure science, induced the actual change in dominance:

> American universities became exposed not only to scientific values, but to the commercial values of the dominant business community in the gilded age. . . . Because of the entrepreneurial attitude to learning, the great industrial fortunes of the 19th century were turned over to the endowment of education . . . accompanied by the assumption that industrial capitalism had much to contribute to the way in which knowledge was produced and disseminated in America . . . the intellectual function of the university came to be progressively defined as the creation and diffusion of knowledge valued in relation to its technological utility. Renaissance humanism and classical culture played no part in an industrial scheme of values and they came to occupy a smaller and smaller part of the curriculum in all but the most patrician centers of learning.[30]

Part of the contemporary rebellion of youth, Conway concluded, consisted of affirming that intellectual excellence can be demonstrated by intuitive and expressive achievement in a way that has equal validity with the rational problemsolving of the older curriculum. "Who has the right to say what truths shall be pursued in graduate schools? . . . To make the definition of truth in our confused times a generational prerogative is to invite the kind of academic turmoil in which we all live."

A supplementary history of what amounts to the same battle over utilitarian vs. humanistic values in the universities of nineteenth-century Western Europe points to the problems created by an excess of educated men in Germany and France particularly, where a chronically underemployed intellectual "proletariat" with purely literary education was said to create social and political instability which played an important part in the 1830 and 1848 revolutions.[31] Uncannily contemporary in spirit was the remark, for instance, of one Charles Dupin, who, writing in 1825, said of the literary graduates, "Their intelligence, formed along no precise lines, remains without application."

Evidence has been presented that the large number of lawyers, journalists, and teachers in the radical wing of the middle class proved that a superfluity of educated men created political instability. Another interpretation may be equally valid: the larger the aggregate of educated men, particularly humanistically educated, the more certain will be the pressure for reform. As applied to the situation in the mid-nineteenth-century Germany, however, reform apparently meant a narrow nationalistic fervor which can only be interpreted as a foreboding of ultimate German tragedy.[32]

The view of the contemporary university as a service facility for preparation of cogs in the industrial wheels was further expanded by Edgar Friedenberg.[33] Not only is technological utility the *raison d'être* of the contemporary university, Friedenberg said, but in providing vocational opportunity in a society holding personal advancement—"making it"—in highest esteem, it neglects to provide a place where young people can develop a sense of personal value commitment and a basis for moral judgment. "These, indeed," he said, "infuriate our society, which prefers decorum to morality and success to either." Administration tinkering with administrative boards and committees in universities would be unavailing, he warned, because the problem was not structural but moral, and had to do with the co-opting to technocracy which the university accomplished by "standing astride the only legitimate highway to advancement."

The discussion of historical irrelevance led inexorably to further explorations of the moral and social values inherent in the social system and to appropriate means and ends in social change. The literature now burgeoned with diffuse commentary on such basic social questions.

Nathan Glazer, obviously skeptical of the developing events, summed up one side of the larger argument: "In the end one must judge whether the student radicals fundamentally represent a better world that can come into being, or whether they are not committed to outdated and romantic visions that cannot be realized, that contradict fundamentally other hopes and desires they themselves possess and that contradict even more the desires of other people."[34]

Lipset, meanwhile, took issue with the means employed by students:

> Many intellectuals react to the emphasis on social science and the concomitant belief in gradualism, expertise, and planning with a populist stress on the virtues of direct action against evil institutions and practices. . . . The view that there is an inherent conflict between the values of intellectuals and those of the market place has sustained an anti-capitalist ideology among many humanistically inclined intellectuals and has affected students preparing for such pursuits. . . . Hence, there is now an international revolutionary movement of students and youth that expresses in almost unadulterated form the ethic of absolute ends. These youths are almost completely uninhibited and uncontrolled, since they have no relations to the parties that have some sort of interest in adhering to the rules of the game and accept the need for compromise. The New Left groups also have no clear concept of any road to power, of a way of effecting major social change. They are ready and willing to use tactics that violate the normal democratic game. . . . Clearly the idea that youth adhere to an ethic of absolute ends while older generations adhere to the ethic of responsibility would appear to be valid.[35]

It is hardly necessary in the post-Watergate era to comment on the fairer vision of hindsight: surely no one in the United States still believes that the ethic of absolute ends is a folly only of the young and the New Left. Neither is there much faith that those in power adhere to the rules of the game.

What was frequently characterized as youth's search for new values (the positive expression of "historical irrelevance") had its defenders, too.[36] The clash of views was not simply the result of a conflict between conservatives defending the status quo and radicals pressing for change and university action in its behalf.[37] Nor was it entirely a contest between liberal, radical, or revolutionary means of attacking the obvious ills of warfare, racism, or poverty.[38] Much of the discussion could be compared to the difficulties of "trading in common coin" when dealing in an international market with no accepted medium of exchange. Dealing in social values, each contributor sought to define his terms to maximize his argument. The requirements and components of one writer's "freedom," for example, were markedly different from another's. Even beyond the problem of common understanding of terms, there was an elusive pursuit of the significance of student discontent, perhaps exemplified in an account given by Stephen Spender of the mood of the French students during the Sorbonne uprising in 1968:

> In fact part of the talk was an attempt of the students to explain to themselves the situation in which they were free to talk about freedom while they did not feel free. They were free it seemed only to define their sense of the lack of freedom. There were moments when this led them to think . . . that to have apparent but ineffective freedom might be a worse state than to have none at all. Students look to writers like Marcuse to analyze and explain—to "justify"— their sense of frustration which they feel in a world in which they are a privileged minority, and where they enjoy a great deal of freedom. They want it explained to them that the whole democracy, with its governing class, big business, mass media, is a vast conspiracy of powers that makes their freedoms illusory.[39]

No one, it seemed, could be altogether certain of his ground on *terra incognita,* and there was no road map to guide those seeking change; no systematic data were available to allow the kind of quantitative, structured exploration of alternatives that modern social scientists feel most comfortable with. Large-scale social theory itself was lacking; "the intellectual bankruptcy of the Left" was the expression used, in fact, to explain the incoherence of the militants. The rationalization was that Western intellectuals produced no systematic new political thought since Marxism, which proved to be inadequate in its application to developed industrial states. Finding themselves oppressed by the dehumanizing characteristics of advanced industrial bureaucracy, the change-seekers had nowhere to go, theoretically speaking, and were reduced to expressive, incoherent militancy, devoid of positive social and political action.[40]

What Joseph Califano described as a "crisis in belief," a feeling among dissident students that they knew only what they didn't like (materialistic pressures, conformism, manipulation), but didn't know what they wanted, was taken up by many writers.[41] Student vagaries, often seen by distraught observers as theatrical, romantic, or absurd, were sometimes referred to as "chiliastic," or as "antinomian" to give then an historical reference. ("Chiliastic," like its Latin equivalent, "millennial," derives from a Greek root meaning 1,000—that is, the expected reign of Christ on earth for 1,000 years; "antinomian" refers to an interpretation of the gospel which holds that moral law is inoperative since faith alone is necessary to salvation.) Tom Burns, discussing the chiliastic stance, saw it as a desire to exclude the world, particularly the world of institutionalized order, in favor of spontaneity, immediacy, and unfettered action in an existential present.[42] Nathan Adler described the antinomian idea as an abandonment or reversal of social controls which has repeatedly occurred in the course of history at times of transition from one type of social order to another.[43] In France, for example, the Revolution of 1830 brought disillusion and despair, especially to the wildly romantic, anticonventional children of the generation which had fought in the Napoleonic wars. It was, in the words of Alfred de Musset, a time when people suffered from the twin injuries of the heart: "all that had been no longer was, all that would be was not yet."[44]

More recently, attempts were made to fill in the theoretical void. Richard Flacks, for example, elaborated a process by which social and cultural revolution would take place through a lengthy conversion of institutions to new values and through model communities (he called them "liberated zones") established in youth ghettos. Invoking essentially Marxian dynamics (adapted to post-Marxian conditions), his change-agent would be the "new working class" (intelligentsia), which he would hope eventually to see merged with what Feuer would call a carrier movement into a coalition that could eventually deal politically with state power. Flacks labeled the crisis in advanced capitalism a contradiction between the technological capacities and the social organization of society. He claimed that radical youth formed an avant garde of the new working class, and was more clearly forming a vision of a viable postindustrial society in which primary vocational activities would be focused on production and distribution of knowledge and art, on provision of a vast array of human services, and on collective efforts to create maximally beneficial communal and natural environments. Further, as students leave the university and move into the larger society, the movement would transcend itself and the action would begin to take place in the many institutions of society.[45]

The mobilization of faculty opinion and appeal to faculty support, examples of which are described in chapters following, bear out at least the unstable nature of some of the unchallenged values of the past, and the beginnings of their re-examination in the locus of the university.

If historical irrelevance of protesters assumed primary importance as a cause of unrest in the view of one group of commentators, and the obverse search for new values by the young was offered by another group, a third distinct emphasis in the literature was on the more narrow institutional factors, particular problems and failings of universities and colleges under siege, and of higher education in the context of the times.

In spite of a reported 135 instances of campus protest during the 1970–71 academic year,[46] and at least 760 campuses affected during the Cambodia and Kent State reactions of the previous spring—to say nothing of the much heavier violence of 1968 and 1969 (of 2,300 colleges and universities, 145 experienced violent and 524 experienced disruptive disorders in 1968 alone), relatively few comprehensive case studies made their way into print, and these usually involved the larger and bloodier incidents.[47]

Much more frequent in the literature were analyses of general institutional factors thought to contribute to student protest. As illustrative a catalog as any was that of Leon Eisenberg: the university has grown larger and consequently more bureaucratic and impersonal; small group and tutorial sessions have been replaced by computer assignments, large lecture halls, and televised instruction; funding mechanisms make each scientist an entrepreneur in supporting himself and his research and weaken faculty loyalty to the university and its students; faculty advancement has been based on number of papers published and grants obtained rather than on capacity to inspire the young; and the university has been assigned the role of producer of a managerial class rather than that of a haven for personal development. In addition, there was the widespread disenchantment with the university's role in loco parentis, students charging that they were infantilized by the rules and so on, and universities claiming an inability to control in fact the students for whom they had accepted responsibility.[48]

The many dimensions in which universities and colleges affronted the ideal of a democratic community could hardly represent, however, a practical basis for an onslaught of the nature of the student revolt. Closer to the core of the controversy was the seething dialogue among academics about the functions and purpose of the university. This issue has already been discussed somewhat in the context of the students' search for new values. The issue moved faculty even more than students. One group of 100 scholars, calling itself the International Committee on the University Emergency, decried the "mounting challenges to academic freedom . . . when universities are threatened, university teachers must act; they have an obligation to defend the university's integrity." Increasingly, the scholars felt, political criteria were being used to evaluate academic performance. "To turn universities into engines of political action or into cockpits for political controversy, is to make it impossible for them to perform their indispensible functions in education and research." This group of influential academics affirmed that "freedom of rational discourse and judgment of professional competence are not only the lifeblood of the universities themselves, they are a trust which the universities hold for the larger society."[49]

The legitimacy of this trusteeship, administered over the years under a "gentleman's agreement" that allowed the university to be governed in what Clark Kerr called "a series of semi-autonomous layers" (the trustees having authority over investments and property, the faculty over curriculum and the students over extracurriculum) is precisely what was called into question by student dissidents and their faculty sympathizers.[50] Hard-liners on student protest issues often defended the self-perpetuation of values in the university which was accomplished through autonomy within department and discipline in hiring and firing. The legitimacy of the functions or purposes of the university as delineated within these closed units met little resistance in the past. Yet the literature reveals the pain of many sensitive academics who understood the forces that made faculty or administrative initiative toward reform improbable, but who at the same time could not condone the irresponsible tactics and impractical, even incoherent, goals of the radicals.

The fragility of the university was a frequent variant theme. Daniel Bell, taking issue with Zbigniew Brzezinski, thought that the authority of the university was not a civil authority but a moral one, foreclosing confrontation politics, but demanding "the fullest commitment to being a participatory institution."[51] Many observers feared the destruction of the university by a backlash right wing reaction as much as by its leftist provocateurs. "The recklessness of some in threatening the university, the last remaining platform for rational dissent; their [the young] isolation from the mainstream of the community—all combine to offer the right wing a prime and long-sought opportunity to smash the university in the name of protecting it," said Leon Eisenberg. "Our difficult task is to defend the legitimacy of student criticism at the same time that we find a way to make students aware that more is needed than sloganeering."[52]

Again, although the idea of the university as a microcosm of the larger society was not generally accepted, there was a recognition that the problem of political (participatory) vs. professional control and governance in the university foreshadowed a pervasive problem facing society in the future: how to reconcile the requirements of democracy with those of advanced technology. Although university and larger society were clearly not considered parallel in nature or function, those observers who looked upon the university disturbances as a quest by intellectual youth for new social values in the outside society tended to have a longer and more temperate view. "We need not, however, take their [the students'] current incivility as a mark of congenital and incurable barbarism" said Howard Becker, "but rather as a tactic that will be succeeded by a new civility appropriate to the new balance that will eventually be reached"[53] by status realignments in the larger society.

As for the dispute among the faculty about the appropriate role and functions of the university, it has often been assumed that these remained unchanged throughout the modern history of the institution. But, as Everett Lee Hunt wrote a year before Berkeley,

> It is not likely that a faculty will ever agree about its functions . . . one reason is that they are influenced in different degrees by their changing roles in education. Older professors in colleges that were once church-related still feel . . . that they should be concerned with inculcation of moral principles (now usually referred to as "values") and the development of character. . . . The aim that succeeded the pastoral one was the informational function, the transmission of the cultural heritage of man. The third and newest function of the teacher, which emphasizes research, is rapidly replacing the others.[54]

Behind the functions, regardless of their label, was the question of funding—the relentless search for money to fuel the operation. Significantly, between World War II and 1970, the federal government had become the source of 25 percent of all funds spent by institutions of higher learning.[55] That the tax-paying benefactors should want greater participation in institutional decision-making was not surprising, but led to the very problem mentioned earlier of appropriate division of decision-making responsibility between political and professional interests. Resolution of this problem is closely tied, in the last analysis, to defining future primary functions of colleges and universities.

If the universal questions concerning social values and the institutional questions involving university role and function in contemporary society appeared as a result of complex interaction of many factors, there seems little question that the impetus for their rapid development came from two specific issues: the response to black aspirations for equal opportunity and the United States' involvement in Vietnam. In his nationwide study of the scope of organized student protest in 1967–68, Richard E. Peterson found that the Vietnam War was the single issue most frequently cited as having triggered student activism.[56] In other countries, however, as many observers have pointed out, other specific issues precipitated student action. The effect was that of a centripetal force in which protest directed at specific issues in different countries generated its own dynamic, and bore more or less rapidly as specific issues warranted, toward more central, universalistic issues.

Most onlookers, whether critical or sympathetic to the students, agreed on the essentially *political* nature of student activism—its basic involvement with questions of power and strategy and the importance to its outcome of the *political* response.

PROTEST AND RESPONSE:
AN INTERACTION PERSPECTIVE

Although much less attention was directed to questions of process in campus conflict than to issues and participants, the small number of case studies completed, including those of commissions of investigation, pointed increasingly to the significance of the provocation/response dynamics and to failures of communication in escalating disputes, gathering support, inciting violence, and effecting polarization. What seemed to be even more fundamental at the time was the concern with questions of rights and responsibilities among all campus inhabitants, an acknowledgement of the tender agreements on which campus relationships rested in less populous days.

What emerged particularly from the case studies was the debilitating effect of uncertainty for all parties when physical force was used on any side—as though a game were being undertaken without any understanding of what the signals meant or of what plays would lead to winning or losing.

"How could an administration, tolerant to a fault and even avuncular in its responsiveness to students, albeit in a fumbling way, become, after a series of fitful indecisions, so punitive as to make a fortuitous conflict with the police seem to be the culminating event in a chain of purposeful confrontations?" asked Daniel Bell about the Columbia events.[57] "The administration above all failed to understand the *dynamics* of the student protest: that whatever reasons there may have been for early police action, when the buildings were seized by the hard-core SDS members, the subsequent surge of political support on the part of 500 other students—most of them liberal, moderate, pacifist, and not members of SDS—effectively changed the *political* character of the situation."

The use of the civil police force was a particular bone of contention. In the Columbia incident, the consensus appeared to be that whereas immediate use of police to clear buildings occupied by radicals might have reduced the scale of the catastrophe, their later use, after administrative rigidity had pushed the moderates into the radicals' camp, proved to be tragic. The route to tragedy, apparently, was the destruction of the moderate position and enlargement of the scale of the dispute by intransigent response on the part of the administration.[58]

At San Francisco State, McEvoy and Miller reported similar enlargement of the scale by enlistment of the police, and the tragedies of Kent State and Jackson State further exposed the dangers in use of outside force.[59] These dangers were the subject of much attention by the President's Commission on Campus Unrest as well as the Carnegie Commission on Higher Education, both of which cleared the air by spelling out conditions required for the positive relationship between law enforcement agencies and campuses that they saw as a vital replacement for the "campus as sanctuary" philosophy widely held before the confrontations. No doubt a major contribution to the police/campus conflict was the confusion over the right or rationale of campus exemption from the general laws and civil law enforcement.[60] As was evident at Berkeley, however, even the university police force, activated at the wrong moment, could fuel a conflict, as when they suddenly seized the leader of the Free Speech Movement at a convocation which until that moment had served to ameliorate student-administration relations.

The use of legal procedure such as the injunction was introduced with great hope to stop occupation of campus buildings, but its effectiveness or importance was little reviewed.

Most important were two developments: first, the spontaneous easing and eventual halt of campus incidents and second, the procedures which were established in many schools for waging dissent in an orderly manner. It is altogether possible that the first development was encouraged by the increasing tendency of state legislatures to pass legislation intended to bring student misbehavior clearly within the scope of civil authority.[61] But unquestionably, the increased democratization of many universities and colleges in governance and parietal arrangements, and the ending of American involvement in the Vietnam War deprived radical leaders of the momentary issues which had mobilized support, and as history shows, the power of inflammatory oratory to hold attention is usually short-lived. When there is no crisis, it is hard to command a crowd. It was also pointed out on the occasion of the passage and the ratification of the twenty-sixth amendment to the Constitution, granting the vote to eighteen-year-olds, that youthful dissenters now had the privilege, and should exercise the responsibility, to seek change through the electoral process before taking to the streets to cry "foul!"

On procedure, two important commissions underscored the right of students to dissent, and indeed appealed for public understanding of the benefits to society of youthful dissenters. The Carnegie Commission on Higher Education made its report on *Dissent and Disruption,* sharply differentiating between the two, supporting dissent and recommending that disruption incur application of the general laws. To promote this procedure, the report included a model bill of rights and responsibilities, suggested the development of effective consultation and contingency planning in event of disruptions, recommended the creation of judicial procedures, including use of the general courts, and the hiring of an ombudsman to handle complaints by any campus inhabitant. "Faculty members with tenure, as well as trustees and administrators, all of whom have substantial authority and security, should not inhabit protected enclaves above and beyond the rule of law nor shielded from the legitimate grievances and requests of other elements of a campus. . . . Too many campuses have faced the inevitable as though it were the impossible; have acted impetuously where the most careful advance thought is essential; and have stayed with traditional approaches despite quite new conditions," the report concluded.

The commission's report essentially seconded similar recommendations which had been made previously as a part of the report of the President's Commission on Campus Unrest. That report also emphasized the need for universities to develop effective methods for responding to student and faculty grievances and to develop contingency plans for handling conflict so that the options are not narrowed quickly to capitulation or the use of force whenever disorder occurs. At the same time, the President's Commission (Scranton Commission) emphasized repeatedly that campus unrest is not itself a social problem but a natural and desirable consequence of renewal in the life of the mind. Here, too, throughout the comprehensive report, the functional aspects of conflict and dissent were clearly differentiated from the unacceptability of disorder. Although the report received short shrift by the President who had appointed the Commission, its findings and recommendations were well received by a wider public.

Further attention to the importance of procedures in conflicts was given by Max Heirich, who used extremely detailed observations of the conflict at Berkeley in 1964–65 to formulate and propose an explanatory theory of collective action.[63] Starting with a specific action, Heirich's theory explored variables at four different levels of explanation, each one carrying the investigator to more distant and more generalized factors implicated in the original action. At the first level, he noted perceptions of the actors (what they see that leads them to act); at the second, the perceptual processes which define a specific belief (how do people come to see things as they do?); at the third, the immediate conditions (when will this happen?); at the fourth, the organizational trends (who will respond to what?). For each level of explanation, hypotheses were framed directed toward answering why the action occurred. Eventually Heirich used the theory and the Berkeley data he had gathered to explain how the conflict spiraled and generated its own dynamic through options involving action/perception/reaction—spiraling escalation. Through a hypothetical formulation of rational options open to opposing parties in a dispute, possible consequences of different combinations of options were suggested. Through a continuum of six steps which yielded options either serving to end or continue the conflict, the theory exposed a process by which a conflict may become enlarged and refocused around more central value-strains within a system at issue, eventually bringing into question the legitimacy of authority relations within the system.

Even though its application to disputes in general may be limited, the

Heirich model is noted at some length because it indicated the trend toward more sophisticated inquiry into process questions concerning social conflict. Since Heirich's data concerned a student confrontation, it fell into the net of studies on student unrest. However, other researchers interested in mathematical sociology and in political science have also been fascinated with questions of option choices and consequences in conflicts, and there seems to be little doubt that progress can be made in establishing procedures which would allow many kinds of conflicts to be waged without violence or unnecessary damage.

Analyses of procedure in conflicts have contributed to the understanding that all sides to a conflict can act rationally in response to differing perceptions, that blame need not be assigned to one side or another, that the transactions between various factors are complex, and that the choice of action strategies by all those involved can be decisive in determining the consequences.

If there is general agreement by writers that the student disorders resulted in new procedural advances, it is accompanied by widespread disagreement about the substantive implications of the protests. Altbach and Laufer, editing a volume of essays on the subject, noted that two positions emerged. While all of their contributors conceded that the major causes of student protest lay in the social and political issues of the day rather than in the narrow institutional issues, there was disagreement over the "interpenetration" between higher education and political, economic, and social institutions, and the extent of that interpenetration.[64] Those analysts who saw the university as an adjunct of social and political institutions in the larger society were inclined to view student protest as related to the systemic social problems of advanced industrial societies. Those who did not accept a systemic outlook were inclined to look for other causes of student disaffection. The latter group generally cast an optimistic eye on the future, seeing little portent of a gathering storm. The first group, however, in varying language and scenario, presented another outlook, one of growing dissension and unpredictable outcome.

The Altbach and Laufer summary is fairly representative of the general cleavage in the literature following a few years of calm. Those who see higher education as a systemic accomplice of the major political and social and economic institutions of society also see a confrontation shaping up between what can loosely be called "technism" and "humanism." "The most obvious fact about students' relationships to society is that they are being trained to fill various roles after graduation, and that most students are being prepared for jobs as 'intellectual laborers.' . . . The very mechanisms necessitated by the change to an economy in which intellectual labor is used on a mass scale serve both as ways in which students are alienated from their studies and as ways in which students become aware of the fate awaiting them after graduation," wrote Samuel R. Friedman.[65]

"Yesterday's problem has abated, but I think that we shall see it recur in an altered context and perhaps in sharper form. What we have been witnessing, since 1964, is the first stirrings of a whole new generation of social problems under the heading of 'education and society,' " was the way Albert K. Cohen put it.[66]

"The real student revolt by the vast majority of college students is just beginning," Gerald M. Schaflander predicted.[67] The underlying contention common to outlooks of this kind is that while advanced technology allows and even demands mass education, at the same time it renders the masses who are educated dissatisfied with their ensuing lifestyle, morality, rewards, and gratifications. Significant for the future, one study indicated a strong relationship between student activism in the civil rights movement during the 1960s and later choice of occupation, with activists highly concentrated in the academic profession. Such a finding would suggest a snowballing awareness and analysis of social issues by future students as they learn from their teachers, who were yesterday's activists.

IN SUMMARY

Within the decade since the Berkeley event burst upon the academic world, one can trace through the research literature a growing sophistication in thought. The initial preoccupation with the personalities and backgrounds of dissenters through survey and interview reports, attendant as it was with the suspicion that dissenters were pathological, yielded in time to a more probing search for causes and issues; then with the validation of dissent itself and some serious debate involving the merits of the issues, some few studies began to turn to moral, rational, and practical methods of dealing with legitimate dissent.[67]

Perhaps the relative paucity of contributions related to process can be charged to the difficulty of any single observer verifying continuous or simultaneous events in different arenas; for whatever reason, a number of questions concerning faculty and administration response, effects of rumor, role of media, and negotiating processes were not as well explored as other facets. The papers following are a partial attempt to fill the void.

In the last analysis, it will remain to the historians to dissect the student protests and to place them in appropriate perspective. Having witnessed the swiftness with which several million clamoring students subsided into avid vocationalism and competition for individual professional success, a contemporary writer may be excused for not daring to "put it all together" just yet.

NOTES

1. Tom Burns, "The Revolt of the Privileged," *SSRC Newsletter,* No. 4 (November 1968): 5-11; "The Revolt of the Privileged: A Postscript," Manchester-Edinburgh University Study, Working Paper No. 1, n.d.

2. See, for example, Alexander Astin, "Personal and Environmental Determinants of Student Activism" *Measurement and Evaluation in Guidance* 1, no. 3 (Fall 1968): 149-62; M. B. Smith, "Morality and Student Protest" (Paper given at the annual convention of the American Psychological Association, September 1968); Jeanne Block, Norma Haan, and M. B. Smith, "Socialization Correlates of Student Activism," *Journal of Social Issues* 25 (November 1969): 143-77; M. B. Smith, Norma Haan, and Jeanne Block, "Social-Psychological Aspects of Student Activism," *Youth and Society* 1, no. 3 (1970); D. C. Westby and R. C. Braungart, "The Alienation of Generations and Status Politics: Alternate Explanations of Student Political Activism," in Robert S. Sigel, ed., *Learning about Politics: Studies in Political Socialization* (New York: Random House, 1968). Also, Richard E. Peterson, *The Scope of Organized Student Protest in 1964-1965* (Princeton, N.J.: Educational Testing Service, 1965); Richard E. Peterson, *The Scope of Organized Student Protest in 1967-1968* (Princeton, N.J.: Educational Testing Service, 1968); Richard Flacks, "The Liberated Generation: An Exploration of the Roots of Student Protest," *Journal of Social Issues* 23, no. 3 (1967): 52-75; Richard Flacks, "Student Activists: Result, not Revolt," *Psychology Today,* no. 1 (October 1967): 18-23, 61; Richard Flacks, "Social and Cultural Meanings of Student Revolt: Some Informal Comparative Observations," *Social Problems* 17 (Winter 1970): 340-57; Seymour Martin Lipset, "Student Politics and Higher Education in the United States," *Comparative Education Review* 10, no. 2 (June 1966): 320-49; Seymour Martin Lipset, "The Activists: A Profile," *The Public Interest,* no. 13 (Fall 1968): 39-51; Kenneth Keniston, "Psychological Issues in the Development of Young Radicals," in *The Dynamics of Dissent,* Scientific Proceedings of the American Academy of Psychoanalysis, vol. 13, ed. Jules H. Masserman (New York: Grune & Stratton, 1968): 82-97; Kenneth Keniston, *Young Radicals* (New York: Harcourt, Brace & World, 1968); and Seymour Martin Lipset and Philip Altbach, *Students in Revolt* (Boston: Houghton Mifflin, 1969).

3. Richard Flacks, "Student Power and the New Left: The Role of SDS" (paper presented at the Annual Meeting of the American Psychological Association, San Francisco, September 1968); Leonard L. Baird, "Who Protests: A Study of Student Activists," in ed. Julian Foster and Durward Long, *Protest! Student Activism in America* (New York: Morrow & Co., 1970), pp. 123-133; Lipset, "The Activists," note 2, pp. 50-51; William S. Aron, "Student Activism of the 1960's Revisited: A Multivariate Analysis Research Note," *Social Forces,* 52, no. 3 (March 1974): 408-14.

4. For indirect support of this finding, see excerpts of the keynote address delivered to the sixty-eighth annual convention of the National Catholic Educational Association by the Reverend Theodore M. Hesburgh, partial text appearing in *The Boston Globe*, April 30, 1971, in which Father Robert Drinan is quoted by Hesburgh as saying: "In my fourteen years in the Civil Rights movement, in and out of government, I have met surprisingly few Catholics, although our schools educate millions annually, presumably in Christian values relevant to the problems of our day. I do receive a surprisingly large number of hate letters from Catholic ethnics every time I put in a good word for blacks or Chicanos. . . . The young, thank God, largely do not share these ugly prejudices of their elders. . . . We have the wonderful opportunity of reversing past studies which show our students to be singularly undistinguished in their values relating to human equality following years of Catholic education." The finding is reported in Astin, "Personal and Environmental Determinants," pp. 160–62.

5. Baird, "Who Protests," p. 131. Although the date of the survey upon which the study is based is not given, it appears to have taken place sometime during 1966–67.

6. Flacks, "Who Protests: Social Bases of the Student Movement," in Julian Foster and Durward Long, *Protest! Student Activism in America* (New York: Morrow, 1970), pp. 140, 144.

7. In a study of Columbia University faculty attitudes toward the Spring 1968 student strike, Stephen Cole and Hannelore Adamsons found also that Jews and apostates, Democrats and Socialists, children of professionals, women, and the young were most likely to support the demonstration. See "Professional Status and Faculty Support of Student Demonstrations," *Public Opinion Quarterly* 34, no. 3 (Fall 1970): 389–94.

8. Lipset and Altbach, *Students in Revolt*, "Introduction," p. xix. See also Martin Trow, "Reflections on the Transition from Mass to Universal Higher Education," *Daedalus* 99, no. 1 (Winter 1970): 1–42; and Max Heirich, *The Spiral of Conflict* (New York: Columbia University Press, 1971).

9. See, for example, Riley Dunlap, "Radical and Conservative Student Activists: A Comparison of Family Backgrounds," *Pacific Sociological Review* 13, no. 3 (Summer 1970): 171–81; and Milton Mankoff and Richard Flacks, "Changing Social Base of the American Student Movement," *Student Protest*, ed. Philip G. Altbach and Robert Laufer (Philadelphia: American Academy of Political and Social Science, 1971), p. 395.

10. A number are reviewed in a paper by Lewis M. K. Long, "A Typology of College Students with Special Attention to the Student Activist," prepared for the Southeastern Psychological Association Meeting, New Orleans, February 1969.

11. Richard E. Peterson, "The Student Left in American Higher Education," *Daedalus* 97, no. 1 (Winter 1968): 293–317.

12. Lewis S. Feuer, *The Conflict of Generations: The Character and Significance of Student Movements* (New York: Basic Books, 1969).
    For critiques of Feuer, see Seymour L. Halleck, "Hypotheses of Student

Unrest," in Foster and Long, *Protest!*, pp. 105–22; and Robert Liebert, *Radical and Militant Youth* (New York: Praeger, 1971), p. 166.

13. See, for example, Morton Levitt and Ben Rubenstein, "The Student Revolt: Totem and Taboo Revisited," *Psychiatry* 34, no. 2 (May 1971): 156–67, particularly p. 163: "We are not entirely happy with the Oedipal explanation . . . because we patently cannot at this time offer that which is crucial to the argument, the 'particularities.' . . ."

14. "A new generation, for us, always starts again with Oedipus," said Erik Erikson in "Reflections on the Dissent of Contemporary Youth," *Daedalus* 99, no. 1 (Winter 1970): 175. "Each new child appears to be a potential bearer of the Oedipal curse, and parricide remains a much more plausible explanation of the world's ill than does filicide," he remonstrated.

15. For comments on the failure of writers on student activism to pay attention to the phenomenon of rightist activism, see Lipset, "Introduction," in Lipset and Altbach, *Students in Revolt*, p. xxii.

16. See, for instance, Martin Oppenheimer, "The Student Movement as a Response to Alienation," *Journal of Human Relations* 16, no. 1 (First Quarter 1968): 1–16; Edward Sampson, "Student Activism and the Decade of Protest," *Journal of Social Issues* 23, no. 3 (1967): 1–33; Bertram S. Brown, M.D., "Alienation and Revolt: Rebels without a Cause?" a dialogue held between Dr. Brown and the Reverend William Sloane Coffin, Jr., at the Fourth Annual New York Congress for Mental Health, New York City, October 1968; D. L. Westby and R. C. Braungart, "The Alienation of Generations" in Sigel, *Learning about Politics* (see note 2); Alice R. Gold, Lucy N. Friedman, and Richard Christie, "The Anatomy of Revolutionists," *Journal of Applied Social Psychology* 1, no. 1 (1971): 26–43; Samuel Lubell, "That Generation Gap," *The Public Interest*, no. 13 (Fall 1968): 52–60; and Kenneth Keniston, "The Sources of Student Dissent," *Journal of Social Issues* 23, no. 3 (1967): 108–37. An analysis of alienation also appears as part of a more comprehensive study in Theodore Roszak, *The Making of a Counter-Culture* (Garden City, N. Y.: Doubleday, 1968). See also Robert Kavanaugh, "The Grim Generation," *Psychology Today*, October 1968, in which activists are divided between "malevolent dreamers" determined to overthrow all authority with little regard for means or consequences and "benevolent dreamers" who, having passed through their identity crisis, pursued nonmaterialist goals with high idealism.

17. Erik H. Erikson, *Identity, Youth and Crisis* (New York: Norton, 1968), Chapter 6, "Toward Contemporary Issues: Youth," p. 242.

18. Roszak, *Counter-Culture*, pp. 58–66.

19. Kenneth Keniston, *The Uncommitted* (New York: Harcourt Brace, 1965); Keniston, *Young Radicals* (see note 2); Keniston, "Sources of Social Dissent" (see note 17); Keniston, "You Have to Grow Up in Scarsdale to Know How Bad Things Really Are," *New York Times Magazine*, April 27, 1969.

20. Keniston, "Development of Young Radicals," (see note 2), pp. 84–88. Robert Liebert, in *Radical and Militant Youth* (New York: Praeger, 1971), also reports

that a series of interviews he had with fifty Columbia students conducted during the disorders of spring 1968 revealed that a predominance of activists were characterized by "principled morality."

21. Erikson, *Identity*, p. 172.

22. Richard E. Peterson's study of the scope of protest in 1967–68 revealed no increase in proportions of activists within student bodies on campuses, but the number of colleges reporting student left groups almost doubled between 1965 and 1968. See Peterson, *Organized Protest in 1967-1968*, Table 3.

23. Talcott Parsons, *Essays in Sociological Theory* (New York: Free Press, 1954), Chapter 5, "Age and Sex in the Social Structure of the United States"; S. N. Eisenstadt, *From Generation to Generation* (New York: Free Press, 1956).

24. See, for instance, Sampson, "Student Activism" (note 16) and Lipset, "The Activists" (note 2); and Lubell, "Generation Gap" (note 16).

25. Nathan Glazer, " 'Student Power' in Berkeley," *The Public Interest*, no. 13 (Fall 1968): 3–21.

26. Bennett M. Berger, "The New Stage of American Man—Almost Endless Adolescence," *New York Times Magazine*, November 2, 1969.

27. From a commencement address delivered at Michigan State University in the Fall of 1969 by Kingman Brewster, Jr. For a similar argument, see Martin Trow, "Reflections on the Transition" (note 8), pp. 27–28: "the discipline and the faculty itself are divided on the relative importance of technical training, on one hand, and a broad general education and familiarity with the literature of other fields of study, on the other. This reflects an older struggle within universities between gentlemanly, aristocratic attitudes toward learning and the conception of the discipline as a body of knowledge that grows by patient systematic inquiry employing the technical apparatus of scholarly and scientific research. The disdain for 'narrow technical studies' or professional training, as well as for the kinds of research that lead to a successful academic career, is common both to the gentlemanly conception of the university as well as to these (a new breed) graduate students. . . ."

28. Flacks, "Social and Cultural Meanings of Revolt" (note 2), pp. 345–57.

29. Jill Conway, "Styles of Academic Culture," *Daedalus* 99, no. 1 (Winter 1970): 43–55.

30. Ibid.

31. Leonore O'Boyle, "The Problem of an Excess of Educated Men in Western Europe, 1800–1850," *Journal of Modern History* 42, no. 4 (December 1970): 471–95.

32. See Priscilla Robertson, "Students on the Barricades: Germany and Austria, 1848," *Political Science Quarterly* 84, no. 2 (June 1969): 367–79.

33. Edgar Z. Friedenberg, "The University Community in an Open Society," *Daedalus* 99, no. 1 (Winter 1970): 56–74.

34. Glazer, " 'Student Power' " (note 25), pp. 20–21.

35. Lipset, "Possible Effects of Student Activism," *Students in Revolt,* pp. 506–21.

36. See, for example, Keniston, "You Have to Grow Up in Scarsdale" (note 19).

37. See George F. Kennan, *Democracy and the Student Left* (Boston: Atlantic-Little Brown, 1968) for a contradictory point of view.

38. For a defense of the liberal, nonviolent political approach to such problems, see Sidney Hook, "Who is Responsible for Campus Violence?" *Saturday Review,* April 19, 1969. For a short history as well as a vigorous defense of student radicalism in the United States, see Jerome Skolnick, *The Politics of Protest* (New York: Bantam Books, 1969). For a justification of violence carried out by students, see Richard E. Hyland, "In Defense of Terrorism," *Harvard Crimson,* October 22, 1969.

39. Stephen Spender, *The Year of the Young Rebels* (New York: Vintage, 1969), p. 104.

40. See Burns, "Revolt of the Privileged" (note 1).

41. Joseph A. Califano, Jr., *The Student Revolution: A Global Confrontation* (New York: Norton, 1969).

42. Burns, "The Revolt—A Postscript" (note 1).

43. Nathan Adler, "Kicks, Drugs, and Politics," Address, Psychology Section, Western Regional Meeting, American Public Health Association, Oakland, California, June 1969.

44. Alfred de Musset, *Confession of a Child of the Century* (New York: Current Literature Publishing Co., 1910), p. 20.

45. Richard Flacks, "Strategies for Radical Social Change," *Social Policy* 1, no. 6 (March/April 1971). The book by Flacks, *Youth and Social Change* (Chicago: Markham, 1971) expands on the same ideas.

46. See *The Chronicle of Higher Education,* May 31, 1971, p. 1.

47. See Foster and Long, *Protest!,* for seven case studies selected because they represented the more unusual incidents: Indiana, Wisconsin, San Francisco State, University of Colorado, Princeton, Howard, and Ohio State.

48. Leon Eisenberg, "Student Unrest: Sources and Consequences," *Science* 167 (March 1970): 1688–92.

49. Reported in *The Chronicle of Higher Education,* Nov. 30, 1970, p. 3.

50. Clark Kerr, "Governance and Functions," *Daedalus* 99, no. 1 (Winter 1970): 108–21. For examples of the arguments of student dissidents and their faculty sympathizers, see Friedenberg, "The University Community" (note 33); Conway, "Styles of Academic Culture" (note 29); *Dissent and Disruption* (New York: McGraw-Hill, 1971), a report and recommendations by the Carnegie Commission on Higher Education; or Leon Eisenberg (note 48), who noted, "let it likewise be recognized that compliant silence is also a political act. . . ."

51. Daniel Bell, "Columbia and the New Left," *The Public Interest,* no. 13 (Fall

1968): 61–101. Zbigniew Brzezinski, "Revolution and Counterrevolution (But Not Necessarily about Columbia!)," *New Republic* 158, no. 22 (June 1, 1968): 23–25. Brzezinski felt that the problem was that authorities did not act quickly and effectively enough.

See also Charles Frankel, *Education and the Barricades* (New York: Norton, 1968), pp. 78–79: "It is not easy to exaggerate the fragility of the understandings on which a university depends. Universities have to be so organized that force and violence are never present in them. . . . In politics, as well as its intellectual affairs, its manners outside classrooms as well as inside them, have to give a place to reason which reason does not have in other domains of human activity. The use of any tactic which substitutes physical pressure or emotional duress for reason is an assault on this basic ethic."

52. Eisenberg, "Student Unrest" (note 48), pp. 1691–92.

53. Howard S. Becker, ed., *Campus Power Struggle* (Chicago: Aldine, 1970), p. 11.

54. Everett Lee Hunt, *The Revolt of the College Intellectual* (Chicago: Aldine, 1963), p. 160.

55. See Kerr, "Governance and Functions" (note 50), p. 112.

56. See Peterson, *Scope of Protest, 1967–1968,* Table 1.

57. Bell, "Columbia and the New Left" (note 51), p. 95.

58. See *Crisis at Columbia: Report of the Fact-Finding Commission Appointed to Investigate the Disturbances at Columbia in April and May, 1968* (New York: Vintage, 1968); Jerry L. Avorn and members of the staff of the *Columbia Daily Spectator, Up Against the Ivy Wall: A History of the Columbia Crisis* (New York: Atheneum, 1969); Ellen Kay Trimberger, "Columbia: The Dynamics of a Student Revolution," in Becker, *Campus Power Struggle,* pp. 27–55; Allen Barton, "Student and Faculty Response to the Columbia Crisis," Bureau of Applied Social Research, Columbia University, June 1968.

59. James McEvoy and Abraham Miller, "Crisis at San Francisco State," in Becker, *Campus Power Struggle,* pp. 57–77. For an analysis of the Kent State crisis, see Philip K. Tompkins and Elaine Vanden Bout Anderson, *Communications Crisis at Kent State* (New York: Gordon and Breach, 1971).

60. Carnegie Commission on Higher Education, *Dissent and Disruption: Proposals for Consideration by the Campus* (New York: McGraw-Hill, 1971); *The Report of the President's Commission on Campus Unrest* (New York: Arno Press, 1970).

61. *The American Association for Higher Education College and University Bulletin* 23, no. 3 (November 1, 1970) reported that over the previous two years, thirty states took legislative action of some type relating to campus unrest, of which twenty-two enacted laws requiring penalties or fines or imprisonment upon conviction.

62. Carnegie Commission, *Dissent,* p. 37.

63. Heirich, *Spiral of Conflict* (note 8).

64. Philip G. Altbach and Robert S. Laufer, eds., *The New Pilgrims* (New York: McKay, 1972), "Introduction," pp. 1–9

65. Samuel R. Friedman, "Perspectives on the American Student Movement," *Social Problems* 20, no. 3 (Winter 1973): 283–99.

66. Albert K. Cohen, "The Social Problems of the University: Two Crises of Legitimacy," *Social Problems* 20, no. 3 (Winter 1973): 275–83.

67. See, for example, Kenneth Keniston, *Youth and Dissent* (New York: Harcourt Brace Jovanovich, 1971), a compilation of essays written over a decade of dissent.

3/The organizational context of protest

James L. Norr

The scope and intensity of student protest of the 1960s created a
dramatic departure from behavior previously expected of college
students. Seven student generations and three decades of campus
quiet separated the protests of the sixties from the pacifist demonstrations
against military build-up in the late 1930s.[1] The locations of these
collective political actions were distinctive, and to understand student
protest of the sixties, one must know where it emerged. Demonstrations
began in 1964–65 on some two hundred and twenty college campuses.
That figure represents more than a fifth of the four-year colleges in
America, and it indicates a scope of activity beyond the highly publicized
events at Berkeley, Chicago, Columbia, Michigan, and Wisconsin.[2]
Moreover, these protests did not occur randomly, but at campuses with
certain similarities. These campuses had organizational features that
actually fostered the emergence of protest. How these campuses differed
from those that were quiet reveals much about the nature and meaning of
student unrest.

This identification of the organizational context of protest
complements the perspectives on student unrest in other chapters. The
cultural and historical forces that account for the timing of protests are
dealt with elsewhere in this volume, but especially in Chapter One.
Concern for colleges and universities as organizations is a level of analysis
between the two major foci of Laufer and Light's opening essay—
institutional change in families, higher education, and society politics on
the one hand and the effects of these changes for socialization, personalities, and actions of individual students and faculty on the other. These
two spheres intersect on the campus. The organizational context of
student protest describes the main arena for student confrontation with
faculty, administrators, and outside groups. Knowledge of this arena

provides background needed for understanding the evolution of protests as detailed in the accounts of tactics, by Light, and of factions, by Spiegel. Specifying the nature of the organizations where students, faculty, and administrators interacted makes these essays more meaningful.

HYPOTHESES FROM PREVIOUS RESEARCH

Beyond acknowledging the obvious fact that student protest did, indeed, occur on college campuses, few researchers have studied the campus context of student unrest.[3] Although they do not deal directly with organizational context, studies from each of the four major stages of research identified in Levin and Spiegel's review imply certain characteristics of American institutions of higher education were crucial for the emergence of student protest. These studies suggest important organizational features to investigate.

CHARACTERISTICS OF THE PROTESTERS

The most direct inference from the studies made of pioneer student protesters is that demonstrations are likely to emerge on campuses where college or student selection patterns result in large numbers of activist students.[4] The larger the student body, the greater the possibility of large numbers of activists. Beyond that, activists tend to have better grades, higher social status, and more interest in the politically relevant subject areas of the social sciences and humanities than nonactivists.[5] High average college-entrance test scores and concentrations of majors in politically relevant fields of study indicate students recruited for academic quality and political interest. A good indicator of student body social status is more difficult. But it seems reasonable to expect high status students not to be discouraged by high tuition and expenses of travelling out of state to go to college.

ISSUES PROTESTED

Studies of the issues protested emphasized the political character of student unrest and its relation to national political debates, especially on issues of social justice and the military. This line of research suggests protest emerges on campuses where faculty and students are concerned with social problems and are politically active. These should be the campuses with students involved in the civil rights movement, the Peace Corps, college political organizations, and getting controversial speakers on campuses.

Large, research-oriented universities tend to be more politically active. Faculty members engaged in research, especially in the social sciences and humanities, are likely to be involved with current social problems.[6] Large campuses with a diverse faculty and student body holding a wide spectrum of political views generate issues around which groups can mobilize. Such diversity, related to the number of majors available to undergraduates, should increase student political activity. Large size can also create an atmosphere of impersonality and lack of concern for student interests. Larger universities are more likely to have a research-oriented faculty and to make use of large numbers of teaching assistants. Greater visibility of research can provoke questions about whether resources should be allocated to teaching or to research. Students who perceive that their own interests are being sacrificed are more likely to engage in protest.

DYNAMICS OF AN EVOLVING PROTEST

A large student body and a high proportion of students living off campus increase isolation and decrease communication between students and faculty and administrators, thus heightening the possibility of political mobilization and protest.[7]

Tolerance of political debate and activities by administrators and faculty is a necessary condition for political mobilization. Student protest is a form of political expression, albeit a noninstitutionalized form. As such it is not likely to take place where the prevailing attitude of authorities toward established forms of student political expression is one of intolerance. Protest will not occur where the cost of action is too high. Where administrators think student organizations should not publicly avow unpopular viewpoints or engage in political action, where the appearance of controversial speakers is questioned, or where student political organizations are not permitted, there is likely to be little political activity and, consequently, little protest.

Faculty quality, secular control, and location outside the southern United States should increase political tolerance. High quality faculty tend to be more tolerant and politically active.[8] Colleges serving limited, parochial interests are less likely to be tolerant of diverse political views than campuses with a cosmopolitan orientation. Secular colleges appeal to a wider spectrum of students and faculty than denominational colleges and should be more tolerant. Also, religious organizations in general tend to be less tolerant, and survey studies show a consistent negative relation between religiosity and individual tolerance.[9] Colleges and universities located in the South are expected to be less tolerant than those in other regions. The South is more provincial than other regions, and agricultural and traditional conservative values institutionalized in the South are antithetical to tolerance.

HISTORICAL AND CULTURAL ANALYSIS OF STUDENT UNREST

Campuses in the forefront of institutional changes in higher education should be the first to experience protest. American higher education has become a national, integrated, and stratified system dominated by the major Ph.D. granting universities which emphasize meritocratic, universalistic, cosmopolitan, and professional values.[10] It is the large secular universities which command greater resources of money, books, and equipment, and attract better students and distinguished research oriented faculty members who tend to have tolerant attitudes. This fourth stage of research on student unrest provides additional support for the major expectations developed from earlier studies. A low degree of tolerance, political activity, and protest can be expected at institutions which are: small, not research oriented, not able to recruit distinguished faculty, and more oriented toward local or special interest groups such as those in the South, under religious control, and emphasizing training of teachers, engineers, and other non-arts-and-sciences professionals.

METHODS

To investigate these hypotheses we assembled data for the 1,000 four-year, accredited colleges and universities in the United States on: the emergence of the first war-related protests in 1964–65, student involvement in the Peace Corps and the civil rights movement, campus political activity, tolerance, and organizational features.[11] Two questionnaire studies of deans of students, college presidents, student body presidents, and student newspaper editors provided the measures of protest on war-related and other issues, involvement in the civil rights movement, campus political activity, and tolerance.[12] College directories and organizational reports supplied information on student involvement in the Peace Corps, location of the institution, denominational affiliation, faculty quality (salary levels, percentage of faculty with doctorates, and peer ratings of graduate faculty), relative numbers of teaching assistants and full-time research faculty, number of available undergraduate majors, size of student body, distribution of majors across fields, average entrance test scores, tuition and fees, percentage of students from out of state and percentage of students living on campus.[13] These data have substantial advantages over the prior, very limited studies of organizational context.[14] More accurate representation of the study population and inclusion of more relevant variables increase the credibility of the results.

Correlating protest with the indicators of organizational context is the first step in assessing the hypotheses developed from the research on student unrest. In addition to providing an understanding of the context of student unrest, verification of hypothesized organizational determinants of protest generated from other perspectives would increase the credibility of these other analyses. The organizational predictors of protest are related to one another, so we go beyond the zero-order associations and examine multiple regressions including all the predictors simultaneously. This procedure makes possible an evaluation of the direct impact of each variable and some understanding of the causal relationships among the variables.[15]

PROTEST, POLITICAL ACTIVITY, AND TOLERANCE

Campuses where war protests emerged in 1964-65 were likely also to have protest on other issues and to have students involved in other political causes. There are significant positive correlations between war protest and protest over college policies (r = .24), the proportion of students working and demonstrating for civil rights (r = .38), and the proportion of Peace Corps applicants (r = .34) and volunteers (r = .36). Civil rights activity and involvement in the Peace Corps share with protest the quality of being activist political expressions. Each activity requries conscientious questioning of existing systems and taking an active stand on behalf of an ideal. Such activities are found at the same campuses because they are similar and are influenced by similar organizational features of colleges and universities.[16]

The best single predictor of protest is an index of the level of campus political activity (r = .55). A protest, however short-lived, is a political organization needing people to carry out leadership and other organizing functions such as internal communication and acquisition of such resources as money, space, paper, media coverage, and outside support. The more political activity present on a campus, the more likely it is that people with these skills will be available. Political activity sensitizes people to a set of beliefs and ideologies. With such a shorthand way of perceiving events and attaching blame to appropriate other parties, collective political action is less likely to occur.[17] In addition to providing training in political roles and relevant ideologies, experience in campus political activities also provides occasions for students to act as a group and become aware of their collective identity.

Political tolerance on a campus affects both the level of political activity and the emergence of protest (correlations of .43 and .34 respectively). Tolerance increases the likelihood of protest primarily by affecting the level of political activity.[18] Rules against political acts and prohibitions against the presence of political organizations or personalities on campus depress the level of political activity and make protest less likely to occur. Students can form political organizations only if those in power allow them to do so. If the sanctions for acting are perceived as too costly, students—or any other group—will not act. Protest does not occur at the most restrictive colleges.

STRUCTURAL CHARACTERISTICS AND PROTEST

Relations among the structural characteristics and tolerance of political views, political activity, and protest are summarized in Table 3.1 Correlation coefficients show the direction and size of the total effect of each feature of college organization. All hypothesized indicators of organizational context are significantly correlated with protest, political activity, and tolerance in predicted directions with only one exception. The percentage of students living on campus is not related to degree of political activity or protest (i.e., the correlations are not significantly different from zero). The features of colleges with the greatest effects, as shown by the largest zero-order correlations, are: level of political activity, tolerance, faculty quality, size, and student academic potential.

In discussing the impact of structural characteristics on tolerance, political activity, and protest, we touched on some of the associations among the structural variables. Such associations are most likely with features related to size, diversity, and quality. Large campuses tend to have high quality faculty (r = .53), more majors available to undergraduates (r = .72), and a greater proportion of teaching assistants (r = .54). Where there are more majors available to undergraduates, there is a greater proportion of teaching assistants (r = .57). A high quality faculty is associated with students of higher academic potential (r = .52), more majors available to undergraduates (r = .51), relatively more teaching assistants (r = .56), and a greater proportion of faculty engaged in full-time research (r = .47). Schools with high tuitions tend to recruit better students (r = .63) and more out-of-state students (r = .60). And where there are more out-of-state students, more students live on campus (r = .53).[19] This set of interrelationships prompts the following questions: Which structural characteristics have a direct impact on protest? Which characteristics have an indirect impact on protest because they affect either tolerance or political activity? And which structural factors are correlated with tolerance, political activity, and protest only because they are related to other factors? The regression analyses summarized in Table 3.1 provide some answers to these questions.[20]

Quality and cosmopolitan orientation are major determinants of faculty and administrators values reflected in tolerance present on campus. The absence of negative sanctions for student political acts represents a commitment to tolerance of dissent and acceptance, if not encouragement, of the questioning of existing social policies. More

TABLE 3.1 ORGANIZATIONAL CONTEXT OF PROTEST (N = 700)

Indicators of Organizational Context	Total Effects: Correlation Coefficient (r)[a]			Direct Effects: Standardized Partial Regression Coefficient (b*)		
	Tolerance	Political Activity	Protest	Tolerance	Political Activity	Protest
Denominational Control	-.36	-.17	-.12	-.40[b]	-.01	-.02
Location in the South	-.26	-.13	-.18	-.27[b]	.02	-.06
Faculty Quality	.37	.56	.49	.19[b]	.11[b]	.20[b]
Size	.21	.45	.33	.06	.30[b]	.02
# Available Undergraduate Majors	.17	.44	.32	-.02	.09[b]	.05
% Teaching Assistants	.21	.44	.31	.01	.10[b]	-.04
% Full-time Research	.15	.29	.25	-.01	.00	.02
Politically Relevant Majors	.14	.22	.15	.13[b]	.16[b]	.01
Student Academic Potential	.28	.38	.33	.04	.09[b]	.03
Tuition & Fees	.16	.20	.18	-.03	.06	.03
% Out-state	.15	.16	.14	.10[b]	.10[b]	.05
% Living On-campus	.13	.05	.01	-.01	-.02	-.06
Tolerance	—	.43	.34	—	.22[b]	.07
Political Activity	—	—	.55	—	—	.35[b]
				$R^2 = .33$[c]	$R^2 = .47$[c]	$R^2 = .37$[c]

[a] All correlation coefficients $> |.05|$ are significant, $p < .05$.

[b] Regression coefficient is significant, $p < .05$.

[c] Coefficient of determination is significant, $p < .01$.

distinguished faculty, and those who work in the social sciences and humanities rather than in professional, education or technical fields tend to hold these values. They are more likely to be present at higher quality, nationally-oriented universities. For faculty at these institutions, questioning the *status quo* is important in both scholarship and politics. The value of tolerance is institutionalized at the top colleges and universities, the stratum of American higher education characterized by secular control, location outside the South, and a high quality faculty. These three characteristics have the largest regression coefficients for tolerance.

In addition to the direct effect of tolerance on political activity, three structural characteristics with an impact on tolerance also increase political activity directly. The proportion of students majoring in politically relevant areas, faculty quality, and the percentage of out-of-state students all have significant regression coefficients for political activity as well as for tolerance. Another four characteristics increase campus political activities, but have little impact on tolerance of diverse views. Large size, diversity of available undergraduate majors, percentage of teaching assistants, and high entrance test scores all have regression coefficients that are low for tolerance but substantial and significant for political activity. These seven features increase recruitment of activist students and the ease with which people can mobilize for political action. By increasing political activity, they indirectly foster the emergence of protest.

Size has the greatest direct impact on political activity ($b^* = .30$). A large student body means more political activity both because there are likely to be more activist students present and because more people holding diverse opinions makes it easier to assemble sufficient numbers for a meaningful demonstration.

One result of greater size is diversity in the number of majors available to undergraduates. It is this kind of diversity, resulting from greater size, rather than from bureaucratic impersonality, that is most important for protest. Size, number of majors, and use of teaching assistants have little effect on the emergence of protest beyond their impact on the level of political activity (regression coefficients of .02, .05, −.04 respectively). In fact, use of teaching assistants tends to lessen the likelihood of protest when level of political activity, size, and the other relevant variables are simultaneously taken into account in the regression analysis. Faculty research seems to be another aspect of diversity increasing political mobilization by focusing attention on relevant issues. These data do not support the interpretation of involvement in research increasing the likelihood of protest because of faculty disengagement from undergraduates. Rather, the opposite conclusion is more probable.

Greater faculty research means undergraduates are more likely to be highly involved in a greater diversity of ideas, including politically relevant issues, through faculty activities.

Student activists are disproportionately recruited from the group of better-than-average students. Like their faculty counterparts, these students have a greater commitment to intellectual values and to questioning the *status quo*. Liberal political views of faculty and students and their work in comparing and questioning social and political arrangements make disciplines in the social sciences and humanities more likely to have activists among their ranks. Their attitudes contrast sharply with the conservative, establishment and service orientations of students in professional, educational, and technical fields. Colleges where there are heavy concentrations of majors in social sciences and humanities and low concentrations in professional, educational, and technical fields consequently have more political activity. Out-of-state students are another source of activist recruits. Out-of-state students tend to be of higher social class and are less provincial in their outlook—two factors characteristic of the pioneer student activists. High tuition was also thought to make for higher status and thus more activist students, but its direct effect, separate from other variables, is close to zero.

The variables with the greatest direct impact on political activity are large size, quality faculty, and tolerance. They indirectly increase the likelihood of protest by increasing political activity. While other characteristics of colleges and universities attract large numbers of activists, size is the most important recruitment factor. Size and tolerance have the two largest independent effects on the level of political activity. Faculty quality has the largest total impact on political activity ($r = .56$). Most of that effect, however, is indirect; faculty quality increases political activity because it increases tolerance of diverse views. Only about one-fifth of the impact of faculty quality is separate from tolerance ($b^* = .11$) and increases political activity directly. High-quality faculty members themselves take part in the debate of national social and political issues, and their example and direct encouragement are important in getting students involved.

Our interpretations of these regression analyses are depicted in the model shown in Figure 3.1. The emergence of protest requires more than the presence of activists. Organizational features of a campus play an important and separate role. A cosmopolitan orientation resulting from such factors as secular control and location outside the South increases tolerance and, thus, indirectly increases the level of political activity and protest. Tolerance almost completely accounts for the effects of a cosmopolitan orientation, so that there are few direct effects on either political activity or protest. Features of college campuses reflecting size and diversity of interests do not affect tolerance but do affect campus political activity. Quality features increase political activity directly as well as indirectly by influencing the amount of tolerance present on a campus. Tolerance only increases the emergence of protest by its effect on legitimate campus political activities.

FIGURE 3.1 CAUSAL MODEL OF ORGANIZATIONAL CONTEXT OF PROTEST

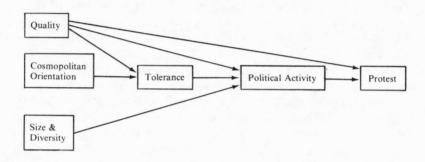

About half the effect on protest of structural features is indirect and results from the effects these features have on tolerance and political activity. There are some direct effects not accounted for by tolerance and political activity so that other intervening variables need to be added to the model. Faculty quality shows the clearest additional impact on protest.[21] This suggests the importance of incorporating the critical determinants of faculty support of protest as discussed by Light in Chapter Five in addition to the effect of faculty quality on tolerance and levels of political activity. The small additional effects of the region in which a college is located and the percentage of students living on campus suggest that some indicators of patterns of student interaction and the level of political activity in the surrounding area might be important variables to be included in an expanded model of protest. The discussions of protests as evolving social events in the other chapters of this volume indicate directions to pursue to improve the explanation of protest.

IMPLICATIONS

These findings are strong support for the implications of student unrest studies focusing on issues, tactics, historical and cultural trends, and the viewpoints of students, faculty, and administrators. Our results increase credibility of the analyses undertaken from these other perspectives found in the companion chapters of this volume.

The similarity between the organizational context of campus political activities in two recent historical periods and student unrest in the 1960s further strengthens the credibility of the results and interpretations we have presented. In the 1930s many students were sympathetic to labor's efforts to organize, in much the same way as students of the 1960s espoused the cause of Negro civil rights. There were trips to coal mining areas where students were harassed by local officials, a scene repeated thirty years later in the freedom rides. With the reemergence of Germany as a military power in the 1930s and the fear of war in Europe, students turned their attention from domestic issues to the international scene and began supporting pacifist causes, including the removal of ROTC from universities. This shift from domestic to international issues parallels the shift of the 1960s from civil rights to war-related protest, even to the focus on removing ROTC.

The height of the 1930s pacifist protest on college campuses was reached in 1934 and 1935. According to the most complete report of this period, 25,000 students left their classrooms on April 13, 1934 in a nationwide strike against war preparations. The next year, approximately 175,000 participated in similar demonstrations. At least 132 colleges and universities had demonstrations in 1934–1935.[22]

Sixty per cent of these colleges reporting a demonstration in 1934–1935 had a war-related protest in 1964–1965 as contrasted with only sixteen per cent for those with no recorded demonstration in the earlier period. We do not have direct data on the organizational characteristics of the colleges with protests, but there is evidence of the persistence in features of size, quality, location, and control over time.[23] The high correlation of protest in 1934–1935 with protest in 1964–1965 as well argues for the importance of the distinguishing organizational context of college campuses.

A second source of support for our findings and interpretations is Lazarsfeld and Thielens' study of social scientists at colleges and universities during the 1950s, *The Academic Mind.* A basic finding of *The Academic Mind* is that large, high-quality, secular colleges and universities were more likely to be characterized by tolerance. Each of these structural characteristics had an independent effect on the level of tolerance of social, especially political, non-conformity.

Faculty members who were tolerant were also likely to be politically involved, left or liberal, professional and cosmopolitan in their orientations, and productive in research. Lazarsfeld and Thielens argued that large, high-quality, secular institutions provided the resources and desirable working conditions which attracted distinguished, tolerant social scientists. It was at these institutions that there were more accusations against faculty for non-conformist political actions. Taking accusations as indicative of actual political behavior, we may argue that tolerance, quality, size, and secularity increase political activity.

The similarities between American higher education in the early 1950s reported by Lazarsfeld and Thielens (1958) and the situation in the middle 1960s is especially suggestive. In both cases, large, high-quality, elite institutions were both more tolerant and more politically active on national issues. And in both cases these institutions came under increasingly heavy attack from conservative and parochial elements in the society.

The structural features highlighted in this analysis of protest characterize relations of a campus as an organization to its environment. To explain levels of tolerance, political activity, and protest, the most important relationships have to do with control and access to resources which are distributed unequally, such as distinguished faculty, bright students, and research monies. Quality and a cosmopolitan orientation indicate where a college or university is in the higher education stratification system. The nature of the current system and the forces that created it are delineated by Laufer and Light in Chapter One. The higher its position, the more nationally valued resources such as high quality faculty a college has, the more tolerant it is. Involvement in intellectual pursuits that bring national prestige also means institutionalization of tolerant values. Tolerance encourages student political activity both by allowing student political groups to form and operate and by encouraging students to take a questioning and politically active stance.

Political activity is not solely a result of quality, a cosmopolitan orientation and a climate of tolerance. Also important are organizational features that affect student recruitment and generate politically relevant issues, especially the size of the student body. The level of political activity tends to be higher on a campus if the college has been successful in attracting students with activist attitudes. This is more likely for large, research-oriented universities and for colleges with high academic standards. In other words, political activity is likely to be high on campuses where there are large numbers of bright, politically aware, and nationally oriented students—students who resemble faculty members in their commitment to tolerance and questioning of existing conditions.

The emergence of student protest is influenced by two characteristics of social interaction at a college: tolerance of diverse views and the level of campus political activity. These two internal characteristics are, in large measure, determined by the external relations of a college or university and its success in acquiring resources vis a vis other organizations and its environment. Protest, political activity, tolerance, quality, cosmopolitan orientation, size, and diversity all reflect campus relations to the nationally stratified system of American higher education with its associated value system.

The similarity in the patterns of relationships of the 1930s, 1950s and 1960s underscores the importance of organizational context in collective political action. Cultural and unique historical situations may affect the total volume, intensity, or violence of protest. At the same time, fairly stable features of colleges and universities influence the probable location of collective political action. Relationships between protest and organizational context found in earlier time periods are likely to exist in the future. The focus on the organizational context of protest in this chapter offers a perspective to view the interface between changes in the larger society and changes in students and faculty, the actions of major contenders in protests, and the evolution of these conflict events detailed in other chapters.

NOTES

[1] See Wechsler (1935) and the historical discussions of student unrest in Chapters One and Two of this volume.

[2] Here and throughout this chapter our concern is with the emergence of war-related protest. The basic relationships reported here are similar for protest on other issues (see Norr, 1971). Also, it is important to distinguish between explaining the *emergence* of protest and explaining either protest *intensity*—the level of involvement—or protest *violence*—the means of conflict used. Factors crucial for the emergence of conflict may not be related or may be related in different, including opposite, ways to the intensity or violence of the conflict. Dahrendorf (1959) predicts that conditions necessary for the emergence of protest tend to *lessen* the intensity and *lessen* the violence of conflict. In this analysis we deal only with the emergence of protest.

[3] There are some exceptions such as Blau and Slaughter (1971), Scott and ElAssal (1969), and Peterson (1966; 1968). However, each of these studies has serious difficiencies in either the restricted nature of the sample so that few or only selected types of colleges are represented or the limited number of variables included so competing hypotheses cannot be rejected or the dependent variable not being the emergence of protest but rather the seriousness or numbers involved in the protest.

[4] The relative proportion of activists in the student population may not be as important as the absolute number. The latter governs the availability of a "critical mass" of similar minded students who can give each other a sense of group identity and are able to staff, at least minimally, organizational roles required for political mobilization.

[5] See Levin and Spiegel's summary of this research in Chapter Two of this volume as well as Lipset and Wolin, 1965; Westby and Braungart, 1966; Matthews and

Prothro, 1966; Flacks, 1967; Bay, 1967; Keniston, 1967; Feldman and Newcomb, 1969.

[6]Lazarsfeld and Thielens, 1958; Lipset, 1970; Lipset and Ladd, 1970; Schuman and Laumann, 1967; Jencks and Riesman, 1968; Light, 1974.

[7]If student residences are distant and dispersed rather than close by the campus, cohesion is likely to be a problem, and there will be less political activity. See Heirich (1971) for an extended discussion of other environmental and timing factors that affect channeling of information necessary for political mobilization.

[8]See references in footnote 6.

[9]Stouffer, 1955, Lazarsfeld and Thielens, 1958; Lipset, 1960; 1970.

[10]Jenckes and Reisman, 1968; Light, 1974.

[11]The universe frame was taken from the Office of Education, *Directory of Higher Education*, 1961–62. Excluded were the federal military academics, seminaries, art schools, proprietary colleges and colleges with less than 100 students. Failure to respond to questionnaire items generated missing data on some variables, so that the effective sample is 700. See Norr (1971) for additional details on the study population and quality of the data.

[12]Peterson, 1966; Williamson and Cowan, 1966. The measure of protest includes striking; marching; sitting-, sleeping-, lying-, or teaching-in; or engaging in petition or letter-writing campaigns. The index of campus political activity includes the number of student political organizations and outside speakers, and participation in civil rights activities in the South in the preceding summer and in new-left student groups. The tolerance measure includes policies discouraging or prohibiting: discussion of controversial issues, political actions, and the presence of controversial speakers or political organizations on campus.

[13]American Association of University Professors, 1965; American Council on Education, 1964; Carter, 1966; Cass and Burnbaum, 1968; Hawes, 1966, Office of Education, 1959; 1961; 1965a; 1965b. For details on sources, coding, and index construction, see Norr, 1971. Because of its skewed distribution, size has been transformed to the common logarithm.

[14]See footnote 3.

[15]Details on the assumptions of these procedures, their relevance for these data, and similar results from alternative methods of analysis are available in Norr, 1971.

[16]Patterns of association similar to what we report below for war related protest are found between features of organizational context and involvement in civil rights and Peace Corps.

[17]Heirich (1971) shows in considerable detail how these aspects of political activity influenced the emergence of protest at Berkeley.

[18]The major effect of tolerance on protest is through political activity. Most of the effect is indirect. The direct effect of tolerance is quite small, $b^* = .07$. Eighty-nine percent of the total effect of tolerance is mediated by level of political activity.

Political sanctions at a college influence the probability of student protest mainly by affecting the amount of the more institutionalized forms of political activity. If the administration makes the costs of engaging in political activity high, then what are thought of as normal political activities are not likely to be present.

[19]There are no correlations among any of the structural characteristics greater than .50 in absolute value in addition to these that we have just reported.

[20]The analyses reported here assume a causal ordering, namely that structural characteristics are causally prior to tolerance, political activity and protest; tolerance is prior to political activity and protest; and political activity is prior to protest. For a discussion and some evidence for these assumptions, see Norr (1971); also cf. Heirich (1971), Darhendorf (1959), Blumer (1955), Gamson (1968), Smelser (1963; 1964), Turner (1964a; 1964b), Coleman (1951).

[21]Our results for quality and size differ from Scott and El Assal (1969) who report the effect of quality disappears when size is controlled. The greater importance of size over quality in their study most probably results from their restricted sample (only sixty-nine public institutions were included) and a different dependent variable—the *number* of demonstrations. On accounting for emergence versus scope and intensity, cf. footnote 2.

[22]Wechsler, 1935.

[23]Few colleges have changed regional location or denominational control, although some change among Protestant colleges may be expected in the latter. There has been a trend through the 1960s and 1970s to eliminate the following requirements (two of which must hold true for a college to be coded Protestant): religious representation on the governing board, chapel attendance, or a course in religion or the Bible. Carter's (1964) evidence suggests persistence in quality rankings over time, and our own data show high correlations for size and research orientation over time.

REFERENCES

American Association of University Professors. 1965. "The Economic Status of the Profession, 1964–65." *AAUP Bulletin* 51 (Summer): 270–301.

American Council on Education. 1964. *American Colleges and Universities,* 9th edition. Washington.

Bay, Christian. 1967. "Political and Apolitical Students: Facts in Search of Theory," *Journal of Social Issues,* XXIII, No. 3: 76–91.

Bayer, Allan E. and Alexander W. Astin. 1969. "Campus Disruption During 1968–1969." *American Council on Education Research Reports,* Vol. 4, No. 3.

Blau, Peter M. and Ellen L. Slaughter. 1971. "Institutional conditions and student demonstrations." *Social Problems* (Winter): 475–487.

Blumer, Herbert. 1957. "Collective Behavior." In J. Gitteer (ed.), *Review of Sociology.* New York: Wiley.

Blumer, Herbert. 1955. "Collective Behavior." In A.M. Lee (ed.), *Principles of Sociology.* New York: Barnes & Noble.

Boulding, Kenneth E. 1962. *Conflict and Defense*. New York: Harper and Row.

Brown, Donald R. 1967. Student Stress and the Institutional Environment. *Journal of Social Issues*, XXIII, No. 3: 92–107.

Carter, Allan M. 1966. *An Assessment of Quality in Graduate Education*. Washington: American Council on Education.

Cass, James and Max Birnbaum. 1968. *Comparative Guide to American Colleges*, 1968–1969 edition. New York: Harper and Row.

Clark, Burton R. and Martin Trow. 1966. "The Organizational Context." In Theodore Newcomb and Everett K. Wilson (eds.), *College Peer Groups*. Chicago: Aldine.

Coleman, James S. 1951. *Community Conflict*. New York: Free Press.

Dahrendorf, Ralf. 1958. "Out of Utopia: Towards a Re-orientation of Sociological Analysis." *American Journal of Sociology* 64 (September).

Dahrendorf, Ralf. 1959. *Class and Class Conflict in Industrial Society*. Stanford: Stanford University Press.

Feldman, Kenneth A. and Theodore M. Newcomb. 1969. *The Impact of College on Students*. 2 Vols. San Francisco: Jossey-Bass.

Flacks, Richard. 1967. "The Liberated Generation: An Exploration of the Roots of Student Protest." *Journal of Social Issues*, XXIII, No. 3: 52–57.

Gamson, William A. 1966. "Rancorous Conflict in Community Politics." *American Sociological Review* 31 (February): 71–81.

Gamson, William A. 1968. *Power and Discontent*. Homewood: Dorsey Press.

Gross, Edward. 1968. "Universities as Organizations: A Research Approach." *American Sociological Review* 33 (August): 518–44.

Hawes, Gene R. 1966. *New American Guide to Colleges*, 3rd edition. New York: Columbia University Press.

Heirich, Max A. 1971. *The Spiral of Conflict: Berkeley 1964–65*. New York: Columbia University Press.

Jencks, Christopher and David Riesman. 1968. *The Academic Revolution*. New York: Doubleday.

Kahn, Roger and William J. Bowers. 1970. "The Social Context of the Rank-and-File Student Activist: A Test of Four Hypotheses." *Sociology of Education* 43: 38–55.

Keniston, Kenneth. 1967. "The Sources of Student Dissent." *Journal of Social Issues*, XXIII, No. 3: 108–137.

Kruskal, Joseph B. 1968. "Special Problems of Statistical Analysis. II. Transformations of Data." *International Encyclopedia of the Social Sciences* 15: 183–191.

Ladd, Jr., Everett Carll. 1969. "Professors and Political Petitions." *Science* 163 (March): 1425–1430.

Lazarsfeld, Paul F. and Wagner Thielens, Jr. 1958. *The Academic Mind*. Glencoe: Free Press.

Light, Donald W. Jr. 1974. "Introduction: The Structure of the Academic Professions." *Sociology of Education*, 47 (Winter): 2–28.

Lipset, S.M. 1960. *Political Man*. Garden City: Doubleday.

Lipset, S.M. 1966. "Student Opposition in the U.S." *Government and Opposition* 1 (April): 351–74.

Lipset, S.M. 1970. "The Politics of Academia." *Perspectives on Campus Tensions.* Washington: American Council on Education.

Lipset, S.M. and Philip G. Altbach. 1966. "Student Politics and Higher Education in the United States." *Comparative Education Review* 10 (June): 320–49.

Lipset, S.M. and Everett Carll Ladd, Jr. 1970. "And What Professors Think." *Psychology Today* (November): 49–51.

Matthews, Donald R. and James W. Prothro. 1966. *Negroes and the New Southern Politics.* New York: Harcourt, Brace.

National Science Foundation. 1967. *Federal Support to Universities and Colleges, Fiscal Years 1963–1966.* Washington: U.S. Government Printing Office.

Office of Education. 1959. *Education Directory, 1959–60.* Washington: U.S. Government Printing Office.

Office of Education. 1961. *Education Directory, 1961–62.* Washington: U.S. Government Printing Office.

Office of Education. 1965a. *Education Directory, 1965–66.* Washington: U.S. Government Printing Office.

Office of Education. 1965b. *Faculty and Other Professional Staff in Institutions of Higher Education—Fall Term 1963–64.* Washington: U.S. Government Printing Office.

Sampson, Edward D. 1967. "Student Activism and the Decade of Protest." *Journal of Social Issues,* XXIII, No. 3: 1–33.

Scott, Joseph W. and Mohamed El Assal. 1969. "Multiversity, University Size, University Quality and Student Protest: An Empirical Study." *American Sociological Review* 34: 702–9.

Schuman, Howard and Edward O. Laumann. 1967. "Do Most Professors Support the War?" *Trans-action* (November): 32–35.

Smelser, Neil J. 1963. *Theory of Collective Behavior.* Glencoe: Free Press.

Smelser, Neil J. 1964. "Collective Behavior and Conflict—Theoretical Issues of Scope and Problems." *Sociological Quarterly* 5 (April): 116–22.

Stouffer, Samuel A. 1955. *Communism, Conformity, and Civil Liberties.* Garden City: Doubleday.

Turner, Ralph H. 1964a. "Collective Behavior and Conflict—New Theoretical Frameworks." *Sociological Quarterly* 5 (April): 122–32.

Turner, Ralph H. 1964b. "Collective Behavior." In Robert E.L. Faris (ed.), *Handbook of Modern Sociology.* Chicago: Rand McNally.

Wechsler, James. 1935. *Revolt on the Campus.* New York: Covici Friede.

Westby, David L. and Richard G. Braungart. 1966. "Class and Politics in the Family Backgrounds of Student Political Activists." *American Sociological Review* 31 (October): 690–722.

Williamson, E.G. and John L. Cowan. 1966. *The American Student's Freedom of Expression.* Minneapolis: University of Minnesota Press.

4/Directed resistance: the structure of tactics in student protest

Donald W. Light, Jr.

G iven the impressive uses of nonviolent protests in the United States over the past twenty years, there has been surprisingly little analysis of how nonviolence and passive resistance work. In her introduction to *Conquest of Violence* (1965:v), a lucid exploration into nonviolence, Joan Bondurant writes:

> The suffering and sacrifice of recent years in civil rights movements around the world have made no advance towards a philosophy of conflict. . . . Why, indeed, have civil rights movements given rise to so little reflection upon the nature of the politics of nonviolence? Perhaps we are bound by a paralysis born of intensive preoccupation with the pressing issues of the day.

Moreover, few sociologists have attempted to substantiate theories of conflict with empirical studies.[1] Here I shall explore the formal properties of certain nonviolent conflicts and apply them to a recurring social form, student protests on college and university campuses. To regard protest as a social form abstracts it from the concrete setting of people and passions; yet looking at it this way enables us to see what people and passions obscure, and thereby complements the other chapters of this book.

Thinking about nonviolent protest brings to mind Mahatma Gandhi. Because he practiced nonviolent direct action so masterfully, Gandhi's thoughts provide the framework for a study such as this one: what kinds of strategies, from his point of view, have American college students used?[2]

Mahatma Gandhi distinguished two major kinds of nonviolent direct action, *satyagraha* and *duragraha*. *Satyagraha* is a technique of pursuing truth through the selfless, total commitment of the participant. One must retain strict adherence to the truth and never waver from it, yet readily admit that one's approximation of truth may be limited or erroneous. It is possible to seek truth only through nonviolence; for only in nonviolence can one display the love of one's opponent and the good faith which seeking common truth requires. *Satyagraha* (truth-seeking) assumes that each party holds a limited view of the truth and that together both parties can find a larger truth; yet one must be ready to die for one's truth rather than to compromise in the face of blind attack. For Westerners, reconciliation means compromise; for Gandhi, reconciliation requires finding a mutual truth.

Whereas *satyagraha* involves interaction with the opponent, *duragraha* (nonviolent harassment) regards the opponent as an obstacle. One engages in *duragraha*, says Gandhi, from weakness (the wish without the power for violence) or as a preliminary to violence. The nonviolent appearance masks a violent intent. Gandhi observed that *duragraha*, in the case of irreconcilable differences, merely leads to a bitter stalemate or to violence; for no effort is made to seek larger truth. In contrast the technique of *satyagraha* is designed for just such a basic difference in the truth. *Duragraha* weakens respect for law and confidence in democratic processes. Gandhi, in using *satyagraha*, respected law and due process even though he broke the law when he thought it necessary.

This discussion makes it clear that virtually no Americans use *satyagraha* as a technique. Civil rights demonstrations, student protests, and other such phenomena employ *duragraha* and display the attitudes which accompany it. We shall equate *duragraha* with "directed resistance," because the usual term "passive resistance" fails to connote the aggression often involved.

When directed resistance *(duragraha)* succeeds and does not lead to violence or a stalemate, the success rests on there being shared values between those protesting and the group they protest against. For *duragraha* works when people inside the community employ it. That is to say, the protesting party depends on support from its opponents or from the surrounding community to bolster its weaker position. In the short run, this appears to be democratic; the community "votes" for one side or the other. But if (as is often the case) those using directed resistance do not accept a "vote" against them, the technique is not democratic. Democracy's core lies in working out differences to attain a larger unity; directed resistance turns to the community only when its ends are thereby served.

Since the success of directed resistance depends on shared sympathy, its effectiveness will vary with the issue being protested. Thus early protests for civil rights and free speech won the day, because of an underlying consensus about such rights. Essentially, the protesters had dramatized false practices of these communal values. Beginning in 1966, a national series of protests against cooperation with the Selective Service shifted the focus from an area of high consensus to one of mixed perspectives. Some felt that higher education naturally worked with the government on matters of national importance; to them cooperation with the Selective Service was a simple matter of bookkeeping. Yet as protesters raised a range of probing questions about the Vietnam War and the role of higher education in it, many members of the academic community agreed that the university must reexamine its ties with government. Another major shift began in 1968 as Indians, Chicanos, and blacks demanded special programs for admission and study. Guilt mixed with resentment as the communities responded to these new pressures, and such protests were only partially successful. Overall, this period of protest in American higher education witnessed a move from issues of *rights* to those of *power*.[3] When the weak challenge the strong, and the issue is power itself, *duragraha* rather than *satyagraha* is likely to prevail.

Yet of all issues, nothing so consistently unites an academic community as serious disruption of university life, especially by physical invasion. This means that if one party can define the situation as a disruption or an invasion by another party, the community will unite against the disrupters even on issues peripheral to that disruption. The Berkeley protests in 1964 illustrate this point. The issue of free speech received only some vague sympathy from faculty and students. Charges that the military-industrial complex was co-opting the university failed to evoke popular support. But the invasion of the campus by large numbers of police to attack and arrest students precipitated great community feeling, not only against the intruders but also in favor of the free speech movement and its rhetoric.

That disruption elicits the strongest response is unfortunate; for it puts a premium on making ends of means (amnesty for one side, "unwarranted force" for the other) and loses sight of the original goals of reform. When university officials and faculty react primarily to protest disruption, however, they are responding to the latent violence Gandhi noticed in directed resistance. Over the decade of the 1960s, such response brought this violence out.

The historical trend from rights to power is paralleled within the development of conflict on campus. As Max Heirich's analysis suggests (1971), each expansion of conflict brings with it a rephrasing of demands which challenge the organization and its tactics. Power and tactics become the issues. This analysis provides not only an explanation of how conflict develops during one crisis but also a way to understand the historical evolution of the protest movement during the 1960s (see the Scranton Report 1970: Ch. 1). Three "evolutionary forces" which shaped this history—the spiral of backlash, the frustrations of superficial reform, and the tendency for more seasoned protesters to speak for new ones—reflect the underlying nature of *duragraha* (see the Scranton Report 1970: Ch. 2).

Directed resistance

In considering the nature of nonviolent protest, we shall begin with a general sequence of events which illustrate the decision-points for each party. Usually the matter begins when a group of students (with faculty) complain that a policy or practice is unjust. A series of negotiations follow, lasting from a few weeks to years, which may or may not lead to satisfactory changes. At any given phase of these negotiations, the students may retire.[4]

Sometimes unsuccessful negotiations lead to an ultimatum. Its rigid nature changes the entire tone of the negotiations, and usually the administration balks at the "effrontery" of the demands. At times, the authorities agree to meet the demands. If, however, the administration resists, the students must decide whether they want to demonstrate. Out of pride and past frustrations, they usually begin a protest. It should be emphasized that protests are rarely undertaken lightly. In almost every case they unveil serious, often long-standing, inequities and "fossilizations" that could have been remedied long before.

Administrative response to protest is typically shaped by the ultimatum: "We will not negotiate under coercion." The protest continues. If the administration negotiates, the protest may or may not end, depending on the outcome. If negotiations fail or if the administration refuses to negotiate, the protest will continue, and usually the officials will threaten the use of force to end the demonstrations. The introduction of force by either side increases tension and shifts the focus from the initial issue(s) to those of power and violence. Threatening force usually stiffens the posture of the other side, although sometimes the opposition will retire.

If the protest continues, both sides prepare for violence, and it is virtually impossible for the administration not to employ the force it threatened to use. The major alternative is for both parties to announce the agreement which ends the protest. Once force is used by the administration, the protest will either end soon or escalate into larger waves, with the process repeating. Such multiple protests greatly disrupt the university but often result in little change on the major issues. This is true because multiple, escalated protests reflect tremendous rigidity and resistance to change on one or both sides.

These stages of protest, outlined, above, are often collapsed. For example, when a student group presents an ultimatum, or even when the group is airing its complaints, the authorities may all at once halt negotiations, have the leaders arrested, and impose a curfew. Or a student group may move from a complaint to demonstration so rapidly that the intermediate stages are barely recognizable.

Figure 1 outlines elementary decision points and strategies in student versus administration conflicts. One can trace any particular outcome through the figure; estimated probabilities have been added to suggest the likelihood of each strategy set. To date, no large-scale research has determined the actual probabilities of protest strategies. However, this model does complement Max Heirich's elaborate analysis (1971) of the Berkeley conflict in 1964. While his theory starts with organizational conditions leading to conflict, this model begins with conflict under way and outlines patterns of strategies. Heirich's analysis is complementary in that it concerns the conditions leading to different strategies.

Amid the possible outcomes, six are especially frequent. The first occurs when an "unjust" policy or practice is satisfactorily negotiated. Little publicity results from such early success, and although studies of protests neglect it, negotiated settlement occurs frequently.[5] Close analysis is needed of when and how potential protest issues are settled quietly and effectively. Instances of this outcome occurred after the assassination of Martin Luther King. Black students at many American colleges demanded more black professors, courses in Afro-American studies, more black students with accompanying scholarships, and other changes. Many administrations resisted these "arbitrary, unreasonable, belligerent demands." At some universities, however, the senior officers believed that the demands were just, if indeed not too little or too late, and they made costly efforts to implement the changes.

Another outcome postpones a successful negotiation to a more painful period. An "unjust" policy or practice is not satisfactorily negotiated, and the students present an ultimatum. The administration then balks, and a protest begins. Faced with a protest, the officials work out a settlement which ends the conflict for the time. This outcome reflects an initial intransigence which is overcome after the situation worsens, and often faculty are the key new element. For demonstration greatly increases "the likelihood of the issues in conflict between activists and administration being taken up by the faculty and student body as a whole" (Morgan in Foster and Long 1970: 371). From informal observations, it appears that administrations which balk at an ultimatum rarely

FIGURE 4.1   ESTIMATED PROBABLE OUTCOMES OF
STUDENT VS. ADMINISTRATION DISPUTES

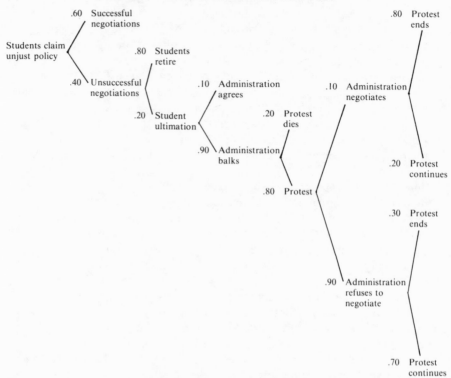

have the courage to negotiate later.[6] They feel that if they make any concessions, they are "capitulating" and that students will feel free to disrupt university life to get whatever they wish.

A third outcome worth noting follows the stages of the second up to a protest, but the authorities refuse to negotiate under such "coercion." Instead, they threaten to use force, and sometimes the threat of force suffices to break up the demonstration.[7] More commonly, however, the threat of force stiffens and expands the opposition so that actual force is used to break up the protest. This constitutes a fourth outcome, more frequent than the third.

A fifth outcome is a multiple escalation. When using force fails to end the protest, new demonstrations occur, largely around the issues of violence and force. They can easily expand outside the campus to involve the city or nation. The demonstrations at Berkeley in 1964, Waseda in 1966, Rome in 1966, Berlin in 1967, and Columbia in 1968 followed this form.[8] These five outcomes, plus the stand-off discussed later, constitute major forms of directed resistance.

FIGURE 4.1 (CONTINUED)

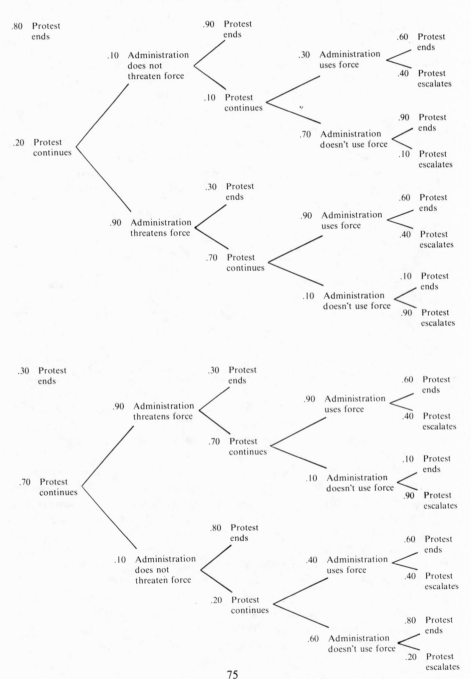

75

Directed resistance is a nonviolent confrontation of an aggrieved party against those in authority; it occurs when other, legitimate means of protest fail, and they fail because the authorities regard the demands as "impossible." While *both* parties may be nonviolent, at least the aggrieved party is. However, the aggrieved may be very aggressive in seeking and provoking the enemy. Thus the authorities can be more passive in behavioral terms that the aggrieved.

In directed resistance, the idea of two parties takes on a special meaning, for the aggrieved party sees itself at some level as part of the same community as the party it opposes. It is the technique of the insider, which is why the hundreds of student protests and the thousands of participants produced so little violence. If the aggrieved party does not assume common bonds, it does not use directed resistance but rather sabotage, assassination and guerilla warfare.

Directed resistance, then, is a tactic of persuasion and requires that each side try to define the situation for the larger community. The aggrieved define it in terms of an unjust policy or action; the authorities justify their policy and define the situation in terms of unreasonable disruption by the protesters. (The relevant "community" for each side is not entirely the same and may change, usually by expanding.) The protest, as it becomes established, takes on the features of a game with utility curves for each side. Those curves change as the issues change. For example, if the authorities succeed in persuading the community that the protest is unnecessarily disruptive, it will win over the community, because that issue stimulates greatest sympathy. If, however, the authorities arrest the protesters quickly, the definition of the situation may change to the unnecessary use of force, as it did at Berkeley in 1964 and Harvard in 1970. Such escalation, brought on by the authorities, also increases cohesion among the demonstrators and attracts sympathetic bystanders to their ranks.[9]

When directed resistance begins, and at each subsequent stage, the authorities judge the strength and sincerity of the conflict. Once the protest issues are considerd insincere and fabricated, negotiations cease. A bogus protest may be disregarded if it is weak. A strong protest deemed insincere, however, leads to severe conflict; for how can authorities negotiate bogus issues? If the issues are regarded as real, negotiation is likely in a protest of any size, so long as disruption does not grow until it obscures all other matters.

Real issues of contention come in two basic forms, those so basic as not to be open to compromise and those which are negotiable.[10] When protesters issue "non-negotiable demands," they serve notice that basic assumptions and values underlying a relationship must change. By selecting nonviolent resistance, they indicate a deep desire to preserve that relationship, not destroy it. Such people come closest to practicing *satyagraha;* for when confronted with the usual intransigence which follows non-negotiable demands, they maintain their position.

THE STAND-OFF

The Berkeley protests of 1964, in addition to foreshadowing the primary issues of 1966–68, suggested a new and effective strategy for college administrators. From Berkeley, many administrators learned not to complicate the issues. Berkeley's officials had gotten into a quagmire by sending in police to arrest students and extending their acts beyond the original issue. Underlying this feeling that it is best not to complicate matters is a law of nonviolent conflict. *The more passive party has a distinct advantage in persuading others of the justness of its cause.* Berkeley's officials failed, not by raising new issues, but by raising issues which made them appear much more aggressive and violent than the free speech movement.

This advantage of relative passivity helps to explain why authorities try to make protesters appear more aggressive than they are. For example, when authorities break up a sit-in, they will describe those sitting in as active and minimize their own aggressiveness. When limp sitters are seized and dragged off, the official announcement will say, "Students blocking entrances and obstructing traffic were removed by the police." By the same token, protesters will respond to arrest and violence with self-righteous, though perhaps genuine, shock.[11]

The *law of passive advantage* suggests that if the authorities are passive, the protesters will be defined as the aggressors and thus start at a disadvantage by their very act of protesting. This implication breaks down only when the protest issue, like Gandhi's salt campaign, has wide sympathy in the community. Then the authorities will appear weak and ineffectual.[12] Directed resistance yields a stand-off when the authorities refuse to take action against those resisting but *also* refuse to yield to the demands made. In a typical case, the aggrieved party resists, and the authorities cry foul. They claim they stand ready to negotiate as soon as the demonstrators cease their "irrational and coercive actions." In this case, the demonstrators usually end the protest themselves, and authorities lightly reprimand them. If the authorities remain passive until the aggrieved party ends the demonstration, a policy change is less likely than if the protest ends forcibly. Chances of policy change are decreased, because the termination of the stand-off requires that the authorities' definition of the situation prevail.

The stand-off, known to some as "the Chicago plan" (after a case mentioned below and described in the next section), has laws of its own. There is an inherent *law of capitulation*, namely, that the protesting party must "see the light," "be reasonable," and stop the demonstration before negotiations can proceed.[13] In one corner stands the aggrieved party which claims that certain matters are unjust and that the authorities refuse to change them or even talk about them. In the other corner sits a gentle but energetic party which claims it is more than ready to talk but which refuses to be bludgeoned into talks. As time passes, the authorities repeat that they are willing to negotiate, that the resisters must show their good faith and fair play by stopping their protest and joining in negotiations. In time, even those members of the community who are sympathetic to the protest issue begin to feel that the demonstration has served its purpose. "You've made your point. Now stop demonstrating and negotiate." As time passes, the authorities emphasize that they are losing patience, and the community feels that the protesters "are more interested in demonstrating than in finding a solution to this problem." Such psychological warfare weakens the aggrieved party; for internal cohesion depends on a clearly defined enemy.

The stand-off therefore has a built-in time limit. The longer the stand-off lasts, the more ground the protesters lose. The stand-off itself structurally favors the authorities because their definition of the situation gains credence.

The stand-off, because of this time limit, is an unstable form of directed resistance (see the Scranton Report 1970: 139). Carried to the end, it leads to capitulation by the protesting party. In the case of Students Against the Rank at the University of Chicago in 1966, this took about three days. A different stand-off protest at the University of Chicago in early 1969 lasted sixteen days; one at Brandeis University in January 1969 ended in capitulation after ten days. Short of capitulation, the stand-off can transform itself into aggressive resistance or violence by the frustrated demonstrators, an outcome more frequent as relations worsen. After a thirteen-day sit-in at Sir George Williams University in February 1969, protesters abruptly destroyed $2 million worth of property as a way of relieving the stand-off pressures of inaction. Or, the stand-off can change to open violence on both sides if the anger of the authorities also rises under pressure. Finally, the authorities can retaliate as a matter of deliberate policy, perhaps by arresting the students or by breaking up the protest.

This last alternative is the most frequent, but the fact that it was preceded by a stand-off redefines the retaliation. If the authorities arrest or haul off demonstrators near the beginning of the demonstration, they may lose community sympathy and appear as intransigent, rigid dictators, just as the protesters described them. At the same time, they will probably make the protesters more entrenched, more cohesive, more determined. If, however, the authorities call in the police after waiting some time for the protest to end and after making several overtures to negotiate as soon as the students stop demonstrating, then the action will seem justified. Before, they would be seen as assaulting aggrieved members of the community with unreasonable force; after a stand-off, the same action will be considered as subduing irrational belligerents who refuse to be reasonable or to negotiate. The community may even come to see it as the authorities' duty to remove a disruptive element from the community.

The social psychology of the stand-off inflicts severe wounds on the protesters. It quickly splits the group into the "all-or-nothing militants" and the "let's negotiate moderates."[14] The stand-off takes away the enemy. The protesters unite as a fraternity to fight against the forces of evil, and suddenly those forces yield; the experience is like that of punching the tar baby. Moreover, the opponent claims he is not against them and will negotiate now. He argues that only the protesters themselves prevent their wishes from being fulfilled. Members of the fraternity begin to sense that they are their own worst enemy.

The protesters gradually sense that their "disruptive" acts have overshadowed their basic demands in the eyes of the community. They find that the faculty is preoccupied with the disruption at the expense of basic issues. The students become dispirited as they see the community become hostile. Note, however, that the time limit in the stand-off is not the same for the protesters as it is for the community. In recognizing their unpopularity, the protesters lag behind the community. This differential means that if the authorities send in police in the middle of a stand-off, they may have community support yet enrage the protesters and make them more determined. All of these effects from disciplinary action depend on the severity and scope of the action. As a general rule, the more severe and/or larger the disciplinary action, the longer the authorities must tolerate the stand-off to justify it.

The stand-off tends to have a regular aftermath. In a stand-off, the protest issue is less likely to be taken seriously by the administration, especially as time passes and their definition of a disruptive situation prevails. When a stand-off completes its natural course, the students are left with a sense of failure and internal disunity. There often seem to be no channels left for them to communicate or express the deep sense of injustice which still remains concerning the protest issue. While the administration has won the battle, it is not clear of trouble unless it makes concrete steps to settle the protest issue. Usually, though, it takes only minor, vague steps, perhaps establishing a joint investigating committee. Students then become bitter and hardened, and the next protest is likely to be longer and uglier.

Mention of uglier protests serves as a reminder of limits to the propositions so far offered. It is true that the stand-off by its very nature favors a patient administration and exposes protesters to demoralization. Yet administrators are not necessarily cool, students are not necessarily unresourceful, and a "settlement" overwhelmingly to one side's advantage may only postpone trouble. Hopefully, there are limits to the sympathy an administration can attract. We would like to believe that if a university in America had participants shot at a sit-in, the act would be reviled no matter how provocative the protesters, but the actual reaction to killing students at Kent State and Jackson State makes us doubtful.

The definition of the situation sets boundaries to conflict even as types of conflict affect the definition of that situation. For example, the psychology and dynamics of the stand-off did not appear in the 1968 protest at Columbia University, because Columbia's administration did not use stand-off tactics. Despite an official emphasis from the second to seventh day that violence would be avoided at all costs, police action was a major element from the first day.[15] In fact, the on-campus demonstrations began in response to the arrest of a student by city police. From the third to the tenth day, large numbers of city police were present on campus, and barricading against massive assault began on the second day. The Columbia crisis, then, was *not* a new phase of student protest as so many people believe, but structurally revealed patterns quite similar to those of Berkeley.[16]

If the focus of a protest turns from the original issues(s) to use of force, a stand-off posture of "let the students get tired" will not succeed. Strategically an administration like Columbia's should either rapidly compensate for whatever force was used or forcibly end the protest. The former has clear advantages in negotiation if the issues are respected. If students are serious about having their demands satisfied (rather than wanting a maximum of disruption and destruction), it is tactically preferable to avoid issues of violence and force as long as possible.

One of the most interesting protests occurred in 1966 at the University of Chicago when students objected to ranking men for the Vietnam draft. Historically that event opened the era of demonstrations against university compliance with the federal government. Over a score of them from coast to coast began in the first days of the Chicago sit-in, and many followed later (see Long in Foster and Long, 1970). Moreover, it was the first pure case of the stand-off.

STUDENTS AGAINST THE RANK

No one at the University of Chicago expected a sit-in that spring of 1966. Even a junior member of the faculty who knew many leaders of the protest said, "I was in Woodworth's about ten days before the protest, talking to another faculty member about how there would not be a Berkeley at the University of Chicago. . . ."[17] Of course there were warning signs. Are there ever no clues in retrospect? But the signs were not seen, partially because people at Chicago associated large protests with Berkeley, and the University of Chicago did not seem like Berkeley. The University of California at Berkeley is part of a mammoth state university system which accepts a wide spectrum of students, while Chicago is private and highly selective. In 1964, the Berkeley campus alone included 27,000 students, two-thirds of them undergraduates, and about 1,800 faculty members. At the University of Chicago, about 9,000 students, one-fourth undergraduates, study under 1,080 faculty members in venerable "Gothic" buildings which look centuries older than they are. The Berkeley faculty is research oriented, and the University of California as a whole has a graduate research tradition. Although Chicago has proportionately fewer undergraduates, its College (a distinct division) has a great tradition of teaching and close student-faculty relationships.

The entire tone of the two campuses contrasts sharply. Chicago is small, quiet, gloomy, with many single figures moving within private worlds against harsh weather along city blocks. The University of California at Berkeley dominates its environment, and one sees clusters of students throughout Berkeley, lots of motion, and an openness which California weather induces. No one knows how much campus atmosphere affects protests, but the predictions that there would be no sit-in at the University of Chicago were made on just these kinds of comparisons.

Faculty and administrators at the University of Chicago also felt that the educational and political atmosphere of their campus differed from that of Berkeley. They accepted the image which discontented students on the Berkeley campus had so graphically portrayed in the mass media of impersonal, abusive, computerized education. And because of the behavior of Berkeley's administration during the 1964 protests and before, most students and faculty at the University of Chicago felt that Berkeley's administration was personally unresponsive and politically restrictive.[18]

In contrast, the University of Chicago boasts of a grand tradition in the liberal arts. The College, developed by Robert M. Hutchins when he was Chancellor, fostered many innovations in teaching, some of which were widely copied. It featured a personal education with faculty who had been selected especially for the College and who loved to teach. The

"Hutchins ideals" still live at Chicago, and during the year 1965–66 extensive discussion and planning had taken place about restructuring the College so that its offerings would be still more relevant to the modern world. Politically, the students did not feel constrained, and they frequently made admiring remarks about how the faculty had fought the loyalty oath in the 1950s.

BACKGROUND TO THE PROTEST

How, then, did a major protest arise at the University of Chicago? The question can never be answered directly, but part of the answer lies in the handling of a faculty report issued the winter before the sit-in. The adminstration lauded the report, which recommended basic policies on housing, and put it on the agenda for official approval. Immediately students on the left began to accuse the administration of railroading the report through, trying to implement it before students could read it. Although the student newspaper devoted many pages to the report and its discussants, student pressure continued, and the approval of the report was postponed. In reality, the faculty committee who issed the report had spent hundreds of hours listening to students' opinions on housing, and the report acknowledged the students as the source for most of its good ideas.

In short, the experience revealed an ingrained, intense, and not wholly rational distrust of the administration.[19] Students focused their suspicion mainly on the administration, not on the faculty who wrote the report, and they felt that administrators did not listen to them.

Finally, in May 1966, undergraduates staged an illegal "sleep-in" on the campus lawn to protest the housing policies. They were met by administrators who brought out refreshments and asked what the students wanted. Almost all the student demands were shown to be incorporated in the new housing policies, an illustration of the extent to which the housing committee had tapped student sentiment on living arrangements. With nothing to protest and rain besides, the sleep-in quickly fizzled.

Two weeks later the sit-in began, and many student leaders said that the failure of the sleep-in had increased feelings of frustration and impotence which made students determined to have a large, successful protest. The administration had "seduced" them once with punch and friendly conversation, but it would not happen again. The basic distrust and antagonism demanded some expression.

The example of Chicago illustrates a fundamental prerequisite for protest. Protest occurs when the authorities are seen as arbitrary and unresponsive; for basically *protest is a unilateral response to an arbitrary force.* As the comparison of the Berkeley and Chicago incidents shows, this perceived rigidity is more important than the commonly attributed causes of protest, such as university oversize, size of classes, poor quality of teaching, inadequate facilities, and political restrictions. Many institutions suffering from one or more of these problems have had no large protests, whereas some small, liberal, high-quality institutions have.

A sense of institutional rigidity can arise in different environments, because student activists on a given campus are part of a national movement and have a national consciousness. They are cosmopolitans, not locals, and they tend to set local problems or characters on a national stage.[20] The one quality which consistently makes universities and colleges protest-prone is academic and/or social prestige. Such institutions are more likely to have large numbers of children from upper-class intellectual homes. These students are most prominent among political radicals.[21]

GRADES AND THE DRAFT

At the University of Chicago, a major, substantive issue soon emerged to consolidate student hostility toward the administration. Since 1964, the attention of liberal students had shifted from civil rights to the expanding war in Vietnam. In 1965, radical leaders stated that the white civil rights movement was dead, and the black power movement grew in its place. The Students for a Democratic Society (SDS) turned to injustices of the war, holding in the summer of 1965 a conference on the draft. During that fall, SDS held numerous though poorly attended meetings at the University of Chicago to discuss the inequities of Selective Service. At the same time, the national office of SDS moved to Chicago near the university.

During the winter quarter, some members of the College staff began to question the use of grades in relation to the draft. This was a *faculty* problem, whether grading a student carried a moral burden of judging a person eligible for battle—and possible death—in Vietnam. Some faculty felt this burden and brought up the subject in sections of a famous Hutchins course, Social Sciences II. Thus a number of undergraduates openly discussed in class this moral issue.

Faculty concern over the Vietnam conflict increased. A Faculty Committee on the Problems of Foreign Policy formed and became more active during the first part of 1966. Six faculty members particularly concerned about draft deferment based on grades met with a high university official and made the following recommendations which are summarized here and listed in descending order of preference:

(1) The University should refuse to issue grades to the Selective Service. If this action is claimed illegal, that claim should be examined and challenged.

(2) The University should gather with other top universities to discuss the joint withholding of grades from the Selective Service.

(3) If the University does not want to withhold grades, it should issue a public statement condemning the use of academic information for Selective Service.

(4) If the University does not want to take a position as a body, it should make it possible for faculty not to issue grades.

(5) As a minimum, the University should sponsor a national conference on the Selective Service.

The Faculty Council and its Executive Committee confidentially discussed these suggestions during February, March, and April. The conclusions, issued May 6, included action on the second of these suggestions.[22]

Although a number of students had been concerned about draft deferments, student initiative did not begin until April 1966. A group of undergraduates, many of them not political activists but destined to become leaders of the sit-in, persuaded two young faculty men to give a course entitled The Moral Basis of Political Decisions. Specific political action leading to the sit-in began in response to a press release by General Hershey announcing the Selective Service test and the use of class ranking for college deferments.[23] Throughout April, students held forums and meetings about the issue of rank in class. Attendance at SDS meetings grew rapidly. Radical SDS leaders came to prominence and tried to negotiate with the administration against ranking undergraduate men. The university reiterated its policy of providing class rank to Selective Service boards at the student's request.

Thus a new issue appeared for student protests. Tension shifted from faculty concern about giving grades to student opposition to being ranked. Fundamentally, the opponents of ranking held that in matters of life and death all men are equal. It is immoral to rank one man above another. If a student gets good grades, for example, he is exempted from the army for that reason only, and he exposes fellow students lower in class standing to the draft. Selective Service thereby pits student against student, and the ultimate stakes are death.

In addition, students were feeling guilty about their privileges. Earlier that year the Student Health Service reported a rapid increase among graduate students of "anxiety over privilege." Then undergraduates began to approach a few faculty members, saying that they did not want to compete against others for deferments. Yet these same students did not want to fight in the war and kill. Taken together, the two positions would force them to almost certain induction, followed by refusal of military service. In other words, for moral reasons they would trade an outstanding college education for a prison sentence. The most serious of them were horrified by the choices they faced.

At Chicago, the protesters explicitly demanded that their school refuse to cooperate with Selective Service and implicitly advocated that universities be an independent moral force in society, in this case by condemning evil policies in Vietnam. This demand challenged structural features of university and society which most people take for granted. University attorneys, moreover, claimed that what the students demanded was probably illegal. Protesters at Chicago also wanted a voice in making policy decisions relevant to students. This second demand seems part of the first one in that the students thought they could not trust the university to be morally responsive or to represent their interests.

IMPENDING RIGIDITIES

Because the protest at the University of Chicago raised new and radical questions, few sympathized with it. Most Americans, including academicians, take for granted some kind of cooperation between universities and the government, a relationship which the students felt had gone too far. To complicate matters, the students as a group were confused about the issues, and faculty quickly found illogic in student position papers. Some senior faculty members also found a no-rank stance irresponsible, because it would give students an advantage over those in weaker colleges if they sought deferment through the national Selective Service examinations. Also, some argued, a Negro three blocks away is morally equal to an A student, as is a student with a D average. Therefore one cannot justly oppose rank without opposing student deferments. Not until after the sit-in did the Students Against the Rank persuade its mixed membership to take this fearful but honest stand.

Between the radical nature of the issues and the lack of clear arguments, the sit-in at Chicago could not rally emotional or intellectual support for its position either within the academic community or among the general public. The faculty was disgusted with the sloppy thinking of protesters, and few took the issues seriously. Moreover, the students who had banked on strong faculty support forgot that the draft is an age-specific (but *not*, to the surprise of some, a sex-specific) issue. Unlike constraints on speech, the draft does not affect faculty directly. The faculty on the whole ignored the demands of the sit-in, and many felt that rank was a bogus issue created by radicals in order to gain greater student power in the university. Ironically, most of the faculty and administration strongly opposed the sit-in because it disrupted university life and breached the tradition of free speech. Protesters could not have been more disillusioned. While they suffered for morality, life, and death, the university was preoccupied with order. On the other hand, those opposing the sit-in felt the students were acting like bad and confused children.

Although the issues and their social context were important in defining the nature of the conflict that soon followed, other forces shaped the sit-in at the University of Chicago and its outcome. The students, frustrated by attempts to negotiate, rallied to form a group, Students Against the Rank (SAR), and decided to sit in the administration building if computation of rank was not dropped or at least postponed until fall. Conflict is ultimately a power relationship, and students had felt powerless before a seemingly arbitrary administration.

One miscommunication particularly intensified this impression of intransigence. An April 12, 1966, the Faculty Council met and, as the ruling body on academic affairs, officially decided (with slight changes) that information on rank would be released only at the student's request.[24] Like many such bodies, the council distributed its minutes just before the next meeting to avoid rumors and to refresh its members' memory of the previous meeting. Consequently, *many faculty and most senior administrators did not know for several weeks that a policy on rank had been made.* By confidential agreement, those who knew could not tell. Since no official policy on class ranking for Selective Service had previously been made, no one even knew who had authorized the current practice.[25] Therefore protesting students got "the run-around" from administrators, who either did not know or could not tell. The minutes came out one day before the sit-in, too late to quell rising passions.

The formation of SAR made once powerless individuals feel powerful enough as a group to force their demands on the university. The transformation was exhilarating. The students gained almost a class consciousness. As their movement grew, they became more intense and idealistic, until they demanded a confrontation. As the group became increasingly hostile toward the enemy and internally cohesive through this effort, its members exhibited glee, comradeship, and enthusiasm.[26]

THE PROTEST

The SAR delivered its ultimatum, and university officials recoiled from its blunt, imperative tone. The die was cast, and on Wednesday, May 11, students began to gather for a rally. A heavy rain drove them into the lobby of the administration building and by five o'clock about four-hundred-fifty people were spreading throughout the building. As employees, deans, and officers left, the crowd cheered and jeered. By that night, the students had secured all exits, including the president's private elevator. The university did not resist, and the students were delighted with their instant success.[27]

For two days the sit-in continued full force. Some students left; others replaced them. Yet the peer solidarity, the celebration of community so important to students inclined to join protest movements, ran high. There were many people coming and going—students, maintenance men, the press, and speakers. Day and night a teach-in continued in the lobby, while other areas were designated for eating, studying and sleeping.[28] Students, faculty—both sympathetic and unsympathetic—and administrators spoke about the issues. Visiting speakers debated policies and tactics, finally convincing protesters that the faculty, not the administration, was the object of persuasion and that faculty were as repulsed by the sit-in as administrators. On Friday, May 13, the SAR voted to leave the building of its own accord, with a token force remaining as a symbol of opposition. Over the weekend students organized to canvass each faculty member and to persuade him of the cogency of their views about the rank and student power.

On Monday, May 16, the employees did not return to their desks in the administration building; the administration considered the building still occupied by the token force of protesters. Students were shocked. By leaving the building, they felt they had made a major concession toward conciliation, and they expected the administration to do likewise. Rather than infuriating the students, as happened at Berkeley, the university's firmness dispirited them. That evening SAR met to decide what to do. Respected faculty spoke and told them once again that negotiations were not possible under conditions of coercion. With "childlike eagerness" the students listened and then voted to remove the token force. Officially, they had held the building for over five days, more than they planned. Now they left the building entirely and turned to persuading the faculty to vote against ranking.

For the next week, students opposing the rank talked to faculty members, especially those who held positions on the Faculty Council. On May 24, the council voted 32–3 for a two-part resolution favoring the then current policy of rank, at the same time commending the administration, and recommending disciplinary action against future disruptive acts. On May 27, the faculty senate met for the first extraordinary session in Chicago's history. While not a policy body, it expressed its sentiment with 85 percent in favor of the policy on rank. A minority of faculty and the protesting students severely ·criticized the way this meeting was conducted.

ANALYSIS OF THE PROTEST

What had occurred in the five days of demonstration that led to all these consequences can best be understood in terms of the structure of a stand-off. The administration initially did not take the rank issue too seriously, and to their audience the students sounded at first like complaining, then pleading, children. Very few faculty members or administrators could understand why the rank issue would touch students so deeply, and theories of outside agitators arose early in the controversy (with the nearby national headquarters of SDS, recently moved to the south side of Chicago from New York, as a convenient focus of suspicion). Moreover, the Chicago administration, learning from administrative errors at Berkeley, controlled the conflict by letting the sit-in occur without retaliation. Thus SAR bore the onus of escalation and invasion, and the students appeared to the university community to be rash and unreasonable. Slowly, through informal talks with members of the faculty, through speeches made by guests in the lobby of the administration building, the protesters sensed that the faculty did not understand their arguments and that the university community was overwhelmingly against them.[29] In the end, they grew despondent about the effectiveness of the sit-in, and they capitulated, however bitterly, without a single concession by university officials. As the students began to see themselves and their "coercive" action as extreme, moderate voices gained greater attention, and by the weekend when the protesters decided to leave the building and to canvass the faculty, the leadership had officially changed to a more moderate one.

To understand the undermining experience which led to capitulation, one must recognize two kinds of messages that pass between the parties in an insiders' dispute. There are explicit, public, official statements, and there are informal or private exchanges. At the University of Chicago, persons on both sides of the conflict used the second channel to express feelings and thoughts which differed significantly from their overt statements about the sit-in and its issues. Official university statements reaffirmed the university's position on the rank issue and deplored the sit-in. Meantime, an *ad hoc* council of senior officers met daily, assessing, worrying, seeking solutions. Members of this group met constantly with leaders of the sit-in or spoke at the sit-in as individuals, and informally they conveyed a willingness to negotiate once the students stopped being "coercive." They expressed a sympathy for the students' cause and a repulsion at the military calculation of life. Representatives of the university expressed privately to protesters their failings and those of the institution; yet no such statements or sentiment became part of the official posture.

Students were especially responsive to these sympathetic and concerned communications by esteemed members of the university community. Because many students value intellectual pursuits and plan to get advanced degrees, these men served as career models for them. At the same time, these men told the protesters that the protest was ruining their university, and such remarks touched the considerable loyalty students had for the College if not the University of Chicago as a whole. The general feeling among most protesters was, "We don't want to destroy the university; we just want to stop the rank."

Students Against the Rank, like the administration, issued strong statements; the hard line dominated the written communications of both sides. Informally, however, many moderate students were quite conciliatory in tone as the community became more hostile. Thus one could see how the unity of SAR dissipated as faculty and administrators focused more on the coercion of the sit-in and less on the issue of rank. SAR was united against the rank, not in favor of being coercive or damaging the university. There were even rumors that opponents of the College were using the sit-in to press for an end to undergraduate education.

The effect of redefining the situation in this manner is that a large group of participants emerge who believe in the initial issue (rank), but not in other emerging issues (destruction). On the other hand, a number of participants remain determined to get their demand satisfied at any cost. In estimating the enemy, they distrust the conciliatory tones which university officials use informally and point to the official reiteration of old policy. The emotional experience of a protester in this situation is almost schizophrenic. All around him he hears different voices threatening and coaxing. "Your behavior is intolerable." "We are deeply concerned about the inequities of the draft law." "You are destroying the university." "As soon as you get out of the building, we can talk this over." "Call the police and have them all arrested." "For God's sake, get out before everyone falls at each other's throat."

CONCLUSION

Although the analysis of directed resistance illuminates some underlying structures, the variations of individual cases remain highly subjective, that is, embedded in the acting subjects. This is seen not only here but in what must be the most exhaustive effort to systematically analyze a protest, *The Spiral of Conflict* (Heirich, 1971). There is an unmistakable *ad hoc* quality to the way in which arrows fly around

Heirich's four-level model of "conflict encounters." The ways in which different elements combine at a subsequent level do not form a logical pattern. In addition, the subjective perception of many elements leaves their definitions suspended. "If those who intervene prove unsuccessful in settling . . ." (45). "If authorities create conditions . . ." (47). "If intervention produces neither of these outcomes . . ." (47). One cannot define in advance and predict.

The same problem arises with the other theorist alluded to in this paper, Lewis Coser. Although his general theory of conflict reflects a formal, structural frame of mind, it is largely phenomenological. Such terms as "basic" conflict, "realistic" conflict, and "in-group" or "out-group" cannot be preestablished. Therefore, many of Coser's propositions are not hypotheses but definitions themselves, definitions indexed to the concrete reality, as Garfinkel (1967) would say. This does not mean that the terms used in these various theories are irrelevant; on the contrary, they *reflect* distinctions which real persons and groups make but which elude us in the abstract.[30]

On the level of policy, the implications are clear. Institutions and those running them naturally tend to freeze themselves in routines that foreclose an open mind. They must continually strive to listen and respond to their clients. If nevertheless a conflict arises, the university should negotiate and bring the general community into the process. Assuming the conflict cannot be resolved, the stand-off is the best tactic. There is no question that even if demonstrators obstruct daily activities, the official use of force will polarize the conflict and often increase it (Foster and Long, 1970: 373). The stand-off allows a university to firmly maintain its opposition to coercion without using coercion itself. However, the long-range effectiveness of the stand-off depends on the willingness of the university to negotiate genuine resolutions to genuine grievances.

NOTES

1. Exceptions are Coser (1967) and Heirich (1971).

2. I am indebted to Richard Flacks, then assistant professor of sociology at the University of Chicago, for starting me on this study as part of the Youth and Social Change Project. The theoretical aspects of the paper have been improved by the comments of Lewis A. Coser. Edward Witten, with sensitive pen, measurably improved the style. The study was conducted with the help of a National Institute of Mental Health predoctoral fellowship (#7–FL–MH–23,333–04).

3. Bayer (1970: 17) found that student power was the most common theme of major protests in 1968–69. See also Kerr in Foster & Long (1970). The shift

from civil rights and student rights to mature campus policies and then to uses of power both on and off campus is reflected in Peterson's surveys in 1965 and 1968 (Foster & Long, 1970).

4. Here, as elsewhere, protesting students include faculty who support them, support which is usually vital to the protest.

5. Discussing and negotiating issues is the recommended way to respond to campus disorder (Scranton 1970: Ch. 4). The Henderson Commission drew the same conclusion, stating that directed resistance resulted from blocked communication (1970: Ch. 5).

6. For one example made visible, see "200 Students Win in B.U. Lockout," *Boston Herald Traveler,* April 25, 1968. The lockout lasted only twelve hours.

7. Students at Brandeis University in one incident protested against the presence of an Air Force recruiter and against new university rules restricting demonstrations. The administration threatened punishment, and the demonstration ended in a few hours.

8. There are three standard books on Berkeley: Draper (1965), Lipset and Wolin (1965), and Miller and Gilmore (1965), all now largely superseded by Heirich (1971). At present, the only account of the Waseda demonstrations is Shimbori (1968). My knowledge about the 1966 university strike in Rome comes from conversations with visiting students who were there. For a summary and review of the events at the University of Berlin, see Wechsberg (1967). A couple of books describe and analyze the demonstration at Columbia University: *The Columbia Spectator* (1968) and the Cox Commission (1968). See also Breslin (1968); Liberation News Service (1968); and *The Public Interest* (1968).

9. See Lewis A. Coser (1964: 139–49). When such escalation occurs, both sides divert their attention from the initial protest issues to matters of sheer power and violence—"our" justly sought power and "their" unwarranted violence.

10. See Coser (1964: 48–54, 72–80). The decision as to whether or not a certain conflict is basic reflects the posture of the assessing party. I am suggesting that what judgment is made about the realistic or basic nature of the conflict tells more about the party than about any "objective nature" of conflict. How these judgments are made serve as indices of the attitudes which the opponent brings to the conflict.

11. Throughout this analysis we are dealing with social and structural regularities—Durkheim's social facts—rather than with calculations of individual actors. The authorities sincerely feel, for example, that to sit in a doorway is "blocking," and the gerundive describes the aggression of the act. Likewise, they sincerely feel that the sitters "were removed," and the passive voice conveys the appropriate tone. In a similar manner, protesters who know they are breaking rules or laws for good cause are nonetheless genuinely shocked when the authorities descend upon them.

12. For a summary, see Bondurant (1965: 88–104).

13. The quotations in this paragraph are from interviews of faculty and administrators during a sit-in at the University of Chicago in May 1966. However, similar phrases and stages can be found in accounts of almost any student protest. See, for example, accounts of the protest at Columbia University, April 24–May 1, 1968, in the *New York Times*.

14. We concentrate here only on the structural aspects of the stand-off and not on the numerous ways in which an administration's actions can alter student leadership.

15. This interpretation is supported by Loya Metzger's detailed analysis of the Columbia crisis. Wisconsin provides another case. While a stand-off followed by negotiations successfully resolved one crisis, the early arrest of protesters on dubious grounds hardened opposition in another. See Long in Foster and Long (1970).

16. Frederick M. Hechinger (1968) was one of the few who observed this parallel.

17. This quotation was transcribed from a taped interview, one of several I conducted with faculty and administrators during and after the sit-in. Other souces of information for this case study include participation in the student protest, interviews with leaders of the protest written by faculty and by protesting students, and the undergraduate newspaper, the *Maroon*.

18. See John Searle in Miller and Gilmore (1965: 92–104).

19. Georges Sorel (1961: 26–56) presents a penetrating analysis of the nature of political myths. The main features of such myths can be seen in this case: that they stand as wholes and must not be analyzed into parts; that comparing them to reality is irrelevant, because they do not make immediate claims on reality.

    Quoting Renan, Sorel writes, "A man suffers martyrdom only for the sake of things about which he is not certain" (pp. 44–45). Sorel states that "the myths are not descriptions of things, but *expressions of a determination to act*" (p. 50, italics added).

20. I am indebted to Professor McKim Marriott for this insight.

21. Freedman and Kanzer (in Sampson and Korn, 1970: Ch. 6) argue that while this relation between family background and radicalism holds for early protesters, militant strikers in later years were more likely to come from working-class homes.

22. Toward the end of the sit-in the university announced that it would sponsor a conference on the draft, but no reference was made to the Foreign Policy Committee's list of recommendations. The following fall, the conference was held, and its proceedings are printed in Sol Tax, ed., *Draft* (Chicago: University of Chicago Press, 1967). The conference was boycotted by some protesters because its agenda allowed for no consideration of whether armed forces were necessary or not.

23. For general background on the events of this time and the issues of the draft, see Flacks, Howe, and Lauter (1967).

24. Faculty Council believed that they had changed "policy" from one of sending class rank to local draft boards *unless* otherwise directed by the student to one of sending the class rank only *upon* the request of the student.

    In fact, effective policy was not changed, because no formal policy had existed and because the "new policy" exactly paralleled the old practice. Since the Korean War, sending ranks had been administrative routine, done only upon the request of the student. No one whom I interviewed, from the highest to the most junior offices of the university, was aware of these facts! Administrators kept referring to the university's "past policy" but could not tell me the exact nature of that policy.

    Such unfortunate errors of knowledge are often the basis for mistrust, as they were in this case. Students concerned about the draft could never get an accurate answer on what university policy was, because none existed and because officials defended their vague knowledge with rigid postures.

25. Thus, in reality, the students were correct to attack the administration and not the Faculty Council, for ranking was an administrative procedure, and no one would tell them the faculty had recently made it an official policy. One dean, who was constantly asked about the university's position, related his frustration at knowing that "something" had been decided on April 12 but at not being able to find out what happened from colleagues who had attended the meeting.

    Faculty and administrators were irritated by SAR attacking the administraton. The more generous saw it as stupid; the less generous regarded the action as a deliberate distortion by radical students to perpetrate a mass bid for student power.

26. For a theoretical discussion of the group-forming and group-binding functions of conflict, including the search for enemies, see Coser (1964: 33–38, 87–95, 104–110, 111–119) and Coser (1967: 22–34).

27. Throughout the five floors, little damage was wrought. After the sit-in, the president estimated costs of lost time and rentals at over $100,000 and indirect costs of grants and donors lost at over $1.5 million.

28. One interesting phenomenon in recent student movements is participatory democracy. The Simmel-Coser theory of conflict draws attention to a serious problem for groups in conflict with outside forces. Namely, under such circumstances, great internal cohesion is demanded by the group; little deviance is tolerated (Coser, 1964: 87–104). Yet conflict usually exists within a group, and safety-valve institutions are important for preserving the group. In the case of student protesters, intragroup tensions are increased by the newness of the group, the diversity among its members, and the severe pressures individuals feel during a demonstration.

    Participatory democracy serves to handle these multiple tensions and conflicts at a time when high group cohesion is required. By its principles, any member can speak for as long as he wishes on any issue. All decisions are made by the general body, not by an executive committee. To formulate a plan of action may take many hours of deliberation, but the process insures that the feelings and loyalties of all are considered. This forum is often expanded into a general teach-in; so that when no business of the group presses, others may speak about the issues of the day. This also permits great deviance while retaining overall cohesion of the group.

29. One SAR activist wrote the following summary of an interview with a professor:

> ". . . [and she says *all* her colleagues] are utterly appalled at the incredible stupidity of our tactics in taking the Ad[ministration] Building.
>
> "Not only will she not support us; she won't talk to us until we get out. She says being in here is killing our stand.
>
> "She says ranks are formed and always have been. They're used for many purposes, including job applications for . . . students. Absurd to say, 'Don't form them.' It's unjust to students who *want* their rank sent in not to have such a rank.
>
> "But foremost in everyone's mind is our militant taking over of this building. She says we're fools to listen to soft-heads like . . . [names of faculty]. They're in an even smaller minority of the faculty than we are of the students.
>
> "Don't bother talking to her again while we have the building.
>
> "Also, she says we're ignorant and stupid and childish to protest the Administration. Faculty made the decision, not the Ad. Faculty Senate has no voting power; so it's even stupider tactics to talk to them about voting for us. 'Stupid' was her favorite word for us."

30. The Simmel-Coser theories present another problem for empirical testing. They form a network of propositions so interwoven that empirically *any* outcome can be explained. This is partly the result of the definitional problem stated above: if the conflict reunites antagonists, it was not basic; if it cannot be resolved, the conflict was basic *(post hoc)*. A second problem comes from the network quality of the propositions. If the conflict was not resolved, was it basic (Coser's Proposition #7), or does it indicate a stable relationship (his Proposition #8)? If students protest vigorously and refuse to negotiate, is it because the conflict is nonrealistic (Proposition #3) or because the students are fervent in their cause (Proposition #12)? If one hypothesizes that conflict with out-groups increases internal cohesion (Proposition #9) and one finds a great deal of internal conflict within the protesting group, does that challenge the hypothesis or validate another hypothesis, that the closer the relationship, the more intense the conflict (Proposition #6)?

Beyond these general problems of testing conflict theory, passive resistance and the stand-off exhibit qualities which differ from other forms of conflict. In terms of the Simmel-Coser conception of conflict, these strategies lead to peculiar experiences in which (a) cohesion may *not* form in the face of the enemy, (b) participants may suffer great confusion as they are pulled in different directions by their conflict loyalties, (c) associations may not form, or (d) the group may accept any sympathetic person and exclude few deviants. All of these "inexplicable" actions happened during the University of Chicago protest.

REFERENCES

Bayer, Alan E., and Alexander W. Austin. "Violence and Disruption on the U.S. Campus: A Survey Analysis" in *Politics*, No. 1 (May 1970), pp. 7–26.

Bondurant, Joan V. *Conquest of Violence: The Gandhian Philosophy of Conflict*, Rev. ed. Berkeley: University of California Press, 1965.

Breslin, Jimmy. Column in the *Boston Herald Traveler*, May 3 and May 13, 1968.

Columbia Spectator, Editors. *Up Against the Ivy Wall*, New York: Atheneum, 1968.

Coser, Lewis A. *The Functions of Social Conflict*, Glencoe, Ill.: Free Press, 1964; and *Continuities in Social Conflict*, Glencoe, Ill.: Free Press, 1967.

Cox, Archibald et al. *Crisis At Columbia*, New York: Vintage Books, 1968.

Draper, Hal. *Berkeley: The New Student Revolt*, New York: Grove Press, 1965.

Flacks, Richard; Florence Howe; and Paul Lauter. "On the Draft," *New York Review of Books* 8 (April 6, 1967), pp. 3–5.

Foster, Julian, and Durwood Long. *Protest!* New York: William Morrow, 1970.

Garfinkel, Harold. *Studies in Ethnomethodology*, Englewood Cliffs, N. J.: Prentice-Hall, 1967.

Hechinger, Frederick M. "Reflections of Berkeley," In *New York Times*, May 2, 1968.

Heirich, Max. *The Spiral of Conflict*, New York: Columbia University Press, 1971.

Henderson, Charles D. et al. *The Academy in Turmoil: First Report of the Temporary Commission to Study the Causes of Campus Unrest*, Albany, N. Y.: 1970.

Liberation News Service. "The Siege of Columbia," *Ramparts*, June 15, 1968, pp. 26–39.

Lipset, S. M., and S. S. Wolin. *The Berkeley Student Revolt*, New York: Doubleday Anchor, 1965.

Metzger, Loya F. *Faculty Activism in a Campus Crisis*, Masters' Thesis in Political Science, Columbia University (about 1970).

Miller, M. M., and Susan Gilmore. *Revolution at Berkeley*, New York: Dell, 1965.

Public Interest, No. 13, Fall 1968. Entire issue devoted to universities.

Sampson, Edward E. and Harold A. Korn. *Student Activism and Protest*. San Francisco: Jossey-Bass, 1970.

Scranton, William W. et al. *The Report of the President's Commission on Campus Unrest*, Washington, D.C.: U. S. Government Printing Office, 1970.

Shibori, Michiya. "The Sociology of a Student Movement—A Japanese Case Study," *Daedalus* (Winter 1968) pp. 204–228.

Sorel, Georges. *Reflections on Violence*, Translated by T. E. Hulme, New York: Collier, 1961.

Wechsberg, Joseph. "Letter from Berlin," *New Yorker*. November 18, 1967, pp. 165–216.

5/The dynamics of faculty response to student protest

Donald W. Light, Jr.

A lthough the faculty of a college or university define its character and hold great—but sometimes unexercised—power, they seem almost immune to exposure of student protest. Until the past few years, both participants in protest and social scientists who studied them overlooked the importance of faculty in protest situations. Since professors make decisions which determine the course of a protest and its subsequent repercussions, it is important to know how they respond and to analyze why they respond as they do.

To a great extent, the literature on student protest overlooks these questions to focus on who the protesters are, what kinds of families they have, what the issues of protest signify, and how protests affect the campus, particularly its governance. However, in the late 1960s, a few researchers began to survey faculty for their views on campus demonstration. The resulting information is valuable but limited in several ways. First, the samples are either national but insensitive to the variety of structures in higher education, or local and unable to embrace the larger patterns of dissent. Second, a few researchers misanalyze their own data and produce faulty conclusions. Third, the studies lack a set of propositions about how faculty relate to protest and its institutional setting. It is a mystery why the authors selected the variables they did, except that they constitute the usual list which all studies of faculty employ.

The following pages will outline a framework for thinking about faculty response to student protest. Because empirical knowledge is limited, parts of the analysis must be hypothetical. Nevertheless, this framework may be useful in relating different fragments of data to each other and to a larger whole.

THE DYNAMICS OF FACULTY RESPONSE

The dynamics of faculty response are those basic values and ways of relating to the university world which shape specific responses to student protest in this case and probably to other campus issues as well. As in psychiatry, from which this definition is borrowed, an analysis of the dynamics requires a model which operates at several levels, each more removed from the immediate response but linked to the levels preceding it. Unlike psychiatry, the model will not argue that certain root experiences determine all that follows but rather that the structural relations of faculty to their institution and personal background generate the dynamics of faculty response. This section will outline the dynamics of response, and later sections will analyze empirical findings in light of this framework.

THE STIMULUS—KINDS OF PROTEST

To begin with the immediate object of response, there are several kinds of protest. Logically, protest *issues* range from those directed against the college or university to those against external agents. Among those directed against the university, issues range from those peripheral to faculty concerns (parietals) to those of vital interest (student participation in tenure decisions). Protest *behavior* ranges from nondisruptive to highly disruptive.

While this outline is quite obvious, it does present the full range of stimuli to faculty response. Moreover, it implies that our interest in this subject is narrower than the logical possibilities. Faculty *qua* faculty concern us only when the protest challenges the operation of a college or university. Even if faculty who signed the Irish petition differed by academic rank, the finding would not be important. This holds true for tactics as well. A peaceful demonstration raises no serious faculty issue. Thus, for the purposes of this analysis, the relevant protests have issues and/or tactics which provoke faculty to respond as members of the institution. In terms of tactics, this means protests which employ what faculty regard as disruptive strategies.

How can we construct a model of faculty response to protest? The task appears quite simple. On the surface, faculty respond to two stimuli, the issues or demands and the tactics. If for the purpose of schematic clarity we confine ourselves to positive and negative reactions, we arrive at the following results.

FIGURE 5.1

	Issues	Tactics	Direction of Response
(A)	+	+	Support protest. Assuming disruptive tactics, these faculty are regarded as radicals.
(B)	+	–	Direction of response unclear; depends on degree to which tactics become the issue.
(C)	–	+	Nihilistic/sadistic support of protest.
(D)	–	–	Oppose protest.

Category C at first seems puzzling because it is difficult to imagine many faculty responding this way. Were the tactics disruptive, a professor could feel, "I don't agree with your demands, but I defend your right to present them." But assuming disruptive tactics, the position would be more subtle, that while students are making erroneous demands, their disruptive activities might shake up the institution. Such faculty may conceal their resentment and sadism, thereby making category C less visible than the other three. They may even appear to be in B, saying they deplore the tactics but approve of the aims when those aims embody the tactics. David Riesman identified such people of the McCarthy era who hid their sadism in this way.[1]

Because studies of protest contain no evidence for a category such as C, our attention turns to category B as the most interesting group. Clearly it needs refinement in terms of those who feel paralyzed by their divided response and those who decide with some doubts to support or oppose the protest. Moreover, response will vary by intensity as well as direction of response. Even in the case of those who oppose the issues and tactics of the protest, the question remains as to how far they are willing to go in their opposition. Would they, for example, urge that police be summoned on campus to break up the demonstrations? This question of intensity can be cast in terms of tactics. That is, both the protesters and the institution use tactics, and faculty respond to both sides. When, for example, university administrators have called in the police, they have usually incurred the wrath of many faculty who otherwise oppose the protest. Underlying the complexities of this interaction is the law of passive advantage, as examined in Chapter 4.

THE RESPONSE—STYLES OF REACTION

To probe more deeply into these subtleties of faculty response which no simple model explains, I made a detailed study of faculty reactions to a disruptive protest based on long interviews and participant observation. This seemed necessary, because the most striking feature of studies on faculty response to protest is that not one reports on a personal interview with a single professor. A later section of this chapter will report this research in detail, but for this general analysis we need only the results of that study—the descriptive summaries, which like clinical diagnoses, capture the style of response.

The study distinguishes between four types of faculty reaction. Members of the first group wished to protect their institution, and more than other groups they felt the university to be fine just the way it was. They were, then, *institutional conservatives,* and their attitudes towards the protest and its issues reflect this allegiance too. One could call them hawks, but it is unfair to represent them as fierce. They knew relatively little about the grievances of the students and did not think the worse of themselves for it. The grievances were, they conveyed, manifestations of an unfortunate uprising which of course had to end immediately.

Faculty in the second group were primarily attached to the institution, but unlike the institutional conservatives, they cared for and worked more with students, particularly undergraduates. They displayed no clear principles or course of action. They hedged, not in the sense of a cool calculation against risk but in the more tormented sense of trying to evade the risk involved in strong decision. For this reason such people were not prominent negotiators or diplomats even when as dean or master their position demanded it. As a group I called them *hedgers.*

The third group not only cared for the students as individuals but felt the protest reflected legitimate shortcomings of the university. Thus, they supported the thrust behind the demonstrations. They wanted to make the university a place for personal growth and individual dignity. Generally they expressed much clearer ideals than the hedgers. Yet they feared that disruption would injure the university, an institution which they loved as much as any institutional conservative. Because of the altruistic, affirmative quality of their beliefs, they might be called *humanistic loyalists.*

Finally, a few professors supported the specific demands and the disruptive tactics of the protest. They considered themselves and were regarded by others as *radicals.*

The relation of these four types to categories (A–D) in the initial scheme is self-evident. On issues and tactics, institutional conservatives are (D) and radicals are (A), while hedgers and humanistic loyalists make up two subgroups under (B). The study produced no evidence of category (C). Thus we now have four categories of faculty response which make intuitive sense and which actually exist.

RESPONSE STYLES AND ACTION

However, the more important question is how these styles of

response relate to the actual behavior of faculty. It turned out that the faculty in each group manifested similar behavioral responses. Because this intensive study was based on few cases, the correspondence is not therefore proven, but the relationships will be useful for future research. Specifically, a couple of conservative professors wrote an early petition implying that police should be summoned to end the demonstration. Within a few hours, two hundred professors signed it. All those interviewed who signed the petition construed it to mean that police should be called, and they fit the description of institutional conservatives. On the other hand, the hedgers did little, which was striking because some of them held posts which would normally require them to be leaders of the university community.

It was the humanistic loyalists who actively negotiated between the protesters and the university. Of the numerous faculty who came to the demonstration and who talked with the protesters, most were humanistic loyalists or radicals. In interviews, the former said that they felt themselves to be the vital link between the institution and the students. They wanted to persuade the students that to continue disruptive acts would only injure their cause and the university. They urged that the students would succeed with their demands if they democratically took their case to the campus at large.

Finally, the radicals essentially supported the protest, and most of them joined in the demonstration. They were the only faculty to do so. However, as opposition to the protest mounted, they split into two groups, those primarily interested in destroying the university as presently constituted regardless of personal consequences, and those who felt that the demonstration had already made its impact and who feared the injury of students if they continued. This latter group finally joined the humanistic loyalists in urging an end to disruption.

UNDERLYING DIMENSIONS OF RESPONSE STYLES

Given these four styles of faculty reaction and their corresponding behaviors, specifically what factors distinguish between these different groups? A careful examination of all the interviews and field notes uncovered three variables which define the professor's relation to the institution and to the students. These dimensions are antecedent to the protest, and it appears that they form constraints on behavioral responses.[2]

There is, first, the loyalty of faculty to the university or college. All groups but the radicals expressed this sentiment, and usually in general terms. They believed deeply in the idea of the university and the values of noncoercive, free inquiry which the protest challenged.

Second, each group expressed its relative satisfaction or dissatisfaction with the daily life and policies of this institution. It was the dissatisfaction with campus life which the humanistic loyalists shared with the protesting students that distinguished them from the hedgers.

The third dimension which emerged as central to each group interviewed concerned their relative attachment to or detachment from the students. If the extreme radicals did not care about personal consequences, neither did the institutional conservatives when it came to the protesters. If they were arrested, jailed, sentenced, or expelled, that unfortunately had to accompany a swift end to the demonstration. All other three groups spoke personally about the students, and this seemed to be an important restraint, especially in the case of the hedgers, from their supporting strong measures against the students.

These three dimensions describe faculty-institution relations and shape the manner in which faculty respond to a demonstration. When dichotomized, they form a scale which clearly distinguishes between the four styles of faculty response.[3]

TABLE 5.1
A SCALE OF STYLES OF FACULTY RESPONSE

Styles of Faculty Response:	Faculty-Institution Relations:		
	Institutional Loyalty	Institutional Satisfaction	Detached from Students
Institutional Conservatives	Yes	Yes	Yes
Hedgers	Yes	Yes	No
Humanistic Loyalists	Yes	No	No
Radicals	No	No	No

Besides dimensions of faculty-institution relations, an analysis of the four styles must include the influence of personal characteristics. The social class, origin of a professor, his parents' religion, and his general political orientation are important variables. But our real interest lies in *how faculty act as members of their institution,* so that one always wants to discover how much these background influences get translated into faculty-institutional relations. As we shall see from empirical studies, to a large extent they retain an independent influence.

ORIGINS OF FACULTY-INSTITUTION RELATIONS

Moving back one more level brings us to the structural location of faculty, which is a main source of faculty-institution relations. Within the institution a professor is located by five characteristics: his rank, his length of service, his department, the milieu of his relevant colleagues, and the balance between teaching and research. This balance should be thought of as undergraduate teaching versus research and teaching graduates (see Light, 1973, Introduction).

These variables locate a professor in relation to other faculty, to the institution, and to undergraduates. One of them has a peculiarly independent effect, departmental affiliation. To some degree, the political spectrum commonly observed from sociology to agriculture represents a translation of personal politics into disciplinary choice. But disciplines have an influence on faculty response beyond one's political orientation. They seem to constitute a world view, as the anthropologists say. Disciplinary world views are a fascinating subject for future research.

A second source of faculty-institution relations is the general structure of the institution—its size, its quality, its type of control (private, public, religious), its structural differentiation, and its relative decentralization of authority. Cultural characteristics such as race, region, and type (liberal arts vs. technical institute) may also provide a general framework for faculty-institution relations.

Of these two sources, the nature of different institutions will probably affect response to protest less than will factors which define the locus of a professor *within* an institution, because the latter are more immediate and are common to all higher education. A professor's field or length of service has similar effects on his relation to the university or college regardless of its structure. Following Parsons and Platt (1968), however, we would expect "better," more differentiated institutions to foster a more intense faculty culture, that is, to "allow" professors' attributes to shape faculty-institution relations more markedly than "lesser" institutions.

SUMMARY

The dynamics of faculty response to student protest begin with the characteristics which define where different professors are located in the institution and, to a lesser extent, the nature of the institution itself. These shape the three central relations of faculty to their institution. Combinations of these relationships form a scale which defines four styles of faculty response. In addition, background attributes affect response independently. The differential impact of these variables are most apparent in a disruptive protest over an external-internal issue and least apparent in a peaceful demonstration over a nonacademic issue. Although this model has numerous flaws it may help to analyze the nature of faculty response to protest.

FIGURE 5.2   THE DYNAMICS OF FACULTY RESPONSE
TO STUDENT PROTEST

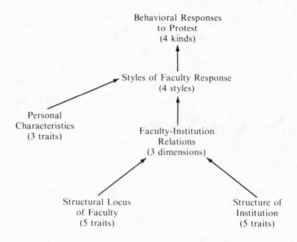

EMPIRICAL EVIDENCE FOR
AND AGAINST THE MODEL

Because the model for faculty response has the advantage of thinking through the relationships between different aspects of the levels of variables, it can organize and relate diverse studies, each of which analyzes only a few of the variables. On the other hand, some parts of the model have not yet been tested. In this case, a systematic review of the literature must yield to the terms of studies actually done. For example, most studies do distinguish between issues and tactics but (excepting Austin & Bayer, 1971; and Bidwell, 1970) not between different kinds of issues and tactics. Concerning types of response, most studies measure attitudes and involvement, simply dichotomizing each. Disruption is most likely to occur over war-related issues (.51) and demands for student power (.51), while violence most frequently occurs over racial policies (.33) (Austin & Bayer, 1971).

As for general level of activity, all reports agree that in the second half of the 1960s many more faculty approved of protest than participated in it, and many more approved of issues than tactics. To convey an overall sense of magnitude, Bayer (1971, Tables 1 & 2) reports that at 85 percent of all institutions, 25 percent or more of the faculty approved of "the emergence of radical activism." At more than half of these institutions over 40 percent approved. However, at only 40 percent of all institutions did more than 4 percent of the faculty "play an active protest role," and at 36 percent of all institutions less than 1 percent participated in support. These proportions vary a good deal from case to case. During the long, painful revolt at Columbia University in 1968, 43 percent of all faculty took an active role, mostly as members of the Ad Hoc Faculty Committee (Metzger, 1970).

RESPONSE STYLES

The materials from which the four styles of faculty response were derived consist of long interviews and field work I did during the protest at the University of Chicago described in Chapter 4. They were gathered during the stage of demonstration which John Spiegel describes as "mounting polarization" (p. 148). Using a case study rather than a broad survey allows the reader to see the four faculty groups together in the same situation, and it also conveys the context in which students make their demands and press for change.[4] In order to obtain the richest material on styles of response, the interviews concentrated on faculty who were involved in the conflict by reason of position or by choice.

The style of interviewing was important for getting full, accurate self-portraits. An open form of the focused interview was used. This form allows the person interviewed to begin with whatever is important to him. He can talk as long as he wishes without interruption and can move to other points as they naturally occur to him. By shaping his own interview, the person interviewed reveals how important different points are and the connections he sees between things without the interviewer— inadvertently through questions—imposing connections which are not there. The interview remains focused, however, by the interviewer making sure that at some time all of the important aspects of the demonstration are covered. Since the order of the interview will differ each time, the interviewer has to explore tactfully each major aspect as it naturally arises and then ask at the end of the conversation about any points never mentioned.

While this set of interviews represents only one case, the classifications produced from it seem broadly applicable for reasons stated before. Certain features of this case, however, do distinguish it from others. The University of Chicago has few part-time faculty and teaching assistants whose presence at Wisconsin, for example, made a great difference. How much difference they would make on this analysis is less clear; for they might have simply expanded the ranks of humanistic loyalists and especially radical faculty. This university is an excellent one, with a full program of research. Being a research university may not affect the *kinds* of responses so much as fill the ranks with institutional conservatives who like the university and their research, but who have little to do with students.

Studies of protest describe the concrete responses of faculty so little and allow them so infrequently to speak for themselves that it is valuable to devote several pages to full portraits of the four styles. To summarize the protest from which they were drawn, Students for a Democratic Society (SDS) organized a protest against ranking students when those ranks were used by the Selective Service to determine who should be drafted. Several hundred students took over the administration building, and the university responded by ignoring them. This effectively ruined the protesters' appeal as an aggrieved party. While most universities, for example Berkeley and Columbia, had counterattacked so that protesters looked like victims of brute force, the University of Chicago did not. This demonstrates the law of passive advantage: the party which appears the least aggressive gains the sympathy of the community in which a conflict occurs.

In the case at hand, the first clear sign of community anger occurred when institutional conservatives wrote and quickly signed a petition to get the protesters out of the administration building immediately, presumably by force. The humanistic loyalists, a much smaller group, feared violence and worked hard to persuade students to leave the building. In sympathy with the students, they argued that such coercion would fail to bring the changes desired.

Realizing that the faculty, not the administration, decided policy, the students ended their demonstration in order to campaign among the faculty. They found that while many professors sympathized with their moral positions, they planned to vote for the administration's position. This frightened students; to them this was so schizophrenic that they felt the university was not just wrong but full of sick people. Some spoke of the moral bankruptcy of the faculty.

In the profiles of faculty response that follow, certain topics are covered for each group. The relative weight given to these problems reflects the emphasis and distinctiveness of the answers made by men in each group. These topics are as follows. What are the apparent and the real issues involved in the protest? What is the University's policy on these issues and is it adequate? How did a communications gap arise over these issues? How did the demonstration take place and what kinds of students do you think participated in it? Who makes the policies under fire? What do you think of the students' demand for more power in making decisions which affect them? What will happen in the future?

Institutional Conservatives

Students were not likely to regard these men as schizophrenic, because they opposed both the issues and the tactics of the demonstration. In fact, however, they focused on tactics and discounted the issues. They considered the protest to be manufactured by SDS, either nationally or locally, even though they recognized that the inequality of grades for the draft had been discussed on campus. "SDS just grabbed it as the opportunity that they were looking for." From then on SDS took over.

> Certainly the initial people were SDS, and they quickly changed the name of the organization, because I think they found some students who didn't want to feel that they were manipulated by outsiders; so they reorganized as SAR [Students Against the Rank]. . . . They know what's going on, but they don't want you to question them about it.[5]

Why was the issue of "complicity" with Selective Service chosen?

> I have certain general impressions, that they are deeply interested in getting students to be more influential in formulating policy on campuses in the United States. And if they saw an issue which seemed to be laden with emotion and to command a certain amount of popular support and which was not local exclusively, that they might seize upon it as a vehicle to advance their more fundamental cause.
>
> This issue has all three properties, that is, it is full of emotions, and it's national, and their view is one which is not inherently absurd. And a fair number of people will find it definitely believable. So if they were looking for an issue, this would do pretty well.

Another conservative put it this way.

> Q. Do you think that the SDS leaders were interested in university ties to the Selective Service?
> A. I don't think initially they were.
> Q. Then why did they pick it up?
> A. Because they thought it was one that could be worked up into a demonstration.
> Q. Why did they want a demonstration?
> A. Well, because that is their business.
> Q. Is that their ultimate goal?
> A. Well, it *seems* to be.
> Q. (Smiling) Sort of a Demonstration, Incorporated?
> A. Yeh. Yeh. Now on the moral issue. . . .

How else, he argued, could one explain a demonstration at the University of Chicago? Every demonstration in the national spate that spring had occurred on campuses which had strong local chapters of

SDS. Moreover, they had not been on the same issues, indicating to him that the issue was chosen for its effectiveness as a rallying point in each locale. His conclusion suggested the ultimate purpose: "I think it was one step in a power play by SDS to get more say in the operation of the university."

When asked to discuss the problems of how the university sent academic records to Selective Service boards, institutional conservatives felt that the university had a good policy. They also found the demonstrators' demands immoral, because they would deny the rights of those students (not demonstrating) who *wanted* the university to cooperate with their local boards. This and other arguments against one-sided positions among the demonstrators came forth in conversations with the first three groups of faculty. However, only the institutional conservatives felt the issue itself was contrived.

Given that the faculty considered the apparent issues of the protest as bogus, what, in their eyes, were the real issues? Two common answers were student power and the general impression conveyed that any question about issues missed the point. What really mattered was the demonstration itself.

Most of these faculty members knew little about the students or the details of the protest. Such knowledge, they seemed to say, was unnecessary; for above all the demonstration was coercive, illegal, and disruptive.

> There's another moral issue which is much more important for me. . . . I can't understand how anyone could regard it as right that coercion be used to decide these things.
>
> I hope very much that the university *never* changes its policy or even discusses its policy while such things are in progress.

The entire sit-in was seen as coming from a handbook, and many of those interviewed alluded to an SDS manual "on how to do it," that is, how to organize insurrection, incite riot, and attack the power structure. To my knowledge, this manual does not exist,[6] and therefore it stands as almost the perfect myth for those who viewed the sit-in as manipulated from outside. But if these men saw the protest as a stereotype from a handbook, real or imagined, their interpretations were a stereotype in the eyes of SAR leaders of how those in power respond, by seeing themselves, the institution, and their students as blameless victims of outside agitators.

Consistent with their views on manipulation, these faculty described how the demonstration smothered reason under its religious, irrational momentum.

> Now in a demonstration of this kind, as soon as it gets to the demonstrating phase, it's clear—and I've seen two of them now, and I guess it's general—all reason goes out the window. The kids get so emotionally involved that they don't listen, they don't reason, they don't think. They're just completely emotional. And that was quite clear here, because they believed things, and they still believe things that are absolutely untrue. They've been told many times that they're not true, and the leaders all know they're not true—that nobody would listen to them, and that there wasn't any communication and there was no opportunity to make their views known.

This flood of words and assertions is almost as irresistible as the protest itself. The speaker continued, illustrating that sit-ins have no substantial foundations.

> Now this was true five years ago when we had a sit-in on the housing policy of the university, and they did come and talk to us before the sit-in, and it was perfectly clear that the cause they had didn't exist. But the sit-in went on anyway for emotional reasons. They already had the steam up, and they really couldn't stop or they didn't want to stop. . . .

Speaking of the present sit-in, one professor said,

> Many of them counted this as a great religious experience, like a revivalist meeting. They went back in the dorms with the sense of having been in a unique group. And some of the students who didn't sit in said, "I missed out on a great experience!"

While this professor correctly identifies the evangelical, communal experience, he uses it to question the sincerity of the sit-in, and (later) the sincerity of the protesters to negotiate. He did not think the protesting students represented students at large. Moreover, negotiation is a rational process and the movement seemed entirely irrational.

> If they were really sincere in wanting a solution to the problem they're demonstrating about, I think this is a sure way not to get it. . . . Everything they did lost support.

Finally, Students Against the Rank was taking a moral stand that every person's life is morally equal. Moral issues cannot be negotiated, and the men in this group sensed that no kind of vote or compromise would be recognized.

As in most protests, communications is a major issue. Demonstrators claimed here as elsewhere that they had tried to communicate their concerns, but that the administration had treated them with benign neglect. Knowing that certain committees of the faculty actually set policy on such matters, institutional conservatives who served on these committees said, "No one tried to talk to me." They concluded that the students picked on the administration because it is easier to demonstrate against than a faculty committee. Moreover, their choice of a demonstration foreclosed all possible communication. In essence, these professors said, "They never talked to us, and if they try now we won't listen."

Institutional conservatives were the only group not to admit the confusion which others saw surrounding the decisionmaking relationship between the administration and faculty committees. One conservative said, "The administration *is* the faculty," without any sense that this viewpoint would confuse others. What he meant is that all senior administrators are professors at the university, and the university involves as many faculty through committees in policy decisions as it can so that no division between the two groups will evolve.

The protest leaders said policy committees seemed to be "dead bodies," and few members attended. Institutional conservatives felt poor attendance reflected "harmony," a lack of issues. But institutional conservatives correctly implied (though never said explicitly) that faculty committees served as buffers which lie in reserve when a controversy arises. Demonstrators felt the administration set policy on ties with the Selective Service. This group of faculty said that the university had a long-standing policy. Here they were incorrect. In fact, administrative practices with regard to the Selective Service had evolved over the years, with no official policy taken until those practices had been challenged just prior to the demonstration.

Given their viewpoint, the institutional conservatives naturally felt that protest leaders, by going to administrators, had falsely contrived a communications gap.

> What I suspect is that the SDS leaders knew always that (pause) after all, they've got full-time people who do nothing but study the system.
>
> I'm sure they knew exactly what was going on, and I suspect that they were not about to tell the mass of students all this information, because that would make their business [of drumming up a protest] much more difficult.

Surprisingly little was said by this first group about the student demand for participation in decisions. Although their prime concern was the maintenance of democratic communications, ironically they gave little attention to demands in this area. Here one saw the crippling effect of the demonstration on this group of faculty. Brilliant, sensitive men, they devoted much of the interviews to condemning every aspect of the protest.

A couple, however, said that undergraduates fell outside university life. Since this group consisted largely of research faculty, one sensed in their conversation an inherent irrelevance of college students for a research institution. The following excerpt contrasts what the undergraduates need with what the university gives them.

> They need to be overseen and checking in and checking out and all that sort of thing. But the pervasive atmosphere of the university is that students are grown up and we're here to teach them, not here to psychoanalyze them, or teach them how to behave at a dance or how to get along with a girl or how to dress, or any of these things.

All faculty interviewed were asked about changes in faculty response as events progressed. Some of the institutional conservatives had been present when leaders stated their ultimatum. One said faculty present felt badly. "They were not hostile so much as sort of distressed that things had reached this point." Once the demonstration began, this group agreed that students lost previous, but dubious support.

> Well, I think that there was a lot of faculty sympathy with the kids, of course sort of unthinking sympathy without quite realizing it, because I think by and large the faculty tend to be antiadministration for no reason at all, except it's a natural phenomenon to be against the administration.
>
> [Yet] I think they [the protesters] misjudged faculty opinion by a very, very wide margin, because they talked to faculty members preferentially who were sympathetic with their point of view, and they didn't talk with the faculty members at large.

As the administration restrained itself from any clear action, institutional conservatives drew up a petition opposing the sit-in and calling for its immediate cessation. Within two hours, two hundred faculty had signed it. Two lines long, the petition made no mention of force or police, but interviews with signers revealed that they understood the petition to imply force if necessary. Hostility was building fast. Then the demonstration ended. In the aftermath, a motion passed commending the administration for its restraint and condemning disruptive acts. In the vote, 60 percent for, 10 percent against and 30 percent abstaining, many institutional conservatives abstained, because they saw no reason to commend the administration.

Looking to the future, institutional conservatives anticipated placating all sides while not making any institutional changes.

> I don't think these committees are going to change the basic structure. They might find ways of involving student participation that we haven't found before. And I think this would be all to the

good. I don't, however, believe that students should participate in the running of the university in any direct sense, because they don't have a commitment to the university in the way the faculty has. They're here for four years and they're out, and they don't have to live under the schemes they might devise. But certainly there are many areas where their opinions ought to be heard and some areas in which they ought to be followed, I think.

Their greatest fear was that the demonstration might discourage senior administrators, whom they all admired.

I've seen some bad administrations in universities in my time, and I think I know one when I see it. And this is a *great* administration. . . . If anything in this sit-in causes a reversal, of this momentum [which the administration has built], it would be a great blow to the university.

The Hedgers

As implied by their name, this group of faculty expressed more complex and ambivalent views on the student protest. Partly by choice, partly by position, these professors had more contact with undergraduates. They participated in both the community of scholars and the community of students. Because of their more intimate knowledge of the college, they did not attribute the cause of protest to outside agitators but to a sense of powerlessness.

It's true, I think, that this university is in one respect very conservative. We've always been terribly free when it comes to free expression, and we don't supervise students' private lives very much. You can say anything. You can invite any speaker you want. We're very free that way. But we're also very conservative, not only in policy but in practice and habit on any matter that has to do with the now-hot issue of student participation.

At the same time, this group thought the issue of the draft was a genuine one. Several mentioned that many faculty opposed current draft laws. All felt the demonstrators really dislike the war in Vietnam.

Turning to the "communication gap," these faculty agreed that university policy had not been clear and that students should have gotten a better response from the deans with whom they talked. Again the interviews reveal overlapping lines of authority. Speaking of action taken in a faculty committee one professor said, ". . . I shouldn't say 'Mr. _____'s policy.' I shouldn't say it. It was the policy which was agreed on by the administration. It was explained to us, and it was endorsed. . . ." When he finished one still felt that this policy came from and was explained by the administrator.

The hedgers also agreed that the faculty committees in question had been on the decline, that their members were out of touch with college students, that one major committee was a shell for a small informal group of faculty-administrators whose work they usually approved, and that the committees were senior and elite.

But the hedgers also thought protest leaders had engineered a communications gap.

> They were being very belligerent, and I think they were doing everything they possibly could to give enough offense so that they would be thrown out. I think it was a deliberate ploy or tactic which they could then use as a *casus belli*. It was straight out of the textbook, I think.

Here they separated the leaders from the majority of demonstrators, not seeing the latter as sheep so much as intelligent, genuine students. While the institutional conservatives did not know enough students to talk much about them, many hedgers did, and a favorite point of conversation was John Holcomb. "Frankly, I didn't think very much of it," said one administrator about one of these early meetings with SDS leaders. "It's partly that the leader of this was [John Holcomb] whom I'd known for a long time, and he seems to me quite an unstable and excitable sort of fellow. He's apt to get excited about a variety of things." Every person who had to deal with him and a few others who surrounded him reported baffling, confused conversations. From both sides, communication seemed impossible, and there were no interpreters. Most frequent was the impression of rigid irrationality.

> His aims are so different from anybody else's . . . well not really. I think that he appeals to a lot of people's unconscious aims, in that his aim has always been to have a big fuss, to have a big demonstration.
>
> He's a really professional demonstrator. I think that's what he conceives his role to be. And that, of course, appeals to the needs of many others, to have some expressive action.

Holcomb had special talents.

> He was so far out in front that they thought he was the general. . . . The loudest, the most vigorous, the only one who could stand up to the avalanche of reason . . . would be [John Holcomb], because he was obdurate and insensitive to reason. His purpose was perfectly clear.

Beyond Holcomb, SDS baffled these faculty. In earlier days, some noted, radicals had led student government. While they kept the Stalinists out of power and out of the National Student Association, the Young Socialists were very involved in power politics. The faculty seemed baffled that SDS was both more active and more anarchistic. It seemed romantic, yet nonideological. But the most salient feature of the New Left for these men was the one manifested in the sit-in.

> I don't want to get too dramatic about this, but one of the things that has always bothered me about the new radicals is that they seem to have no regard for, no appreciation of the values of due process, an orderly procedure. Now that seems to me to be in a way one of the *leading* virtues of Western Civilization.

Hedgers, who were mostly full professors, characterized in a similar manner the junior faculty with whom the demonstrators had consulted. Student activists had greatly overestimated faculty support by talking only to this special group.

> Like the present generation of students, they have a great distrust of institutions. Because they have a great distrust of institutions, they're not really very interested in how they work. I think there is a very important distinction between the New Left and the old left of thirty years ago, where the Marxists were very interested in institutions and their mechanisms, partly so they could infiltrate them at strategic points and control them. And the present ones don't care. They've been brought up on the idea of direct actions and a kind of anarchism.

People in this second group were astonished at the expressions of alienation and powerlessness from some junior faculty.

The demonstration itself led to statements which distinguished this group from institutional conservatives. They thought manipulation could not explain how the mass of students got involved. "Well, you couldn't have manipulated them if they didn't have something they were bugged about." Beyond the issues of rank and power in making policy, there were two subtle but profound forces which these faculty discerned at work among the students. First, they seemed dependent. There was the feeling ". . . that somehow the university is their shield and their protector, and somehow should protect them against the outside world." When they realized that their institutional parents were in collusion with the outside world, they became outraged.

Second, to their surprise, these professors discovered a new embarrassment about privilege.

> But I'm sure most everyone thought and every faculty member I know thought that students in general would have enough of their own self-interest tied up in educational deferments that they would want their class standing sent in. . . .

Who would have ever thought that students who opposed this war, or war in general, would endanger a privilege that kept them out of war?

> And it's interesting that our mental health people . . . mentioned earlier that there's been a rapid increase in the amount of anxiety among graduate students, based primarily on the matter of privilege.

For these and other reasons, the students rallied for a demonstration. One hedger was in his office when the demonstration took over his building.

> Of course we were all prepared. We knew it was coming. We had made advance plans. Everybody had nothing but trivial stuff on his desk. My concern with the secretaries was they they not get panicky. . . .
> Just the impact of having all that racket coming up from downstairs and its gradual spread upstairs—pretty rough! . . . All work stopped.
> And walking down the stairs was not very pleasant. When I went home you had to pick your way, with the klieg lights in your face . . . lots of noise. Cat calls, whatnot at the hated symbol of oppression. . . . And, uh, that's not very pleasant. I did manage to wave as I went out and smile, but uh. . . .
> And I might say it was . . . I feel very strongly, uh, the kind of *desecration* in what they were doing . . . in spite of the care with which they tried to clean up and so forth. . . . That anybody could do that—*just the presence of the filthy mobs.* . . . Yes, it's disgusting. . . . You're never the same after an experience like this.

Unlike the first group of faculty, these men took time to talk about what kinds of students participated in the demonstration; for that was important to them. Neither the man who spoke the words above nor the others in this group thought grubby or bohemian students dominated the ranks of protesters. They found many bright students there, and they showed no surprise, saying such a demonstration was the last place for narrow minds. At the same time, the presence of distinguished undergraduates troubled them; for it legitimated an otherwise abhorrent protest. These students made them take the protest more seriously than John Holcomb had inspired them to do. The ambivalence was well expressed by one professor:

> When you see some of the very best students of the university in there, then we feel they have to be saved at all costs. . . . They may be irrational deep down, but they're rational on the surface.

Yet the impact of the demonstration on these faculty was similar to its effect on institutional conservatives. They bristled and thought of nothing but student coercion.

> I think the main effect of the protest, certainly on me, has been that I
> haven't been able to think as well or as much as I should about the
> basic policy questions.

Since more of this group participated in the university's response to
the demonstration, they revealed in their conversation the dynamics of
institutional response. Legal issues arose immediately, they said. Was the
university responsible if an injury (such as fire) took place? Legalistic
thinking was powerfully put forth in council, they said, and (in this
group's eyes) fortunately not followed. As the faculty and staff struggled
on, one policy emerged, "Do nothing to provoke."

Meanwhile, John Holcomb's impassioned style had become less
relevant to the problems of sustaining the demonstration, and these
faculty felt new needs led to a change in student leadership. Moderates
took over and finally decided it best to end the demonstration and canvass
for faculty votes. But the hardcore radicals kept control of the press with
unfortunate results, they said. Many senior officers of the university and
the community at large took these press releases at face value and thus
overestimated the belligerence of protest leaders.

As mentioned before, many faculty came to speak informally to the
students, including one of the hedgers. Arriving to speak at 11 P.M., he
stayed until 2 A.M. During this time, he reported, his audience of seventy
listened intently to everyone's questions and his answers. If someone
interrupted him, others would hush the student up. Some students were
practically exploding with eagerness to speak, but they would wait their
turn. Never had this professor seen a group work like that. When he left,
he was thanked for coming and told that they had five to six more hours
of debate left!

> I tried to imagine last night when I was driving home what would
> happen if we got the seventy members of the [department] together—
> and that's about the same number as there was—put them into those
> same circumstances and said,
> "Now look fellows. We've got an iron chairman. Dean _____ is
> going to be tough today. You're not going to interrupt each other the
> way you usually do, and we're going to be very courteous. And we're
> going to stay here twelve, twenty-four hours or whatever it takes, and
> we're going to hammer out a new curriculum in that time."
> Q. What do you think would happen?
> A. Oh, it couldn't be done. The faculty would resign.

On the stated issues of the protest, this second group agreed with
many of the views expressed by the first. They supported the administration's policy on cooperation with the draft, and they felt that coercive

demonstrations were intolerable. But we have seen how differently composed are their views from those of the institutional conservatives. Such differences matter, and they appear in perspectives on student participation. The demonstration "made an awful lot of people who would not otherwise have done so to think seriously about the place of students in the university." Another said:

> Student affairs is now as important in the university as labor relations is in the company, and you really ought to know what the hell they think.

Had there been change? Answers were basically conservative and apprehensive.

> Well obviously, the next time faculty votes on this problem their votes will be inevitably affected by the commotion, and I suppose that's a role that students take in decision-making.

> It ought to all work out peacefully, in the sense that it's very hard for people to maintain that they are right and that the university must do what they say in the face of overwhelming opposition and examination.

> But my perception is that there's so much feeling and so much self-righteousness there, that it still will be very explosive.

> The fuse is still lit. . . .

Humanistic Loyalists

In many respects this third group of faculty and faculty-administrators responded like those we just finished describing. However, all of these men taught in the college and by temperament seemed more personally involved with students. This involvement appeared at the beginning of interviews. While others wanted me to start ("Well, where would you like to begin"), these faculty immediately began to talk about a recent encounter, unwrapping the complex problems it revealed ("Before we begin, I must tell you about . . ."). They knew the issues well and described the origins of the uprising the way the hedgers did. Unlike them, however, they did not want to focus on history. Rather, they wished to talk about present problems, the greatest of which was alienation. Their emphasis of this theme was greater and their analysis broader, including the experience of demonstrating itself.

> I think students have been sadly in need of social amenities on campus. . . . It's impossible to calculate how much that had to do with the present disaffection, but I know it had a lot to do with its

continuation. Once the students got into the building and found themselves for the first time with a certain amount of community affiliation, this, in a way, took over. Many of them stayed on because it was pleasant and exciting and fun to know each other, to get acquainted, and to feel close.

Some signs of the envy which John Spiegel describes as part of the dynamics of doves emerged; for these faculty expressed frustrations of being cut off, of being estranged, and spoke in a soft tone about the pleasantries of being in the demonstration. The following quote ends with what may be a personal statement.

Graduate students were furious about their poor teaching, about the indifference of the teachers, furious about the bad housing conditions, furious about a series of rude rebuffs by minor employees in the bookstore and comptroller's office. A general annoyance at the institution, even though you love this place basically too.

Already the causes underlying the demonstration are more detailed here than given by other groups, and this group of faculty added others, such as secrecy.

. . . a general pattern in the administration . . . of not letting people know how decisions have been made and not letting people know when decisions have been made, a pattern of secrecy or seeming secrecy which gave students a feeling that they were shut out and nothing they could do could change it.

More than other groups, faculty in this one emphasized how poorly known—if not defined—the decision-making policy structure was.[7]

The problem was one of communication. The structure of an organization becomes explicit only when there's a problem, and it was this problem that forced many faculty members as well as students to become aware of the nature of the policy-making structures of this institution.

The students were too sophisticated and had enough complaints to be seen as manipulated into demonstrating.

On the basis of this analysis, humanistic loyalists felt that students wanted to protest "even if the draft hadn't existed."

I think it is very unlikely that there is a small group of SDS'ers who meet privately and who are trying to control the things.

These faculty, therefore, thought that students participated in the protest because they were frustrated and wanted to see change. The following exchange about SDS contrasts with the one recorded earlier.

And they finally found one in this, and I don't mean by that to say they're insincere. It was an issue about which they really cared, but I do think they were really looking for an issue.

Q. An issue for what reason?
A. In order to have an organized protest.
Q. Why would they want that?
A. Because it's part of the SDS general goal to transform society by transforming society's institutions . . .

Nevertheless, this group also took the issue of the draft seriously in its own right, and one produced this eloquent statement about a conversation with a radical:

But then he went on and said something I have a great deal of respect for, and he and I found ourselves from radically different positions coming together on one major point: the supreme principle on the matter of the draft was the *absolute equivalence* of value of every human life. . . . There's just no way you can calculate these things. Therefore a draft which pretends that a student's life is worth more, that an A student's life is worth more than a B student's life, that a student's life is worth more than a laboring man's life, is an immoral system.

Beyond this point they parted company.

It is immoral, radically immoral, to have a system in which you calculate with human lives. *But* we all make calculations whether we want to or not, and so we are radically immoral. The problem is to be as little so as possible.

A basic difference lies in that this group is fiercely loyal to the university while radical faculty give first loyalty to beliefs not specific to the university.

And therefore, if I see a tremendous institution like this university which serves other values which are also valuable, and I see it possibly destroyed by my pursuing a particular moral line, then I have a moral conflict and have to make a choice. . . .
And since I put such a very high value on this oasis of an effort to preserve human reason and the free act of inquiry in a world that has never known many such institutions and never will have very many, then I would sacrifice all kinds of things in order to preserve it.

One of the most important features distinguishing this group from the previous two was its response to the protest itself. While most faculty grew angry and said the demonstration precluded any negotiations, this group immediately wanted to talk. When asked how he felt when he heard the demonstration had begun, one professor-dean said,

> Oh, I felt desperate. I felt it was a terrible mistake (to sit in). And I felt that those of my colleagues who said that there is nothing we can do because they've threatened to go in and "this puts us under a coercive situation and therefore anything we do will be interpreted as concession," I felt they were entirely wrong. . . .
>
> I was in favor of a maximum number of talks and communiques. . . . But I still think that the administration made a mistake in giving an air of not just firmness and decisiveness, but of implacableness and of deafness.

This group of faculty took the demonstration as a direct blow to the college and to themselves. Ironically, some of them had been busy with plans for a more open college experience, so busy that contact with students had been abnormally low. They felt guilty and wished to do anything to help both the students and the institution they loved.

> And many of my most beloved students . . . I really reached the point where I wasn't worried about myself at all. About the third day I decided the only way to survive this one was to make quite clear you're going to resign the day it's all over and that you don't have any stake in it whatever.
>
> And I felt completely free about my personal involvement. But I was quite sure that some of my . . . some of the best students were going to be hurt, kicked out, drafted, permanent marks on the records. I don't think students can ever possibly believe how much that kind of concern would have motivated not just me, but . . .

Being of this more open persuasion (and less frightened by the protest), these professors fought hard against the institutional conservatives.

> The image that kept being offered was, "The first thing you know we'll be a South American university, in which the students are able to kick the chancellor out by having a protest movement."

Men in this group found this extreme.

> It seemed to me that meeting with them wouldn't have to be interpreted in that way. We were meeting with them because they were protesting, yeah, but that doesn't mean all right you can have your way. We're open to hear what they have to say and discussions.
>
> The reason the administrative group didn't want conversations to go on with students was that even if you held a conversation and said we will not make any concessions until you get out of the building, that's an implied promise that as soon as you do get out of the

building things will happen. Well, I felt that although a real point, it was something we could afford, well afford to pay.

Since this group lacked passionate commitment to some set of institutional principles, they reported that others saw them as muddle-headed. Over time, however, their influence grew and helped to avert calling in police. Nevertheless, the administration's press statements continued to be written by the more belligerent camp.

The statement to the public made it look as if the university didn't care about moral questions and thought the students were just a bunch of illegal poachers. There's nothing more to be said for them than the fact that they were committing an intolerable act. . . .

I can't help thinking that if the administration had been willing to use imagination and perhaps appear in the early days in the sit-in and talk with students, that a very different tone would have emerged. They might have even averted the sit-in if there'd been some meetings earlier.

If the hard-liners wrote university statements, so did hard-line students write SAR statements.

I think the documents which came out of the building were unfortunate because they tended to harden the line. . . . The literature, in other words, of the students in the building was so bad that it was thought to be good ammunition by the administration just to distribute it. And it was. It made faculty mad.

The humanistic loyalists influenced greatly the demonstrators' own decision to leave occupied facilities. Many students trusted leading members of this group, who spoke firmly about the destructiveness of the demonstration.

The rhetoric of my speech Monday night was to support them as much as I could before blasting them, but I felt like doing nothing else but blasting them. But I felt they needed that support, and they deserved that support.

Another professor said that the protest had done more to raise the moral tone of the university than anything in the past ten years, but students would hardly have guessed this feeling from his speech to them.

In talking with the demonstrators, these faculty also noted a certain childishness.

They're looking for an ideal father. . . . They're very critical in looking for this ideal father. They almost never find him, because they're so critical. They always find the clay feet, and therefore they go from dismay to disillusionment.

From the outside, it is hard to imagine how much some students fear and respect certain faculty heroes.

> I went to a meeting later in the week at which I wasn't allowed to say a word for three hours, because the students were afraid that they would be snowed by my magical remarks. . . .
>
> I finally got the floor and I told them, Look, you're worried about showing deference to professors. You started out saying you never get a chance to talk to professors, and any professor you'd want to talk to has a good deal of deference towards students.

Because they helped to persuade the students to end the demonstration, the humanistic loyalists expressed responsibility to see that significant changes occurred. On the issue of cooperation with the Selective Service, they agreed with other faculty groups. However, they favored more student participation in policy decisions, and they found the final resolutions passed by the faculty too harsh, formal, and implacable. In speaking of future work to be done, they spoke of their frustration with faculty conservatives on one hand and radical professors on the other. Some of them, for example, organized an informal faculty group to draft new reforms, but extremists dominated the meetings and threw them into confusion.

> I've been struck again and again by how radical the difference is between the different types of temperament, quite aside from the intellectual tradition on this matter. There's some of the faculty and a certain number of the students who really would like to have trouble, and they feel cheated if they don't get to have a flare-up.

Nevertheless, these faculty expressed optimism about what gains would be made in the next several months.

Radical Faculty

> If the students are constitutionally outside the decision-making process, then it seems to me that ultimately their only course is to direct action—if they form a body of sentiment within the university. How else do they influence the decision making?
>
> Every single political system has some process of consultation with the lower orders. No authority acts without trying to feel what the lower orders believe. That is not the democratic process; that is not a community. A slave system has some process of consultation. But, in a highly authoritarian situation, they will either engage in some form of direct action to bring pressure on the system or actually engage in rebellion.

The radical faculty was a more heterogeneous group than other groups suspected. Some found a temporary cause in the protest which satisfied psychological needs; others held a deep radical commitment as a way of life. This description focuses on the latter, who were not unaware of the unfortunate presence of the former and the bad name they gave true radicals in the eyes of other faculty. One radical described a "pseudoradical" at an SAR meeting as "bounding up and down as if on a horse and frothing at the mouth as his words were choked by his excitement." Radicals, themselves a small group, felt the campus contained only two or three highly visible men such as the one just described. Both kinds were most heavily involved in college life and teaching, and radical faculty knew student activists the best of any group.

This was the only group of faculty who contributed significant new pieces to the account of how the protest began. They mentioned, for example, a group of radical faculty who had proposed a range of policies for separating the university from Selective Service activities some time ago. The administration did not reply, but adopted parts of them after the demonstration. They spoke of long conversations among fellow teachers about the morality of giving grades when they would be used by the Selective Service. Selection by academic prowess is not only immoral but also amounts to selection by social class. There was also an informal seminar unknown to other faculty which centered on conflicts between humanist values and politics. "Some of them I guess were SDS people, but none of them are people who are viable. They're a different group, and they play a very active role in the demonstration."

This was the only group which took the issue of the university's complicity with the Selective Service seriously. They also were alone in thinking the university's stance was in error. They felt the arguments were subtle, and that few administrators really understood them. Other faculty, including humanistic loyalists, appeared to them to be employing the old habit of displacing the real issue for a psychological one.

> On the whole the root of the problem I repeat is the inability to take the students seriously for what they're saying. The tendency on the part of any administration is to interpret what they are doing in other terms.
>
> The rank issue itself, my strong feeling is, is not seen as real by anyone other than the students and a few faculty. Others think it might have to do with some malaise in the college, or with student-faculty relations, or be due to neglect of the undergraduates in various ways. Maybe it stems back to the housing situation. Or, some of them are more radical and alienated so that it could have been any issue.

To be sure, this group said, there was a malaise in the college and a number of local complaints, but the administration put them into a dishonest framework and ignored indigenous sources of the protest against ranking.

> What I am saying is that the administrators will focus on the other things, that they are sophisticated . . . which is to focus on trouble-makers, manipulators, outside agitators, and a whole bunch of extraneous factors. . . .

Administrators seemed to think that a lot could be solved by just talking to students more, that there were no deeper issues. Other faculty thought there were deeper problems, radicals said, but one sensed they were playing out their own guilt rather than listening to what students were saying.

Radical faculty directly linked student alienation with lack of student power in policy making, and thereby interpreted this second issue of the protest in significantly different ways. First, they did not think a demonstration was inevitable or even that the issue of student power per se could have generated a protest.

> You see, I don't think that the issue of student participation *as such* leads to demonstrations. It's a rather abstract issue. It becomes an issue only as a consequence of students trying to win a certain point at the university on *other* grounds, realizing the limitations of their power. Then you can interpret all this as feeding into changing relationships between the students and the university, but no revolution is simply a revolution for greater participation.

Not only did there have to be a substantive issue, but radical faculty believed that students had interests and needs genuinely different from those of the university. Unlike the second and third groups of faculty, these men did not think the alienation could be eliminated by better college programs or even by giving students more power. Students needed and deserved a voice in making decisions, but their alienation was inherent in their class differences as students.

Being mostly junior faculty, this group also expressed personal alienation and powerlessness.

> But, really, there's a hierarchy of power. The very fact that junior faculty are excluded from the Senate. . . . The attitudes are very associated with it. That is, the most powerful men in the university clearly were the least sympathetic with the student demands.

Did these junior faculty feel they were like students?

> At the *beginning* of the sit-in, I didn't think of it in that way, and that was one of the reasons I had decided that I wouldn't sit in, that I was not like the students. I had other channels to use.
>
> I did decide to sit in, though. . . . I looked around and saw all my students sitting on the floor and saw graduate students sitting on the floor and I said those are the people I'm with.

The final decision was so easy, so deep. The spectrum from students to university officers seems wide, and junior faculty concerned about the draft saw themselves at the lower end. At the far end of the spectrum, they sensed little difference between most faculty and administrators.

The topic of how the protest grew also received different interpretation. Radical faculty were alone in mentioning that before John Holcomb took leadership, delegates from the protest group were sent back to speak with university officials. These delegates came back persuaded by administrative arguments about the legal problems of their position. The general group, however, wanted its view to prevail and did not want any compromises; so they changed spokesmen.

> What struck me was that the kids they appointed as their main spokesmen were the most militant radicals. They were younger and fantastically naive. [It seemed] that when they knew they were going to be in some kind of bargaining situation before the sit-in, they wanted the most intransigent, bluntest, most aggressive spokesmen, rather than someone who would cave in. . . . They had very articulate, young guys, who they seemed to keep in the background for purposes of being spokesmen. Perhaps they didn't trust their rigidity.

This interpretation, for which there is considerable independent evidence, contrasts sharply with that of institutional conservatives at the other end of the faculty spectrum. They thought radical leaders manipulated large groups of students for their own ends; radical faculty maintained the opposite, that students about to protest used certain leaders to achieve their ends.

To this extent, students arranged a confrontation, but radical faculty thought little of arguments that students had intentionally ignored channels of communication just so they could have a demonstration. Rather, these men claimed that the students had tried every route they could before finally electing leaders like John Holcomb, as just described. Although university officials said that faculty make university policy, no one said this before the protest, and moreover administrators *acted* as if they ran the university. At a crucial meeting of administrators and protest leaders, for example, the dean present stated the university's position flatly and left. He never indicated that he was merely the spokesman for a faculty committee. Besides this, faculty committees met in secret, as the humanistic loyalists explained too. Finally, radicals said that the administration almost fused with senior faculty committees, a fact which institutional conservatives applauded and which radicals deplored.

While most faculty thought the demonstration was ultimately unnecessary even if understandable, radical faculty said the students *had* to protest for reasons given in the opening quotation to this section. The response, they emphasized, was big.

> In no case ever do most people organize for anything. I think the fact that something like one-fourth of the undergraduate student body was probably involved directly in this thing represents a very high degree of organization.
> I think that there were perhaps 600 students at one time who slept in or otherwise were highly committed to the demonstration itself, and of the 600, 450 or 300 were undergraduates.

Some faculty with this fourth perspective distinguished between two kinds of demonstrators. A minority of students were political radicals, experienced and interested in challenging the university and its policies. For them the demonstration was an instrumental act to confront a power elite. For most of the students, on the other hand, the protest expressed basic feelings about people (they're human), conflicts (both on campus and abroad), and community (you can talk to people). The protest grew when these students believed that the school was being run like a total institution rather than like a community and felt that communications had broken down. The sit-in itself was a four-day communal act, a deeply personal experience which penetrated the questions of what the world is like and how one should live one's life. Communication improved, not only among themselves in the building, but with teachers who came to speak with them. When in the end the faculty responded only to the instrumental demands, students felt the faculty had never faced the more complex feelings and problems expressed by the demonstration.

The radical faculty group said the demonstration expressed a high moral feeling for the university. "These kids really believe in a community of scholars."

> Any group of academically serious kids, particularly in the last few years, is going to take very seriously the pretentions of the academic institution for being a bastion of stimulus and dissent and independence from social pressure. [It] will want the university *to be like them* and that's not only true here but everywhere.

[This] will be increasingly a major source of pressure on university faculty and administrations: "Why aren't you living up to *our* moral standards?" [This] is a very interesting switch from the past when universities had moral standards.

The tone of these excerpts from interviews correctly conveys that radical faculty were the only group whose first loyalty lay with their (rather than "the") students, not with the institution. Some had joined with the humanistic loyalists in persuading students to end the demonstration, but for different reasons. While the loyalists wished to save the college, radical faculty wanted to save their students. In a singular parallel with all other faculty groups, radical professors also noted "an infantile dependence on the faculty as figures of warmth and desirable to emulate as models. . . ." Radical faculty were very aware that to some degree they had manipulated the students and therefore had a responsibility towards them. The question was how to create a participatory university.

> There's a large problem in figuring out how students participate or should participate. . . . For someone like me who likes a situation in which there is a high degree of grass-roots involvement in an issue, this sort of small committee structure seems to me to be more manipulation than real participation. But real participation, how you institutionalize that is a mystery to me at this point.

If change did not come about, these men and other faculty would have hurt themselves and the college.

> If the students feel that they have been manipulated or sold out by the faculty, even the faculty they most respect, there will be a legacy of bitterness within the college they won't be able to overcome. . . . It seems to me that the next time there's a cause for direct action, however, the students will be much less likely to accept faculty suggestion.

Ending on a note of apprehension is most appropriate for a description of faculty response to protest.

FACULTY-INSTITUTION RELATIONS

These four styles of faculty response are important as predictors of specific actions taken by different groups, particularly when a protest is disruptive. The earlier analysis of these styles into their respective components suggests why. Beyond this study, there is no evidence for these three dimensions of faculty-institution relations, except that many variables used in surveys appear to stand in for them. Consider academic rank. The reason one would predict that senior faculty are more likely to oppose protest (as in fact they do) stems not from something inherent in rank itself, but from the social bond of senior rank that makes its holders more loyal and satisfied than junior faculty. In a similar manner, length of service correlates with conservative response, because one assumes that faculty of long standing have stronger ties to the university or college than do new professors of any rank.

The dimensions of faculty-institution relations also clarify the consequences of calling in the police to end a protest. Only the conservatives are relatively detached from the students and would favor swift action against the demonstrators. The hedgers and humanists fear any drastic counterattack and favor persuasion. The radicals will divide. Those most eager to undermine the institution will favor a bust as a way to radicalize the liberals against a "police state." Radicals who temper their institutional attack with concern for individual demonstrators will argue that the demonstration has made its impact in that the radicals should convert this gain into favorable negotiations rather than risk losing all to a faculty backlash.

Thus, if the administration, without consulting the faculty, calls in police, as at Harvard, or even threatens to call them in, as at Columbia, it will effect opposition from the hedgers, the humanists, and of course the radicals. But a patient administration, in dialogue with its faculty, will eventually find first the hedgers and then the humanists favoring strong measures. In many lesser known demonstrations, however, things never reach this point, because the students get scared or tired and because the humanists and hedgers persuade them to end the confrontation.

This analysis runs counter to the usual wisdom about the Columbia crisis—that much destruction would have been avoided by calling in the police early. This view depicts a patient, suffering (or indecisive) administration hoping that reason will prevail in an unreasonable situation. But the administration had in effect "called in the police" very early by disclosing such plans. This was the fatal flaw, and it polarized everyone. There was no middle ground. In a careful analysis of the Columbia crisis, Loya Metzger (c. 1970) writes:

> What is not emphasized in the numerous recountings of the 1968 Columbia story is the extent to which, from the outset of the demonstrations, the question of resorting to police action was the central stated concern of faculty involvement. (P. 7)

Of those professors who opposed using police, 81 percent became active during the crisis, while the figure for those favoring police was 35 percent (Metzger, Table 5).

Therefore, while many observers believe Columbia used the stand-off strategy, in fact the Columbia case contrasts with that approach. Our model of faculty response makes clear the differences between the two and the sociological logic behind them. In the stand-off, the administration refuses to yield to student coercion but lets the demonstration proceed. In effect, it lets the institutional conservatives build up pressure for strong measures, while the humanists work endlessly to persuade the students that the university cares for them and will make the needed changes. This strategy exhausts the protesters, provides face-saving middle ground and does not polarize the faculty. Only the conservatives are not happy with such "tolerance," but they are not miserable. Although the stand-off may include private concessions to students' grievances, unfortunately this is not a necessary part of the deal.

Little has been said about the dimension of institutional satisfaction. While loyalty and student affiliation shape faculty response to tactics, satisfaction and student affiliation affect response to issues. It is the humanists' and radicals' dissatisfaction with present practices which make them credible in protesters' eyes. This is the dimension which best predicts which faculty will support other kinds of campus reforms, such as changing the curriculum or going co-ed.[8] However, institutional satisfaction needs more refinement for future application, because it is less global than the other two dimensions. The case materials just presented suggest that in a crisis each group of sympathetic faculty will project its own complaints about the institution on to the demonstrators.

PERSONAL ATTRIBUTES

In terms of elementary characteristics, much evidence suggests that personal background influences a professor's response to protest, independent of his position as a member of the faculty. Studies do differ, however, over some characteristics, and in reviewing the literature we shall try to analyze which conclusions are most reliable.

The findings can be quickly summarized. Faculty are substantially more likely to support the issues, if not the tactics, of campus protest if their fathers had a lower-class job rather than a middle-class one. (Faculty from upper-class families, however, are more sympathetic as well.) Although one's own religious affiliation does not predict faculty response, having Jewish origins, particularly in contrast with Catholic ones, predicts sympathy with protests. Although party affiliation has shown some relation to sympathy for protests, political orientation works much better, because many Republicans (and virtually all Democrats) describe themselves as "liberal" (Bidwell, 1970; Cole & Adamsons, 1969; Noll & Rossi, 1966, Table III-2).

Sex and ethnicity do not correlate with any particular response, but age does as one might expect. The effect of age, however, disappears when one controls for political orientation (Bidwell, 1970). Cole and Adamsons (1969) found that age differences of protest support persisted after controlling for political beliefs, and many others have cited this finding uncritically. It certainly is fresh, but it is based on a sample far more limited than Bidwell's.

Of the variables tested then, social class origins, parents' religion, and political orientation are the most influential, and of these political orientation ranks first.

THE STRUCTURAL LOCATION OF FACULTY

No evidence exists to measure the effect on faculty-institution relations of academic rank, discipline and other professional attributes. Instead, researchers have surveyed the simple relationship between such variables and attitudes or participation. The model in this paper suggests that logically such research is measuring indirectly faculty-institution relations. One's position implicitly defines one's location among others who make up the institution, which in turn shapes attitudes (See for example Cole and Adamsons, 1970, 391).[9]

Nevertheless these surveys are informative. To begin with status, as rank and income rise, response is more likely to be conservative. Near the bottom, moreover, a sharp break appears. Junior faculty, instructors, and those earning less than $10,000 are much more likely to be radical when the issues concern campus governance and censorship. But this is not true concerning issues of Vietnam, black students, and matters which affect them less directly (Barton, 1968, Tables 2, 4, 12; Boruch, 1969; Metzger, c. 1970).

Length of service also seems to implicitly measure institutional loyalty. The only study to use it (Wences and Abramson, 1970) found it to be *the* major explanatory variable explaining how faculty view their institution. In this first paper, the authors overinterpret their tables, which show rank and discipline to have independent effect as well. However, in a second paper Abramson and Wences (1970) establish clearly that, at least at the University of Connecticut, longevity is the single most important attribute associated with how stringently faculty vote on penalties for demonstrators. David Riesman, however, notes that this university is one of the most upwardly mobile in the country, so that older faculty are more likely to cling to their institutional ties in face of young, cosmopolitan faculty. By contrast, longevity would not so strongly predict loyalty at Harvard.[10]

The impact of rank and income is considerably reduced when one controls for political orientation (Bidwell, 1970; Cole and Adamsons, 1970). Although Abramson and Wences did not control for political orientation, it might also reduce the impact of longevity. Thus, two or three of the professional attributes have little *independent* effect, and some studies conclude that professional attributes do not shape faculty response, but that background characteristics, such as political attitudes, do. However, promotions and longevity may alter political orientation, thereby making it an attribute acquired both before and after entering the academic profession (see for example Cole and Adamsons, 1970, 391).

This issue of personal-versus-professional influence is an important one in the literature. Cole and Adamsons (1969, 328) state that "reaction to politically relevant issues in a profession will be shaped by socialization acquired prior to entrance to the profession." Given their weak, local sample, the inability to separate the interaction effects just discussed and evidence in their own data to the contrary, this conclusion is overstated.[11]

Although rank has some effect on faculty response (Cole and Adamsons, 1970, 391 and Table 2) and longevity may as well, the professional attributes which shape response most are discipline and colleague response. Both Bidwell (1970) and Cole and Adamsons (1969) present data showing the importance of how one perceives colleagues in one's department. Professors who favor the protest are more likely to act on their sentiments if they feel that colleagues in the department agree, but are strongly held back by collegial opposition. Professors against the protest are somewhat mollified but generally less affected if colleagues differ with them. These patterns persist *independent of other factors,* and Table 5 in Cole and Adamsons even shows colleague attitudes to be significantly more influential than one's political orientation.[12]

Evidently one's department is an important environment for faculty response to protest. By discipline there appears in every study a continuum of protest sympathy and participation from the social sciences to humanities to the sciences, ending with professional schools like engineering and agriculture. While most studies lump together all departments in these large divisions, Lipset and Ladd (1970) and Ladd (1970) remind us that these divisions are not homogeneous. Within the social sciences, for example, approval by department of student activism ranges from 56 to 79 percent. These responses by discipline remain strong even after controlling for such relevant variables as political orientation (Bidwell, 1970).[13]

An intriguing question raised by this research is whether disciplinary qualities socialize those exposed to them or whether a person initially chooses a discipline whose values suit his own? Cole and Adamsons (1969, 1970), among others, argue strongly for the recruitment hypothesis. Lipset (1970) also cites studies which show selective recruitment among undergraduates of different political persuasions. On the other hand, these same authors and Bidwell (1970) offer evidence that disciplinary differences remain even after taking into account the political beliefs of faculty. Drawing on his excellent data, Bidwell concludes, "Differential recruitment . . . does not account for the relation between field and response to student activism." And ". . . personal traits had little effect on their exposure or vulnerability to colleague's attitudes" (pp. 16–16a).

What these differences constitute have received many interpretations. More sympathetic faculty are in disciplines which work with "core ideas," or which are in more "exploratory areas" and thereby do not accept the status quo (Lipset, 1970). Some say that the more "intellectual disciplines" are more liberal. While it is important to analyze underlying dimensions which distinguish disciplinary politics, these efforts help little. What discipline is not concerned with core ideas or exploratory areas or both? One would have trouble arguing that physics is less core or exploratory or intellectual than English. A more reasonable explanation is that the disciplines in which sympathy for protest is found range from those which scrutinize and question human institutions and values to those which do research on nonhuman subjects (the sciences) to those which service our society (engineering, agriculture). Within each division disciplines differ in mysterious and complex ways as Ladd's (1970) interesting data show. Bidwell (1970) has created a "human content" index of disciplines which correlates better than the usual departmental spectrum with response to protest, but what it tells us about differences between disciplines is unclear.

To summarize the entire analysis, these surveys indicate that a few personal and professional characteristics have an independent effect on faculty response to student protest. Our analysis suggests their descending order of important to be: perceived collegial attitudes, political orientation, discipline, parents' religion, and parents' social class. Academic rank, income, and scholarly output have minor independent effects but may affect later political orientation as a professor increases any or all of them.

Finally, we wish to know how often faculty participate in protests and what effect they have. A national survey of activities during 1967–68 found that in 53 percent of all recorded protests some faculty had helped to plan the protest. In only nine percent of the cases did they become leaders; most of the time they lent support (Boruch, 1969). Faculty are more likely to help plan a protest, Boruch argues, if the protest is nonviolent or mildly violent. One might infer a tempering effect of faculty involvement; however, in this and in several other points, Boruch uses faulty statistical arguments.[14] We cannot say his argument is false, only untrue, and it remains an interesting and plausible hypothesis that faculty participation tempers the intensity of protest.

Boruch also found no relation between faculty participating in campus policy-making and informing the administration about protest. One could guess these senior professors involved in policy-making would not be in touch with student radicals, but the author does not interpret his finding. However, providing information *does* associate significantly with faculty or teaching assistants planning and supporting the protest. Among his policy recommendations, Boruch does not mention one apparent inference, that if an administrator wishes to keep in touch with protest activities, it is in his interest to have faculty involved with protest groups.

INSTITUTIONAL EFFECTS

The structure of the institution is the second origin of faculty-institution relations in our model. Again, available research measures these relations indirectly by asking in what kinds of college and universities are faculty more likely to approve of student activism and to participate in demonstrations? These faculty tend to be located in universities more often than in colleges, and in colleges more than in junior colleges; in liberal arts schools or divisions more than in technological ones; in private nonsectarian schools than in public or denominational ones; and in more differentiated institutions more than in less differentiated, as measured by the size of the library, the proportion of Ph.D.'s on the faculty, the school's affluence, and its selectivity for admitting students (Bayer, 1971). There is some evidence that more faculty at black schools are likely to support student activists than faculty at white schools, and that faculty are so inclined more in the Northeast and West than elsewhere (Bayer, 1971).

All these figures are very crude, of course, dividing the nation's 2,500 institutions of higher learning into two or four categories. For example, Bayer's findings on the size of the libraries divides them simply into those with under 60,000 volumes and those with more than 60,000 volumes! Nevertheless, 25 percent of the institutions with the former and 60 percent of the institutions with the latter had over 40 percent of their faculty *participating* in demonstrations, and 32 percent of those with small libraries versus 66 percent of those with more than 60,000 books had over 40 percent of their faculty *approving* of recent student activism.

Of these institutional variables, those measuring quality correlate highest with faculty response. In Bayer's study, percent Ph.D.'s, library size, affluence, and student selectivity had zero-order correlations of .30 to .40 with the proportion faculty sympathetic and participating. Using more refined indices of attitude and involvement, Bidwell (1970) found that measures of institutional quality correlated about .30 with attitudes and .20 with degree of involvement. These effects support the general finding that "better" institutions have more protests and more faculty support for them. Such institutions recruit more faculty who support student activism on one hand but who create a less cohesive, personal student experience (Bayer, 1971, 19; Light, 1973). Both qualities promote student unrest, leading ironically to demonstrations which threaten the structure in which faculty work.

SUMMARY

This chapter has attempted to develop an overall model of faculty response to protest, one which not only shows which variables correlate with faculty response, but also specifies how they relate to each other. To do this required new categories to describe how faculty related to their institution and how their responses varied. The analysis indicates that one cannot understand the character of faculty response simply by determining what percent of senior versus junior faculty (or some other variable) signed a certain petition. Influences on faculty response operate at several levels and from different directions. These relations are more complex than past research has examined. But the model organizes that research and outlines a design for future research, when the occasion arises.

NOTES

1. I am indebted to David Riesman for this insight and many other valuable comments. Richard Flacks encouraged this work, providing good counsel and opening up new areas that altered my career.

2. Lest one think that this model implies that response to protest in the 1960s can be understood solely in terms of institutional relationships, let me emphasize the primary importance of national policies concerning race and Vietnam which offended the deepest values of many faculty and students and which sometimes involved the university in important ways. Moreover, from the perspective of the 1970s we can see how important was the general political tone of the times, for these policies continue without nearly the same response. This essay, in order to keep its task manageable, focuses on those variables which explain not this broad response but the differences in response between different faculty.

3. The phrase "detached from students" is rather inelegant, but does contribute to the overall symmetry and elegance of the scale. A better term would put it

positively, such as "attached to students" or "care for students," but then the first two dimensions would have to be couched in the negative to show the relationships in the diagram.

4. A full treatment of these materials is found in my unpublished paper, "Faculty Images of a University," 1967.

5. To honor the confidentiality which allowed these interviews to be granted, certain names and situations have been fictionalized.

Unless otherwise noted, this and all of the following quotations in the entire essay come from transcriptions of tape recordings made during the ten interviews.

There are well-known problems of transcription. Even with these articulate men, a sentence would be started three or four times followed by several switches in the predicate. In all cases, the speaker was given the benefit of the doubt. That is, the subject (usually the last articulated) which made the most sense for the sentence was chosen, and in general the sentence was transcribed which fit in with the conversation. Nevertheless, speakers occasionally used bad English, with no alternatives, and this was transcribed as spoken. Punctuation was used which conveyed the vocal stops and the oral continuities of the speaker. Underlined words are those emphasized by the speaker. Words in parentheses were added for clarification.

6. After hearing several allusions to the SDS manual on revolution and insurrection, I asked to see a copy. An officer of the university took a copy from his files, saying that he had not had time to read it and insisting that I not take it from the office.

The document was a mimeographed manual on how to start and run a local SDS chapter. Much of the material did not differ from other pamphlets on organizing be it a Boy Scout troop or a women's auxiliary. However, the manual went on to suggest how to challenge and change the university, especially in regard to military contracts which a university might have. It gave advice on how to use literature, it recommended that only one person speak to the press so as to avoid contradictory statements, and it suggested that one know the law before disobeying it.

At no point did the "manual on revolution" suggest that students try to gain a larger role in decision making or revolt against second-class citizenship. Nor were there suggestions, mentioned in conversations about the manual, about the best way to play one administrator off another. The other striking fact was that SAR either did not read the manual or followed its limited advice poorly; for the SAR literature was not well written until the end, the press releases were no better and misleading, and no careful study of the law was made.

7. This point is illustrated in the protesters' statement, *An Outline of Issues and Arguments.*

> We have learned many things in the last four days. One thing that has affected us very deeply is the knowledge that although, as ideally

stated this is a "faculty-run university," by inaction, the faculty has not fulfilled this responsibility. This has been a great source of disappointment and frustration for us. *It took the issue of the draft to educate us about this state of affairs.*

At the same time, we were made aware of the fact that we as students have also been negligent in carrying out our responsibility as concerned members of this community. We fully realize that the bulk of administrative operation *must remain* within the established apparatus. However, it is essential that both students and faculty be awakened to their collective responsibility to voice opinion, and actively participate together in making decisions which *transcend* the day-to-day concerns of operating the university.

8. Cole and Adamsons (1970) and Barton (1968) measured degree of satisfaction in their study of the Columbia crisis. They found it correlated with faculty views even after controlling for political orientation, one of the most powerful variables.

9. This is the obverse of Cole and Adamsons' interpretation of their data (1970, p. 392), and a more accurate one.

10. Private correspondence, August 25, 1974.

11. Cole and Adamsons (1969) predicted that the dominant influence of background variables would diminish as faculty experienced more and more protests. Bidwell (1970) partially tested this hypothesis and found no substantiation for it.

12. Professor Riesman notes that someone should have studied graduate students as well, because faculty often are more involved with them than colleagues and can be influenced by their politics.

13. Cole and Adamsons (1970, pp. 391–93) conclude otherwise, but their choice of "disciplines" casts doubt on their argument. For departmental range they use "pure sciences" (not a department), "political science" (in all studies the most conservative of the social sciences) and "philosophy." As one might expect, only philosophy provides some range of disciplinary response.

14. The correlations between faculty involvement in planning protests and degrees of protest intensity are all significant at the .05 level. Because the correlations are higher for nonviolent types of protest than for physically obstructive ones, Boruch makes his argument. However, he is not justified in distinguishing between two correlations, both statistically significant, unless he does a test of significant differences. This he did not do.

Boruch makes the same error in arguing that faculty are more likely to participate in protests having to do with Vietnam than with those concerned about black studies, governance, and other local issues. While technically not true, his position is supported by Volkwein, who found that of 430 protests studied in 1966–67, faculty participated in 71 percent of those concerning off-campus issues and 38 percent of those concerning campus issues (Morgan, 1970).

REFERENCES

Abramson, Harold J., and Wences, Rosalio. "Campus Dissent and Academic Punishment: The Response of College Professors to Local Political Activism." Presented at the meeting of the American Sociological Association, August, 1970.

Astin, Alexander W., and Bayer, Alan E. "Antecedents and Consequences of Disruptive Campus Protests." *Measurement and Evaluation in Guidance* 4 (1971): 18–30.

Barton, Allen H. "The Columbia Crisis: Campus, Vietnam and the Ghetto." *Public Opinion Quarterly* 32 (1968): 333–351.

Bayer, Alan E. "Institutional Correlates of Faculty Support of Campus Unrest." *American Council on Education Research Reports* 6, no. 1 (1971).

Bidwell, Charles E. "Faculty Responses to Student Activism: Some Preliminary Findings from a Survey of American Professors." Mimeographed. Varra: World Congress of Sociology, 1970.

Boruch, Robert F. "The Faculty Roles in Campus Unrest." *American Council of Education Research Reports* 4, no. 5 (1969).

Cole, Stephen, and Adamsons, Hannelore. "Determinants of Faculty Support for Student Demonstrations." *Sociology of Education* 42 (1969): 315–328.

Cole, Stephen, and Adamsons, Hannelore. "Professional Status and Faculty Support of Student Demonstrations." *Public Opinion Quarterly* 34 (1970): 389–394.

Ladd, Everett C., Jr. "American University Teachers and Opposition to the Vietnam War." *Minerva* 8 (1970): 542–556.

Light, Donald W., Jr. "Faculty Images of a University." Manuscript. Chicago: University of Chicago, 1967.

Light, Donald W., Jr. "Black and White at Brandeis." *North American Review* 254 (1969): 25–29.

Light, Donald W., Jr., Marsden, Lorna, and Corl, Tom. *The Impact of the Academic Revolution on Faculty Careers.* Washington, D.C.: American Association for Higher Education, 1973.

Lipset, Seymour Martin. "The Politics of Academia." In *Perspectives on Campus Tensions,* ed. David C. Nichols. Washington, D.C.: American Council on Education, 1970.

Lipset, Seymour Martin, and Ladd, Everett C., Jr. "And What Professors Think." *Psychology Today.* November 1970.

Metzger, Loya F. *Faculty Activism in a Campus Crisis.* Master's thesis in Political Science, Columbia University (about 1970).

Morgan, William R. "Faculty Mediation in Campus Conflict." In *Protest,* ed. Julian Foster and Durwood Long. New York: William Morrow, 1970, pp. 365–382.

Newman, Frank, et al. *Report on Higher Education.* Washington, D.C.: U.S. Office of Education, 1971.

Noll, Edward C., and Rossi, Peter H. "General Social and Economic Attitudes of College and University Faculty Members." Mimeographed. Chicago: National Opinion Research Center, 1966.

Parsons, Talcott, and Platt, Gerald M. *The American Academic Profession: A Pilot Study.* Mimeographed. Washington, D.C.: National Science Foundation, 1968.

Wences, Rosalio, and Abramson, Harold J. "Faculty Opinion on the Issues of Job Replacement and Dissent in the University." *Social Problems* 18 (1970): 27–38.

6/The group psychology of campus disorders: a transactional approach

John Spiegel

There can be no doubt that the spectacular growth of campus disorders over the past several years has aroused the most intense interest and has stimulated the strongest feelings in this and in other countries. As one of the most popular controversies of our times, it has generated a wealth of publication. Innumerable articles have appeared in the press, in national magazines, and in professional journals, expressing either hostility toward or sympathy with the student uprisings, or perhaps more characteristically, a mixture of both feelings. Congressional committees have been urged by expert witnesses to pursue completely incompatible lines of inquiry and to establish quite contradictory national policies in the interest of terminating the disorders.

In all this varied comment, however, little attention has been paid to the group process and the dynamic interactions, which create the various factions, on and off campus, and set them into such intransigent, antagonistic, and occasionally violent relations with each other. Especially prominent through its absence has been a consideration of the psychodynamics, both conscious and unconscious, underlying the group conflicts. An examination of this sort might be of interest only to specialists, or even suspect, were it not for the peculiar and unlikely behaviors exhibited on all sides during a campus crisis. Many observers of such incidents have noted, though few have put into print, the number of surprising, illogical actions which disfigure the behavior of previously collaborating groups—and of individuals within such groups—whenever activist students use militant or disruptive techniques to obtain satisfaction of demands for change.

Low boiling points and trigger-happy responses, frequently based on the imagery of Western films and television programs, occur at the highest levels of administrative responsibility. During his 1966 gubernatorial campaign, Ronald Reagan, the ex-governor of California, said that the student leaders of the 1964 free speech movement at the Berkeley campus of the University of California "should have been taken by the scruff of the neck and thrown out of the university." Testifying in May 1969 before the McClellan Committee hearings on "Riots, Civil and Criminal Disorders," Eric Hoffer, the longshoreman philosopher, a student of the fanatical "True Believer," said about violence:

> Take Grayson Kirk [president of Columbia University during the Spring, 1968, campus disturbance]. Here they got into his room. They burglarized his files. They smoked his cigars. They used his shaving kit. Grayson Kirk didn't forget himself. . . . I think it would have been a wonderful thing if Grayson Kirk got mad, grabbed a gun and went out there and gunned them down. I think maybe he would have gotten killed, maybe he would have killed two of them when they were jumping up, but I think he would have saved Columbia.

Hoffer's attitude seems bloodthirsty, but the irritability underlying his response is shared by more sophisticated commentators. Irritation with student rebels colors the comments of at least two of the scholars who have recently employed psychoanalytic ideas in accounting for the problematic behavior of the dissidents: Lewis Feuer and Bruno Bettelheim.

In *The Conflict of Generations: The Character and Significance of Student Movements,* historian Lewis Feuer reviews student movements in various countries over the past 200 years. He concludes that the impact of the student movements has been basically destructive except for the rare occasions when their goals have been taken over by the adult world. The mainly undesirable outcomes, according to Feuer, are logical results of the students' unconscious and irrational motivations: hostility toward the fathers of oedipal origin, castration fears stimulating overcompensatory aggression, and homosexual longings stimulating overcompensatory masculinity. As a result of these (and no other, for example, intellectual or political motives), the sons develop an attitude which Feuer calls "deauthorization" of the parents.

In a similar tone, but with a different list of pathological factors, Bruno Bettelheim, the expert on childhood and adolescent disturbances, told the McClellan Committee that student rebel leaders are (partially concealed) paranoid characters. Their followers are adolescents who have been deprived of emotional gratifications and warmth by their parents, and who are looking both for an object on which to vent their rage and for a cause of sufficient intensity to generate the warm group feelings they have missed since earliest childhood. According to Bettelheim, these grievances, left over from childhood, are much more important than the actual issues about which students currently protest.

The statements of Feuer and Bettelheim suffer, in my opinion, from two kinds of errors. First, they both attribute the behavior of activist students almost wholly to preexisting neurotic motives, although it is not at all clear to the neutral observer what is cause and what is effect. It is at least possible that the behavior of dissident students is a response to irrational and excessively disturbing external conditions. Shortly after the conclusion of World War II, Dr. Will Menninger, reacting to his experience as chief of psychiatric services for the Army, dealt with this problem by posing the question. He wrote:

> During the war, we had frequent occasions to contrast the psychiatrist's job in civilian life with his job in combat. In civilian life he attempted to understand and treat the abnormal reactions of persons to normal situations. In military life he attempted to understand and treat the normal reactions to an abnormal situation. One might seriously question if our world condition does not now place many of us in a continuously abnormal situation to which we are having normal reactions, even though these by all previous standards are pathological. To such a turbulent world, one might legitimately ask, what is a normal reaction?[1]

Although the contrast between the reactions to combat and civilian life is somewhat overdrawn, the question is as pertinent now as it was in 1947, perhaps more so. Any attempt to answer it requires the help of method and theory—a matter to which we shall return when considering the transactional approach toward the end of this inquiry.

The second error arises from the exclusive focus on just one party to a complex interaction. It is simply not reasonable to raise questions about the irrational, unconscious motives of students while ignoring the similar implications of the behavior of those members of the faculty and administration who oppose them. Such a procedure prejudges the question as to where the pathology lies, thereby limiting the inquiry to such a degree as to be misleading. By the same token, it raises questions as to the "blind spots" of the observer. When groups find themselves in conflict, it is difficult enough to determine which group is right or wrong, much less which of the groups is "healthy" and which "disturbed."

It was under the condition of maximum inter-group conflict that Freud first turned his attention to group psychology and asked what unconscious processes led individuals to associate in groups, to conform to group norms, to create new forms of behavior, and to involve themselves in adversary relations. *Group Psychology and the Analysis of the Ego,* published in 1921, was prompted by the experiences of psychoanalysts in World War I as military psychiatrists. Freud's approach was not based upon the attribution of sin, evil, or psychopathology to any one group or society as against another. He was interested in the human condition, in the way in which conflicts operating below the surface of consciousness interacted, for all concerned individuals in groups, with external social reality, distorting that reality and thereby rendering it even worse, even more limiting and traumatic than it had to be, given the economic and technological situation of man vis-a-vis nature.

It is in connection with the problems posed by group-formation and the unconscious origins of inter-group hostility that this inquiry approaches its more immediate aim: to describe in rather general terms the phenomenology of campus disorders and to examine the psychological processes which lead individuals to join one or another of the contending groups in the course of these disturbances.

My colleagues and I at the Lemberg Center for the Study of Violence have had the opportunity to observe campus crises at several American universities, and we have been repeatedly impressed with the speed and intensity with which aggression and hostility are released among all parties connected with these affairs. The extreme and seemingly unreasonable behavior evoked by such disturbances has been deplored, condemned, and praised. Although such responses are one, probably inevitable, way of dealing with human problems there is much to be said for a more neutral examination of the process of elicitation of aggressive behavior in reaction to group conflict. At any rate, what the observer faces at the outset is a dramatic and kaleidoscopic series of events featuring the sudden use of physical force, threats of more serious violence, warnings of punishment, cries of outrage, abuses of language, and gaudy exhibitions of contempt, insult, and calumny.

It would be easy to ascribe such sudden releases of inhibition to contagion, feelings being notably infectious when released at high levels of intensity. Although it is undoubtedly a part of the phenomenon, contagion is too global an explanation. Besides, it affords no leverage on the behavior aside from the usual admonitions to "keep cool."

Rather than remaining satisfied with a theory of random release of hostile energies automatically triggered by the illegal acts of rebellious students, I shall argue that, once the stage is set, the suddenly appearing antagonisms and the associated formation of groups in opposition to each other break out along previously determined lines of cleavage in accordance with certain ego mechanisms which are largely outside the awareness of the individual. This line of argument will not ignore the social and political issues so important to the setting of the stage for conflict. On the contrary, my procedure shall be to begin with the psychological factors and then to examine their interplay with the social structural factors.

Since our observations have been drawn from participating in or observing the process of angry polarization within and between groups, rather than clinical or standard research situations, we must be cautious about any formulations of unconscious motivations. But the existence of unconscious factors at work in campus disorders is supported by two easily observable aspects of the response of those concerned in the conflict: (1) the irrationality, often bordering on the bizarre, displayed by persons whose usual behavior toward each other was characterized by good humor, even in disagreement; and (2) the forgetting, denial, or discounting of the irrational behavior once the crisis has passed.

In describing campus polarization, I shall treat it as a crisis occurring in four stages, each characterized by a sequence of actions and reactions. Given the variations in actual forms of disorder from campus to campus, there is a risk of overgeneralization or unwarranted stereotyping in such an approach. Still, whether or not the four stages to be described actually fit all situations is not as important as the advantage gained through imposing some clarity and order on the dynamics of the arousal, escalation, and decline of group hostilities.[2]

PREMONITIONS

The *premonitory phase* is characterized by slowly mounting resentment within a number of students whom I shall call, for the sake of generalization, the "aggrieved" group. Their anger is aroused by the failure of the administration to respond rapidly enough, or at all, to their expressed desire for change within the institution. The desired changes vary from school to school, but in general they revolve around administrative policy with respect to three substantive issues: (1) the quality and pertinence of the curriculum and other institutional arrangements for students of various ethnic backgrounds; (2) policies related to the conduct of the war in Vietnam and the involvement of the university with military research and training; and (3) the rights of students to have a part in the determination of institutional policy of all sorts.

In the minds of the aggrieved group there is no question of the legitimacy of and the pressing need for the desired changes. Within the student body as a whole, however, there is a spectrum of opinion ranging from active support through apathy to opposition. For this reason, among others, the first administrative response to the proposals of the aggrieved group is likely to be perfunctory. Meetings between representatives of the aggrieved students and the administration, if they occur at all, are viewed by the administration largely as opportunities for "abreaction"—for the expression of feelings and opinions, in the hope that this will satisfy them. No real change is expected nor envisioned by the authorities.

After a certain lapse of time without progress or change, the aggrieved students begin increasingly to see themselves in an adversary role vis-a-vis the administration. The current of the times, laden with scenarios of dissent, asserts itself in the thinking of the aggrieved group, sometimes aided by visits from activist students at other universities. Ideas originally defined as suggestions or proposals become talked about as "demands." This hardening of attitudes and the growing spirit of militancy within the aggrieved group leads to changes both in the general student body and in the administration. An increasing number of previously indifferent students identify themselves with the goals of the aggrieved students, though not necessarily with their activities, mainly because these additional students share the resentment at the failure of the administration to consider requests for change with the proper seriousness. A large proportion of the student body, in other words, feels vicariously slighted.

Representatives of the administration are usually aware of the changing attitudes of the students, but they tend to misinterpret them in the light of their own stake in avoiding rapid or abrupt change. The aggrieved students are now seen as threats to the tranquility and maintenance of order within the school. Their supporters are perceived as misled, easily attracted through romantic impulses or merely youthful exuberance to the inflammatory language in which unrealistic or illegitimate goals are clothed. Since the goals of change are still not taken seriously, administrators discount or dismiss the entire effort through a process of labelling designed to split the student body and to rally outside support for the policy of resistance to change. Leaders of the aggrieved group are called "radicals," "anarchists," and a variety of other names. In private conversation they are often identified as spoiled, pampered products of well-to-do, permissive parents, or as disturbed persons in need of psychiatric attention. Their followers among the more moderate students are regarded as essentially fair-minded and well-intentioned (though temporarily infatuated) dupes. This labelling process reflects the growth on both sides of the mistrust and disrespect whose unconscious origins we are about to trace.

Toward the end of the premonitory phase some subtle cleavages begin to appear, both within the administration and among the faculty, though they are still papered over with politeness. Some faculty, usually from the social sciences or counselling services, adopt a sympathetic, liberal attitude toward the changes requested by the students. They then urge, to the distress of others, that the college president, the deans, or whoever stands for officialdom, modify the rigid policy of resistance. These persons have usually been in face-to-face contact with some of the dissident students and perceive themselves as "honest brokers" presenting the students' case with intense sincerity and urgency. As a result of the advocate role of the "sympathizers," the spokesmen for the university now shift their tactics to some degree. Representatives of the aggrieved group are seen and listened to more attentively. Some of their demands are accepted as potentially legitimate. The administrators promise to channel these requests for change through the bureaucratic machinery with which every institution of any size is saddled.

The crisis process at this point is in a paradoxical state. A temporary relaxation occurs because the aggrieved students believe they are finally making progress, while the administrators think they have with some luck defused a potentially dangerous situation. Actually, this is the calm before the storm. On both sides the inevitable disappointment of unrealistically raised hopes is a guarantee of disaster. On the administrative side, the "channeling" procedure, at best a clumsy business, tends to get stalled because of uncertainties and disagreements about the appropriate manner of solving the problem or about whether it should be solved at all. In the students' view, the delays, mixed messages about what is taking place, and the intimations of implacable rigidity behind a surface mask of acceptance, all add up to a dead end: no possibility of progress.

INITIAL DISORDER

At this point, the crisis process moves toward the second phase: the *initial disorder*. Disillusioned, convinced that only the force of a dramatic act of protest can alter the situation in their favor, the aggrieved group begins to plan some form of disruption. At the same time, they elaborate and firm up previously (though tentatively) held hostile beliefs about the character and motives of the administration and of the social system it represents. The resulting ideological creed, for example, that the administration is authoritarian, bigoted, and hypocritical, and that the social system is racist, exploitive, and oppressive, thereupon is used to overcome moral scruples about the legal and ethical justification of the disruption being planned. (In saying this, I am not passing any judgment on the validity or lack of validity of the system of beliefs, but merely describing a continuing process.)

So far all is prologue. The actual disorder that opens the second phase may begin with a series of small but increasingly disruptive demonstrations or with a major act such as seizing and occupying a building. The students usually display contradictory moods which nevertheless fit together. They are excited and aggressive, even abusive, but fairly well disciplined; exhibitionistic but secretive; happy because they are finally taking action but fearful of what it may lead to; defiant and uncommunicative yet letting it be known that they would accept communication. An aura of unity and determination expressed in publicly stated "nonnegotiable demands" masks privately felt uncertainties and divisions of opinions. Despite the disagreements, the aggrieved group is, at that moment, unified through the sharing of norm-violating behavior: they are all in the same boat.

The usual administrative response is shock. Under the impression that the new policy of bureaucratic openness to complaints has mollified the dissident students and reassured the moderates, the administration is unprepared for serious trouble. But neither the realization that they have misjudged the mood of the aggrieved students nor the deeply felt indignation serve any useful purpose. Some action must be taken, if only to relieve frustration and anger. Unfortunately, the administrators are faced simultaneously with two types of decisions, neither of which is easy to make: what to do about the "nonnegotiable" demands and how to deal with the norm-violating behavior. Nor can the two be easily separated, since the message contained in both the illegal behavior and the "nonnegotiable" label is the same: no more stalling; the students mean business!

Faced with this threat, the administrators have only a limited number of clear-cut options. They can:

1. Accept all the demands and ignore the norm-violating behavior. This capitulation by the administration promptly resolves the current situation. It is the least common solution.

2. Ignore the demands and throw out the offenders with the help of the police and other law enforcement agencies. Although this approach has been used, it brings about so many additional problems, particularly strong support for the militants by the moderates, that many administrations are reluctant to use it.

3. Ignore the norm-violating behavior while offering to negotiate the demands. Since this technique can easily be seen by the students as a "put on" (with punishment to follow later), and since, from the side of the administration, it does not meet the challenge of illegal threat by the students, it is likely to result in a protracted stalemate.

4. Meet threat with threat by promising disciplinary procedures and punishments for the future while avoiding a confrontation and ignoring the demands, in the hope that the students will lose the support of their classmates and tire of their unproductive behavior. Since they often do, this method can succeed, at least temporarily.

5. Ignore both the norm-violating behavior and the demands by doing nothing and saying nothing. This produces an unsettled ambiguity and frustration for the students and gives the administration freedom to pursue any policy of punishment or nonpunishment or to sanction, negotiate, or deny any part of the demands, once the students give up. Any administration choosing this inscrutable policy must be certain of support from its various constituencies (faculty, trustees, alumni, and the general public), not all of whom will understand what the administrators are up to. Because of the exacting conditions for its success, this policy is seldom used but it can be devastatingly effective.

Whether or not these policies exhaust the logical (and legal) possibilities for action afforded by the initial situation, most administrations without a history of previous disorder are unable to proceed immediately toward any one policy based upon such an abstract calculus of means and ends.[3] Clear-cut as these policies may be, there is usually too much confusion and emotionalism and too little prior experience within the administration to permit the straightforward implementation of any one of them; also there are too many audiences to be taken into account. Instead, a seesaw struggle takes place around three more intuitively developed positions: (1) a desire to support the goals of the aggrieved students while minimizing any loss of face to the institution for what may be interpreted as surrender. This position is usually called the "soft line" advocated by the "doves"; (2) a desire to defeat and punish the students while minimizing any loss of face to the institution for what may be interpreted as callousness or cruelty. This policy is the "hard line" pursued by the "hawks"; (3) a middle ground, or temporizing position, which attempts to placate both the "hawks" and the "doves," in part, while also partially satisfying the demands of the students—a balancing act which requires great skill, diplomacy, flexibility, and inventiveness, plus some Machiavellian sleights of hand.

Within a university of any size and complexity, it takes some time for these positions to become crystallized in explicit policy. Since this occurs in the conte.t of relentless political in-fighting, the administration is for the time being unable to promote any coherent policy. It is usually forced to delay action while contenting itself with ritualistic statements for public consumption, usually condemning the students' methods ("We can neither condone nor excuse violence . . .") while expressing cautious sympathy for some of their goals ("The students' demands have been under consideration by the Committee on . . ."). It is this period of delay that ushers in the third phase of the crisis.

MOUNTING POLARIZATION

The atmosphere of events now becomes increasingly hectic, acrimonious, and conspiratorial. A state of emergency exists characterized by ad hoc committees, sudden summons to meetings, secret emissaries mediating between rival factions, rumors and counter-rumors, corridor gossip, student manifestoes circulated in and out of print, and the ever-present television crews and newspaper reporters on the lookout for interesting stories, unexpected confrontations, pitched battles, or worse.

Though activities at this point are almost "round-the-clock" and administrators are getting little sleep, the passage of time and the way time is used form the superficial stimuli to the lines of cleavage which now develop. Time is somehow always involved in the justifications which advocates make for their preferred solutions. The "hard line" advocated by the "hawks" maintains that every day that passes without the implementation of the "realistic" policy consolidates the position of the dissident students, encourages them in their unlawful behavior, and affords opportunity for the growth of extracampus support by sympathizers in other schools and in the community. The "doves" fear that the passage of time without an accommodation being worked out will force the students to create some new manifestation of disorder, thus forcing the administration to "crack down," perhaps by calling the police. The "temporizers" while uncomfortable about the passage of time, generally feel that time plays into their hands by wearing down the opposition on all sides to their middle-of-the-road policy. For the aggrieved students, whether occupying a building, maintaining a strike, or staging forbidden rallies, time is a more ambiguous matter. It may exhaust their energies before bringing the administration around.

From attitudes toward time, further polarizations grow by wild leaps into increasingly extreme positions. For the "hawks" any attempts to negotiate with the students *before* those "troublemakers" yield to punishment is anathema—a betrayal of everything the school stands for as an intellectual establishment. It is the end of reasoned inquiry, the death of scholarly detachment, the beginning of the politicalization of the school, and thus the *finis* of academic freedom and the dispassionate search for *the truth*. For them, any decision taken under the threat of force is tantamount to accepting a fascist dictatorship. Nevertheless, they have no compunctions about intimidating "doves" and "temporizers" with dire predictions. In thundering tones and with the visionary fervor of the prophet, they foresee doom in general and schedule deadlines for specific catastrophes. Since, as they say, it is impossible to appease the students' hunger for violence and revolution, they guarantee that, should their policy lose out, in a few days, weeks, or months, another building will be seized, then another and another; next, the students will be running the institution, and in a year it will have collapsed altogether. To buttress the argument, analogies are summoned from all corners of history, with special emphasis on the Nazi and Communist movements.

In addition to such fulminations, the "hawks" can scarcely conceal their contempt for the "doves"—those "bleeding hearts," those "masochists" who, perhaps unconsciously, are out to wreck the university. On their side, the "doves" show a mild but persistent abhorrence of the wrath, and in their eyes, "sadism" of the "hawks." Privately, they tend to believe, for the moment at least, that most of the "hawks" are paranoid personalities. In meetings and public discussions, however, they try to appeal to what remains of the "hawk" sense of reality by portraying in detail the way the aggrieved students have experienced the institution: its irrelevance, its arbitrary rules and regulations, and its unresponsiveness to student needs and especially to the need for shared communication. Such attempts to explain are, nevertheless, preceived by the "hawks" both as attacks upon the virtue of the academy and as apologies for deviant behavior—just what one would expect from such "sob sisters." And, in fact, in their attempt to find some means to penetrate the heavy "hawk" defenses, the "doves" do at times resort to illustrations based on troubled family relations productive of deviant or psychotic behavior in a child. This is a gambit which, predictably, fails with the "hawks" though it may impress the "temporizers."

Being men of the middle, the "temporizers" are not much persuaded by the logic of either the "hawks" or the "doves." More realistic than the "hawks" about the extent of political influence endemic to the university, they are not so afraid of the loss of an already restricted academic freedom. Unlike the "doves," they are worried by rapid social change of any sort, with its turbulence, its constant overhauling of bureaucratic procedures, and its threat of loss of support from conservatives in the outside community. Moreover, they are drawn to the "hawks" position by a shared sense of indignation, though it is based on a different calculation. The "temporizers" had been impressed by the amount of movement shown by the school prior to the outbreak of the initial disorder. They had shared, vicariously or actually, the "liberalization" of American life in recent decades, the partial transformation of habitual "racist," "antistudent," or indifferent attitudes which this amount of movement entailed. Accordingly, they feel offended by the ingratitude of the aggrieved students, who, in their perception, are "biting the hand that feeds them." This feeling is not shared by the "hawks" who feel that too much attention has been given to the students all along; nor by the "doves," who feel that students have had too little attention. The function of this "betrayal reaction," then, is to diminish the willingness of the "temporizers" to listen sympathetically to the students in the course of any negotiations— an effect in line anyway with the "go slow" policy.

The sense of betrayal is shared by many persons in the general public who ask, with genuine annoyance and uncomprehension, "What do these students want, anyway?" or who write to college authorities demanding that no more concessions be granted the students. Naturally enough, the conservative publications provide ample fuel for such sentiments, but even the "liberal" press is apt to respond with the dismay provoked by feelings of betrayal. For example, in an editorial on December 6, 1968, the New York Times said, "Recent episodes at Fordham University, New York University, and San Francisco State College mark a new upsurge in the recurrent effort of a tiny minority to disrupt academic life. College and university officials should have learned by now that it is useless and dangerous to appease or compromise with such disruptive tactics. There is no place and no excuse for violence on the campus." On March 18, 1969, an editorial in the Christian Science Monitor, indulging in the classical phraseology of outrage, said, "There is no longer any excuse— social, political, pedagogical, or theoretical—for college authorities, city officials, or the police to allow rioting, vandalism, terrorism, or just plain nastiness to continue on campuses of higher learning." The Monitor's fit of indignation seems to have swept its editorial staff off its feet; no matter how firm the regime, nor how many college authorities, city officials, and police officers are brought to bear on the situation, it seems doubtful that "just plain nastiness" can be banished from the campus, or anywhere else.

The polarization of the third phase is painful for most participants. Old friends find themselves unable to converse; people who have scarcely met fall into shouting matches; alliances hastily set up come crashing down, often aided by gossip communicated with the best of intentions. Faculty meetings based on *Robert's Rules of Order* become travesties of rational discussion, with members heatedly declaring each other out of order or throwing other monkey wrenches into the parliamentary machinery.[4] Peacemakers by the dozen offer their own special formula for solving everything. The intensity of the frustration of concerted action, the apparent reality of institutional chaos combined with the exhaustion of sleepless nights, produces a sense of "executive fatigue," a state in which no decision seems well considered nor objectively arrived at. The temptation to avoid or withdraw from the struggle is very strong. It is not unusual for some administrators or faculty to threaten to resign in the heat of controversy, though actual resignations are ordinarily reserved for the soberer and more reflective mood of the aftermath of the crisis.[5]

RESOLUTION

Despite the appearance of chaos, the group process is actually moving toward resolution, the fourth phase of the crisis. The manner in which the crisis is resolved varies so much from institution to institution that no general description can be offered. The resolution can be either "hawkish," "doveish," or in line with the middle ground of the "temporizers." No matter which method resolves the crisis, there is likely to be some effort made to establish negotiations with the dissident students. The students, of course, do not acknowledge that such an event is occuring, their demands being "nonnegotiable." Similarly, the university authorities must officially deny that any such thing is taking place since they will not negotiate under threat or force. If not held in secret, such conversations are called "explorations" or "clarification of demands." The function of labelling continues to be prominent throughout the crisis.

There is not time to examine this process nor to discuss the conflicts within the aggrieved group of students which it generates. Suffice it to say that if efforts are actually established to end the struggle without using external force, severe dissension occurs within the student group about how much or little to settle for. Hard-liners, often women adept at shaming the men, remind the group that *none* of the demands are negotiable.[6] Moderates, arguing for a policy of realism, urge settling for what they regard as the administration's best possible offer. Extreme activists suggest escalating the disorder, while those with less taste for prolonged struggle, indicate a reluctance to go on much longer. In the course of the prolonged discussions aimed at resolving these differences, attitudes frequently harden and arguments often end in fist fights. The bitterness underlying such affairs seems to be an example of what Freud called "the narcissism of small differences." In the atmosphere of emergency, small differences in tactics or goals assume huge proportions and are then used to separate the strong from the weak, the "good guys" from the "bad guys," or the true revolutionary from the phony reformist. Here again, labelling and emotionalism rather than precise political or sociological analysis seems the preferred way of solving a problem.

An important aspect of the negotiations, once they start, is the degree to which administration and student representatives at the negotiating sessions miscommunicate. Identical words and expressions mean different things to the two parties. To the extent that this is the case, such sessions really *are* more for the sake of clarification than negotiation. In part, misunderstanding occurs because of the gap in values, beliefs, and experience separating the two groups. In part, the failure of communication is due to the novelty of such occasions and the absence of any traditional or agreed upon style of conduct for the procedures, such as characterizes labor bargaining sessions. But in large part, the communication failures are also the product of unconscious psychological processes, which will be discussed in a moment.

AFTERMATH

The last phase of the crisis process, the aftermath, is formally not a part of the crisis itself. However, there are two related aspects of the aftermath that are relevant to our purposes. The first is the "Rashomon effect," the varying and often incompatible stories that are told of what transpired during the crisis. Interviewers from the media and committees appointed to review the events are frequently surprised by the conflicting narrations of supposedly the same incident obtained from different persons. Certainly this is not a new finding in the history of psychology. The surprise occurs because the discrepancies are so blatant and the witnesses so credible.

The second matter has to do not with inconsistencies in what people remember, but with what they "forget." To be sure, with so much happening from hour to hour, no one can witness, much less recall, the whole spectrum of events. What stands out, however, is the inability of people to remember things that they themselves have said and done, that others retain vividly in mind.

For example, after a particularly frustrating faculty meeting during the height of one campus crisis, a junior faculty member, who was a "dove," engaged a senior colleague in the same department in a corridor conversation. The young man was attempting to defend the legitimacy of the students' occupation of a campus building by drawing an analogy to the labor movement, especially its earlier phases when strikes, picketing, and sit-ins were still matters of controversy. During the faculty meeting, the senior professor had vigorously attacked the seizure of the building, warning of the fatal consequences to the university if it were allowed to continue. During the corridor conversation, he repeated these arguments and, with some asperity, denied the merits of the labor analogy. When the junior colleague continued to press his arguments, the "hawk" grew red with rage, advised the younger man not to address him by his first name, told him he didn't know what he was talking about, then, with a certain dignified, almost classical flourish, turned on his heel (just as in nineteenth century novels), and. abruptly departed. After the crisis had died down, this incident was mentioned to the older man. He had no memory of it, denied that it had ever occurred, and showed mild irritation at the suggestion that he could have behaved in such a fashion.

A similar blank wall was encountered at another university when a journalist attempted to interview a high administrative official about the events of the campus crisis. The interview had started in a jovial, friendly atmosphere and continued for some time in this vein. Through others, the journalist had learned that the president had made vacillating statements on the subject of disciplining the rebellious students, at times threatening severe punishment, at other times suggesting that only mild procedures would be used if the students left the building they were occupying. When the journalist brought this up, without revealing his sources, the atmosphere suddenly cooled. The uncertainty was interpreted by the official as "weakness' and was denied, to the surprise of the journalist who thought there must be good reasons on both sides of the ticklish question of punishment versus amnesty. When he pursued the point, he was accused of being hostile to the university and oversympathetic to the line adopted by the radical students. The journalist was amazed at the situation he found himself in but was unable to extricate himself. The encounter terminated on a note of muted tension and bitterness. The journalist found the whole episode bizarre and difficult to fathom. He was still quite shaken by it when, soon afterwards, he reported the incidents to one of our staff members.

EGO MECHANISMS

We have now come to the point where we can ask: what is it about the crisis that accounts for the forgetting, the exaggerations, and the distorted, hostile interpersonal relations in which participants become involved?

Let us begin with the dissident students who provide the apparent stimulus for the crisis. Since they constitute a group—an aggrieved group—we must examine the identifications that hold the group together and apart from the usual student groups. Obviously an extensive transformation of both the object and the nature of identifications has taken place. In the past, and for many students, still, faculty and administrative figures are accepted as persons with whose values, if not personalities, the student can identify. There is among most students a generally positive orientation toward scholarship, research, and teaching; this is one factor in the large number of undergraduates who apply for graduate training. And in the past, at any rate, students have been able to overlook the paternalistic behavior of their mentors, sorting out in their own minds and discriminating between the best and worst aspects of university life. They usually accept their student leaders as substitutes, junior partners, or intermediate figures in a ladder of positive images pointing toward their own futures. Now comes a gradual, but traumatic disillusion with the university, deep suspicion of its good faith and essential benevolence, and bitterness over the failure of their petition for the relief of grievances. Hence the previously positive side of the identification process is put to severe strain.

In his original discussion of the role of identification in the process of group formation Freud said, "Identification is ambivalent from the very first; it can turn into an expression of tenderness as easily as into a wish for someone's removal." In the same work, *Group Psychology and the Analysis of the Ego,* he said, "The leader or the leading idea might also, so to speak, be negative; hatred against a particular person or institution might operate in just the same unifying way, and might call up the same kind of emotional ties as positive attachment."[7] Though Freud never commented in any detail on the transformation of group identification from primarily positive to primarily negative shared attitudes toward the leader of the institution, we can perhaps employ an observation he made in another context as the intervening link in this process. In the first of the two essays included in *Thoughts for the Times on War and Death,* when speaking of the effects upon the intellectual community of the outbreak of World War I, he said, "Then the war in which we had refused to believe broke out, and it brought—disillusionment. . . . The individual citizen can with horror convince himself in this war of what would occasionally cross his mind in peace time—that the state has forbidden to the individual the practice of wrongdoing, not because it desires to abolish it, but because it desires to monopolize it, like salt and tobacco."[8]

This sentiment, uttered fifty-odd years ago, was widely shared by intellectuals steeped in the humanist tradition and wholly alienated from the militaristic and patriotic fervor which swept the warring nations. In England, Bertrand Russell went to jail for his pacifist, antigovernment writings. Lytton Strachey told the Hampstead Tribunal (the equivalent of a contemporary draft board):

> This objection [to the war] is not based upon religious belief, but upon moral considerations, at which I have arrived after long and painful thought. I do not wish to assert the extremely general proposition that I should never, in any circumstances, be justified in taking part in any conceivable war; to dogmatize so absolutely upon a point so abstract would appear to me to be unreasonable. At the same time, my feeling is directed not simply against the present war; I am convinced that the system by which it is sought to settle international disputes by force is profoundly evil; and that, so far as I am concerned, I should be doing wrong to take part in it."[9]

Such reactions to government policy during World War I appear as pale precursors to the convictions of dissident students concerning the evils of the war in Vietnam. If we remember that such students are self-selected among the general student body on the basis of their intellectuality, awareness of social trends throughout the world, and high standards for political morality, then their sense of disillusion follows logically from the expectations based upon their previous schooling. The germ of the hostile belief system embedded in Freud's and Strachey's comments is, of course, enormously elaborated in the dissident students' "thoughts for the times," in ways that need not be reviewed here. But it seems plausible to assume that the hostile attitude toward the authority of the state and toward all who cooperate with it, including the universities, follows the disillusionment. The withdrawal of respect and admiration replaces love with hate and releases superego constraints where most authority figures are concerned.

As a result, most authorities, intellectual or administrative, are seen in accordance with the model of the state as oppressive, manipulative, and corrupting. Although this perception is magnified by the newly formed negative identifications, it is also close to the truth. Jails and the armed forces aside, schools, colleges, and universities are among the most irrationally authoritarian of American institutions. More precisely, so far as formal organizations are concerned, they are characterized to an unusual degree by decentralized oligarchies: many faculty members are responsible to one departmental chairman, surrounded by his clique of "inner circle" confidants; many departmental chairmen are responsible to one dean who is more loyal, on the whole, to the president and the various governing boards than to the intimate concerns of the departments. The decentralization of oligarchies guarantees feeble communication of mutual concerns. The various departments and their chairmen know or care little about other departments; and the higher administration, erroneously persuaded that departmental freedom and independence are being encouraged, experience a poverty of information about the needs of the department except where their own, usually fiscal, interests are concerned. Thus, despite (or because of) the misleading slogan of "academic freedom" (which literally means freedom to hold and teach unpopular views) the most important policy decisions are made at the top by boards which have little or no contact with staff and line personnel.

The role of the student is beset by similar anomalies. A student shares incompatible features of a hospital, a jail, a retail commercial outlet, and a club. Like a patient in a hospital, the student achieves little good by complaining about the service and he must follow orders. Like an inmate in a jail, the student can be put on probation or punished in other ways for infractions of rules. But, like a customer, he can shop around for consumer products, hoping to accumulate an education with which to impress future employers. Finally, as a club member, he can be granted or denied admission, and he is expected to contribute to and take pride in the elite status of his membership.[10]

As a result of these singular, institutional arrangements, until the advent of the student power movement, students had few rights and little control over their lives.

With the attainment of the partially realistic perception of the administration as the "oppressor,"[11] the student's ego is suddenly assailed with anxiety from three sides. From the environment, the ego must face the real possibility of punishment for the loss of respect toward authorities. From the id there is the possibility of being overwhelmed with rage, including the resurrection of long-repressed oedipal hostilities. And from the super-ego there still remains the possibility of guilt. The loss of positive identification is not as deep nor thoroughgoing as it may seem at first glance. In fact, the negative side of the identification is like a thin, protective armor that requires constant reinforcement. Therefore, guilt feelings must be constantly warded off.

Under these circumstances the ego must be protected. Two defenses are available for this purpose, and used together, they prove fairly serviceable. The first is identification with the aggressor—or, as one might say in this instance, with the oppressor. Anxiety is dispelled in the fashion described by Anna Freud,[12] not through a general identification but by means of an imitation of the aggressor's behavior as perceived by the victim. Are the authorities insensitive, unresponsive, willing to use force (the brutal police, the narrow-minded lower courts) to get their way? Yes.

Then so are the students. Is the aggressor frustrating and evasive? The list could be extended but the point is clear.[13]

That this process is unconscious and not well controlled by reality is revealed in a variety of ways. The hostile, disrespectful, impatient attitudes demonstrated toward administrators is apt to be exhibited in their behavior toward each other. Since the behavior is defensive rather than a spontaneous release of instinctual energy, it is rarely satisfying, and on this account, prompts a continuous search for new objects. It tends to be ritualized—that is, automatically displayed in the presence of any member of the administration. As reality testing is reduced, the students tend to misjudge clues of receptivity and change in their opponents. Opportunities for successfully pressing their advantage are frequently passed up on this account.

Because of the novelty of the defense, it is always in danger of breaking down. The second defense is then brought to the rescue: the principle of negative justice. Each member of the aggrieved group must be known to the others as equally deserving of the retributions of the oppressor, lest group solidarity weaken. Thus, each must provoke in the same way and to the same degree. To maintain such conduct in the face of the positive feelings being warded off—to say nothing of long standing habits—is difficult. To be on the safe side, the aggrieved group needs to keep away from frequent contacts with the administration and to be sure that if contacts are made, at least three members are together, watching each other and helping each other to continue to display the requisite degree of distance, coolness, and unfriendliness.

In *The Strawberry Statement: Notes of a College Revolutionary,* James S. Kunen, who participated in the Columbia uprising, cites an amusing example of this sort of ambiguity in student attitudes. In his role as commentator on the local scene, Kunen had made an appointment to interview Dean Herbert Deane of Columbia, a confrontation to which he looked forward with a certain degree of malice, as well as curiosity. Herbert Deane had provided Kunen with the title of his book. In April 1967, a year before the campus crisis, Deane had made the comment, "A university is definitely not a democratic institution. When decisions begin to be made democratically around here, I will not be here any longer. Whether students vote 'yes' or 'no' on an issue is like telling me they like strawberries." After a long, friendly, and candid conversation with this paragon of academic paternalism in July 1968, Kunen wrote in his diary, "God, what am I going to do? I *liked* Dean Deane."[14]

Nevertheless, at the height of the crisis, the students' defenses produce a rigidly maintained and often affected hostile manner. This is not to say that the behavior is insincere; rather, it is out of control because of the conflicting inner feelings. This is one of the reasons for the poor communication during negotiating sessions, noted above. It is also one of the conscious reasons for the activity of the "doves," who perceive that the students are not presenting their case in the best light and therefore need an advocate.

Despite their defensiveness in the presence of authority figures and the sometimes inappropriate behavior toward each other evoked by the identification with the aggressors, the students generally display warm relations within the group. The libidinal component which has been detached from authority figures is now directed toward the group as a whole. The resulting increase in available affectionate energy and the closeness of personal relations lead to a rise in group morale. Throughout much of the crisis the students' ability to display, wit, humor, and creative activity reaches unusual heights. The occasion becomes memorable in their eyes, and even in the eyes of some outside observers, because of the exuberant energies it releases, and because of some of the comic scenes acted out on all sides.

In *The Strawberry Statement,* for example, Kunen describes an incident which occurred when the Columbia students arrested in the April 29 bust were taken to the Twenty-fourth Precinct to be booked: " 'Up against the wall,' we are told. I can't get over how they really use the term. We turn and lean on the wall with our hands high, because that's what we've seen in the movies. We are told to can that shit and sit down." The police, it turned out, merely wanted the students to sit on the chairs alongside the walls.

The "doves" within the faculty and administration are among those favorably impressed with the novel, creative aspects of student activity. Anxious as they are to be of help, they, too, are under the influence of an unconscious, defensive process: a variant of what Anna Freud has called "altruistic surrender." In their face-off with the "hawks" they are not asking for anything for themselves, as are the "hawks" and the students. Their motives are purely altruistic in that they want to see the students obtain a "fair shake" from the administration. For this reason they undertake, at great cost of energy and possible risk of their security, a strenuous defense of the students' cause. The unconscious motive for this position, however, is envy of the students' aggressiveness. They would like to have the role of the young students for themselves, defying the established authorities, bringing them to heel, and reaping the rewards of victory in the manner of David over Goliath. The oedipal background of such an identification with the challengers, is, again, a part of the constellation of motives. But, in the foreground is the problem of envy too productive of guilt-feeling to be directly acknowledged. Accordingly, to back the challengers, to take the risks without reaping the rewards, to offer themselves up to the wrath of the "hawks" as sacrificial lambs—all these behaviors neutralize the claims of the superego.

Although the voice of the "doves" exerts a strong influence on the outcome of the crisis, it generates severe antagonisms. Its defensive quality is perceived by both students and "hawks." Students feel that "doves" are defending them for the wrong reasons, that is, for their own narcissistic (or "liberal") reasons, and not because of a realistic understanding of the students' position. "Hawks," on the other hand, immediately perceive that behind the even-tempered and apparently reasonable arguments of the "doves" there lies an intense desire to humble them.[15]

This sensitivity on the part of the "hawks," which to the "doveish" mind looks so paranoid, is based upon a strong, narcissistic defense. Although "hawks" show a great deal of variation in personality and background factors, the largest number of them are men who have climbed up the academic ladder from humble origins. They have obtained positions of some power and influence through hard work and the sacrifice of many pleasures, exemplifying in the process the individualistic, achievement values of American culture. Not only have pleasures been postponed, but, in addition, such men have had to endure narcissistic wounds and humiliation in the struggle to rise from an inferior status to one of relative superiority. At last they are in a position to enjoy their hard won privileges—that is, to have power over others, to make the decisions they have accepted from others on the way up. Moreover, in their view, they have been fairer in the exercise of power than have their predecessors. Now, just at this moment, they suddenly find themselves challenged. They are being asked to share their power with the young, with student usurpers lacking all self-discipline and completely callow about the difficulties of obtaining power and the responsibilities of exercising it. To add insult to injury, though they perceive themselves as defending liberal principles, their behavior is called reactionary or authoritarian by their opponents.[16]

Under these circumstances, with pride so largely secured by their careers and in the prerogative of office, the demands and behavior of the dissident students represent direct assaults upon the "hawks'" self-esteem. It is as if they were being forced to return to their humble origins. The narcissistic defense then enlarges the ego by identifying its fate with that of the institution, or even with the country as a whole. If they are to be destroyed, then so is the school and the nation. This view is, after all, not so irrational as it may seem. For the attack upon the "hawks" is an attack upon the structure of power and the hierarchical values of superiority and inferiority concealed behind the individualism that is supposedly the hallmark of our democracy.[17]

So far as the "temporizers" are concerned, their unconscious motives are more varied and more difficult to discern. Some are merely timid and cautious, defending themselves against anxiety through watchfulness and delay of action. Others are really emotionally uninvolved in the struggle, denying their unconscious feelings through isolation. Still others are convinced that compromise and an Hegelian synthesis of opposites are the only effective methods of conflict resolution, techniques that always require time. Because their motives are obscure or undefined, "temporizers" are apt to be made into scapegoats for the frustrations felt by all. Their delaying tactics and shillyshallying policies are seen as the reasons why the crisis remains so long unresolved.

TRANSACTION, INTERACTION, AND SELF-ACTION

This review of the ego mechanisms and defenses elicited by the crisis is not very satisfactory. It is far from a complete inventory of unconscious ego mechanisms and it leaves many problems unresolved. It produces the impression that no group comes off well in the struggle. If there are no obvious villains, neither are there any heroes. Moreover, it places me in an awkward position since I have not explicitly aligned myself with any group. Can the investigator of such situations really remain above the fray, analyzing everyone's motives except his own? Especially if the investigator is also an academic?

The pressure to take sides is intense. Not only one's inner promptings are at work, but also the expectations of others. As has been repeatedly (and regretfully) observed, in the current heated atmosphere it is difficult to maintain a dispassionate, objective position. Moreover, in some quarters, notably among the students, lack of passion is suspect; it is regarded as indicating insincerity or evasiveness.

Despite these pressures, I should like to postpone stating my position for the moment. Rather, I would ask whether there is not a line of argument capable of avoiding an emotional but somewhat arbitrary commitment, on the one hand, and an intellectual withdrawal, on the other. Is there not some mode of analysis which can bring the goals of change desired by the students and their tactics—as well as the goals and tactics of their opponents—into the same frame of reference? Can we devise some language capable of displaying pathology, either within the individual or within the structure of the university, as the outcome of a larger process? Finally, can such an approach indicate the direction in which a possible solution might lie?

I believe that answers to these questions can be found in the transactional mode of analysis proposed by Dewey and Bentley.[18] The writers, one a philosopher, the other a political and economic analyst, started with a critique of theories of knowledge, but, like Whitehead,[19] ended up with a new formulation of process. Process, they said, has been explained as the operation of self-acting entities, or as the result of interaction between entities. They suggested that a more appropriate description would refer to transaction among systems. *Self-action* describes a preset entity, like a clock, all wound up and ready to go at a given signal or stimulus. All the elements of the process are within the entity— the star, the gene, the plant, the personality, the institution—and will simply unfold themselves over time, at least under the right circumstances.

Interaction describes a process in which entities are connected with entities in a sequence of action and reaction, like billiard balls. The patient unburdens herself to her therapist; the therapist makes an interpretation; the patient goes home and for the first time tells her husband what she really thinks of him; the husband calls the therapist in a rage; the therapist notes that the patient is losing some of her inhibitions but, in the process, may be acting out too much. The focus is on the behavior of each entity rather than on the interplay of all as a system.

Transaction refers to a web of complex, interwoven systems within a total field such as the metabolic, endocrine, and neuro-physiological processes that maintain blood sugar at a steady level. Because of the chainlike and reverberating effects, with constant, mutual adjustment of subsystems to each other, such processes cannot be appropriately described by reference to the activity of any one organ or structure. All systems are involved in the behavior of all. On this view, structure (an organ, an institution) becomes both the product of the systems which maintain it and the source (if one is needed) of the activity of some of the systems. The choice of cause or effect is up to the observer—a product of *his* activity—rather than a fixed principle given in the nature of "reality." What is found when the scientist publishes a finding is what he had arranged to look at, because nature consists merely of processes of exchange—that is, of transactions.[20]

To place the processes of campus disorders within this framework, I should like to argue that the descriptions offered by Bettelheim and Feuer and discussed above are examples of cause attributed to self-action. In response to the stimulus of a general, student protest movement, with its stylized list of complaints, the preexisting neurotic problems of the activist students are externalized, and then justified by the movement and its supporters, who see it as interaction. If it is self-actional, then the critiques of Bettelheim and Feuer are the logical correctives.

The description which I have just given, on the other hand, is mainly interactional, specifying the conditions to which the "aggrieved" group responds, the initial reactions of the administration, and subsequent reactions back and forth in ping-pong manner. While less biased and mechanical than self-action descriptions,[21] it is still selective and thus arbitrary. Omitting some factors from consideration may have unduly biased the explanation. But, since any scientific approach is based on the selection of some variables, and the omission of others, how can this deficiency be repaired?

In struggling with the problem in the past, I have proposed for consideration a *field of transacting systems*[22] composed of six foci: the Universe (physico-chemical and cosmic systems), the Soma (biological systems), the Psyche (cognitive and emotional systems), the Group (small face-to-face organizations), the Society (governmental, economic, educational, religious, recreational, intellectual-aesthetic, and family systems), and the Culture (language, technological, value, and belief systems). The foci are arranged, for graphic and representational purposes, in a circle so that all are interconnected. Processes within and between foci are assumed to run in either direction around the periphery, eliminating the need to specify "cause and effect" except for the aims of a particular investigation. Although all foci are assumed to be operative at all times in the smallest or largest phenomenon, as many foci (or parts of foci) as one wishes can be disregarded, provided one allows for the probability of error as a result of the exclusion.

In the interactional analysis presented above, parts of three foci within the transactional field were considered: the Psyche (including unconscious processes), the Group, and Society, at least as represented by educational institutions.[23] Although parts of several other foci could have been plugged into the aggregate of processes,[24] what is conspicuously missing is any consideration of the cultural focus, especially the cultural values governing decision-making processes within the society as a whole and within the university. Bringing this system of values into the analysis is crucial because it is the key to the conflict within the institution as well as to the related conflict within the larger society. To introduce the topic, I shall use the language and concepts proposed by Florence R. Kluckhohn in her analysis of variation in culture value orientations.[25]

The Kluckhohn theory assumes that all cultures (and subcultures) find the same solutions to the problem of group relations and decision-making; they vary, however, in the rank-ordering or patterning of the solutions. The solutions discoverable in every culture are (1) the *Lineal,* in which group relations are arranged vertically, accenting the dominance of the superior over the inferior, with decisions made at the top; (2) the *Collateral,* in which horizontal group relations are stressed, with decisions made by prolonged discussion to reach group consensus; and (3) the *Individual,* in which each person is equal to any other and thus is free, indeed, obligated, to make up his own mind, and to choose his own affiliations, with group decisions taken by majority vote.

The pattern of preference promulgated under the aegis of American democracy is first, the Individual; second, the Collateral; and third, the Lineal Solution. We are all educated in accordance with this pattern: Americans should be independent and unsubmissive, but in an emergency or for team efforts we should all pull together within the collateral group. While authoritarian hierarchies might be necessary evils, our sympathies are with the little man at the bottom and against the bosses.

Despite the widespread acceptance of this pattern as official ideology, if one inspects the actual functioning of our major institutions, one comes across a paradox. Government, schools, most commercial organizations, the economy, the relations between ethnic groups and social classes, are all oriented to a different pattern: The Individual is still first, but Lineality is in the second position, with Collaterality a poor third. The vertical structuring of power is at times so prominent—for example, in our foreign policies generally, and particularly in Vietnam—as to assume a virtual first-order position. The accompanying elitism is usually hidden beneath a mask of individualism, as in the notion of a "meritocracy" (the best float to the top[26]). But, in fact, one finds rule by oligarchy, whether carried out by big city "machines," university boards and deans, or congressional committees dominated by Southern conservatives.

As a result of this paradox, our values (cultural beliefs about the way things should be) do not correspond to our practices (the way things really are). Or, to put the matter more precisely, the value orientations which support our institutions are in conflict with the values represented in our official ideology, and, accordingly, in our ideal self-concept. Such a conflict in values cannot exist without generating some groups organized to expose it and to change the structure of the social system. Nor can it exist without giving rise to intrapsychic conflict, expecially to problems of identity, and more especially where the young are concerned. Which way is the student to direct himself: toward power and success ("making it") or toward fulfillment for the self and others?

Whenever groups are beset by a basic conflict in values, there are only a limited number of ways in which chaos and disintegration can be avoided. The conflict can be denied, concealed, or explained away, in which case all concerned are expected to buy the formula which buries the conflict. If such techniques of persuasion fail, then coercion, involving the use of force and punishment, can be used for those who resist the more "reasonable" methods of suppressing the conflict. For example, those who are older, who are in authority, and whose lifestyle was formed by somehow successfully getting around the conflict (and who therefore feel threatened by being brought to face it again) are likely to start off with some dissembling technique if challenged. They will say that America is the freest country in the world (denial of conflict), or that the challenger has to recognize the difference between ideals and reality (rationalization of conflict), or that the challenger is right, but things are slowly getting better, and he should be patient (delay as a method of conflict avoidance).

Conflicts act like pain or any other irritant. They must either be avoided or resolved. In the past, and to a large degree still, American students have tended to accept the conflict-avoiding explanations proposed by their wiser and more experienced elders. If they no longer accept conflict-avoidance as readily as in the past, it is because the chances for actual resolution now seem better, and accordingly, the value conflict stands out in sharper relief.[27] Once convinced that the time is ripe, students discover that for each conflict-avoiding technique there exists a "neutralizer" capable of exposing the conflict.[28] For example, denial can be met by assertion (the poor, the draftees, the blacks, the Spanish-Americans, the Indians are oppressed); rationalization can be countered by unmasking ("reality" doesn't require that poor people be thrown out of their homes by university expansion); and delay can be interrupted by provoking, which moves the timetable for conflict-facing forward. Even coercion, the last resort of the powerful, can be met by sabotage or defiance, the last weapons of the weak.

Of all these methods for exposing the basic conflict of values, "provoking," "unmasking," and "counter-coercing" are the most disruptive. When dissident students sit in as uninvited guests at a faculty meeting, break up a lecture by seizing the microphone, or occupy a building, they gain nothing for themselves. Their actions are effective only because they are norm-violating—an outrage, which like personal insult or injury, can scarcely be disregarded. Any tendency by officialdom to postpone facing the conflict is dealt a severe blow. When students raid the personal files of university officials and publish letters exposing the discrepancy between the public and private views of these officials, they inflict similar injury to convention and public morality. But, on the other hand, the value conflict can no longer be explained away.

We are now in a position to examine the three-way struggle between "hawks," "doves," and dissident students from a transactional point of view. The neutralizing techniques of the students lay bare the value conflict which has so long been concealed and denied. Every one of the specific "issues" brought up by the students—whether concerned with race, with capitalist exploitation, with the war in Vietnam, with the institution's complicity in the military-industrial complex, with the curriculum or other "student power" issues—all are reflections of the conflict between individualistic, democratic ideals and authoritarian, elitist practices.

Faced with the exposure of the conflict in all its native crudeness, administrators have three choices. They can acknowledge the conflict and embrace Lineality openly, as did Dean Herbert Deane of Columbia ("When decisions begin to be made democratically around here, I will not be here any longer."). They can admit the conflict and endorse the official American pattern, usually through implementing some of the students' demands after a thorough discussion. The third option is to continue rationalizing and denying the conflict while describing the students' provocations as representing the very essence of that arbitrary and authoritarian style which the students attribute to the administration. It is this third position which becomes the core of the "hawks'" opposition to the students' behavior.

Confronted with this situation, the "doves" face a difficult choice. It is hard to deny the sincerity, even the possible validity of the hawks' fear that student provocation imperils the very "justice" they seek. On the other hand, "doves" are well aware of the unwillingness of the "hawks" to face these issues without student pressures. Weighing these two risks, they come to the conclusion that the danger of supporting the students is not as great as claimed by the "hawks," while supporting the "hawks" would guarantee preservation of the status quo.

The "doves" and the student leaders of the "aggrieved" groups are on the side of change. If the above analysis is correct, then the advocates of change are also advocating that the value conflict be brought out into the open. It is in connection with the transactional implications of this process that I should like to state my own position. I have felt it necessary to make the case for my position carefully, and at length, because it does not conform precisely to any of the standard positions and because, as a student of violence, I am expected to pursue the matter to whatever lengths, pleasant or unpleasant, the evidence seems to lead.

My position is that of a therapist. All therapists have the experience of dealing with conflict wherever they find it, within the person, within the family, or within the culture. Their experience tells them that a concealed conflict almost always has unfortunate effects. It also tells them that in the process of therapy, if it is to be effective, the forces that hide the conflict are loosened, and that, as the conflict erupts into the open, the patient, or the family, undergoes considerable pain and discomfiture. It is a time for fastening the seat belts. But only by undergoing this exposure can the systems in conflict be brought into a better state of mutual accommodation. This does not mean that the conflict vanishes but only that the person, the family, or the afflicted organization of whatever type is able to make a better choice between the two sides of the conflict. Resolution of the conflict means that there is knowledge of what is to be lost and gained by promoting one side of the conflict and demoting the other, and that this knowledge can be put into action.

Holding these views, I can reach no other conclusion than that the student leaders are performing a therapeutic function by forcing the value conflict into the open. Of course, there is the danger that some students may become fixated on provoking as an end rather than a means. But this risk does not seem to me to be greater than those encountered in any therapeutic "working through" of conflict.[29]

As in any therapeutic situation, exactly how the conflict of values will be resolved, or even if it will be resolved, cannot now be foretold. We are too much in the early stages of the struggle. In addition, the universities are merely the presenting aspect of a conflict that cannot be resolved until the exposure spreads to all parts of the social system. If past cycles of disorders are any clue to the future, the chances of a real resolution of conflict are not too good.[30] But it is at least possible that this time around the American people will ultimately choose to demote Lineality to the last and least honored position specified by our official values, provided the students and the young everywhere keep up their pressure.

Does this position make me a "dove?" Perhaps, but a dove bearing a scalpel rather than an olive branch.

NOTES

1. W. C. Menninger, "The Role of Psychiatry in the World Today," *American Journal of Psychiatry* 104: 155-163. Reprinted in *A Psychiatrist for a Troubled World: Selected Papers of William C. Menninger, M. D.,* ed. B. H. Hall (New York: Viking Press, 1967), pp. 568-581.

2. I am confident that some critics will argue, with a good deal of justice, that the phase model imposes too much order and clarity on the phenomena. In situations characterized by considerable variation and fluidity, a highly structured and abstract description may lead the unpracticed observer to see the general form in the particular instance when, in fact, it is not there. As a last ditch defense, however, I would claim that the phase sequence has the merit of being easily rearranged to fit altered circumstances, and, finally, that it is a good target. It can be shot down and abandoned easily enough when a better model is proposed.

3. Some administrations dealing for the first time with an initial disorder base their strategy on the correction of an error presumably committed at another university. Thus, the Harvard administration in the spring of 1969 called in the police a few hours after the students had seized the administration building because Columbia in the spring of 1968 had supposedly waited too long before summoning the police, thus allowing time for support to build up

among the moderates for the student rebels. But the Harvard policy worked no better than Columbia's.

4. An amusing description (for those not attending it) of a typically frustrating faculty meeting during the height of a crisis is to be found in *Shut It Down! A College in Crisis,* a staff report on the San Francisco State College disturbances, October 1968 to April 1969, prepared by William H. Orrick, Jr., for submission to the National Commission on the Causes and Prevention of Violence, pp. 52–53.

5. The "walk-out" and the "walk-in" ("sit-in," "sleep-in," "study-in," etc.) appear to be two of the most effective weapons in the whole armamentarium of nonviolent techinques of disruption. To fail to appear at a meeting or to leave in the middle puts an effective stop to action. To appear when not wanted can be equally effective. Seizing a building combines both techniques and is, thus, doubly effective. "Intrusion" and "exclusion," the action bases of these techniques, are universal attention-getting devices, whether used legally or illegally. This is what makes the "we cannot excuse or condone . . ." approach so weak and ineffective as a policy and so hypocritical or comical as a posture.

6. The intransigent attitude of the female leaders seems to arise less from a purely competitive urge than from having abandoned the more traditional feminine role of "peacemaker." Such a role would undermine the whole position of the women within the aggrieved group. But having given it up, the women appear to be particularly sensitized to the possibility of its being taken over by any of the men.

7. Sigmund Freud: *Group Psychology and the Analysis of the Ego,* Vol. 18, Standard Edition. Freud repeated this observation in his letter to Einstein, *Why War?,* and again in *Civilization and Its Discontents,* but in neither instance did he subject the matter to any further discussion or analysis, except insofar as he joined it to the notion of the "narcissism of minor differences."

8. Sigmund Freud: *Thoughts for the Times on War and Death,* (1) "The Disillusionment of the War," Vol. 14, Standard Edition, pp. 278–279. The omitted section gives concrete examples of "wrongdoing" perpetrated by the state.

9. Michael Holroyd, Lytton Strachey: *The Years of Achievement,* Holt, Rinehart and Winston, New York, 1968, Vol. 2, p. 177.

10. There are only a few studies of the forms and effects of authoritarian structure in the universities. Christopher Jenks and David Riesman touch upon the effects in their book, *The Academic Revolution* (Doubleday, New York, 1968). Theodore Newcomb has summarized studies comparing universities with industrial organizations in this regard, adding cogent observations of his own in an article in the June 1969 issue of *Political Science Quarterly,* entitled "University, Heal Thyself." A more general analysis of the authoritarian structure of American society, and of localized rebellion as a way of

democratization, is presented by Michael Walzer, "Corporate Authority and Civil Disobedience," *Dissent,* September-October, 1969, pp. 395–406.

11. To call this perception "partially realistic" is not to say that administrators explicitly intend to oppress students. On the contrary, administrators often feel themselves caught up in a system which they are powerless to change and duty-bound to uphold, despite their own dissatisfactions with it. A study carried out by the staff of the Center for Research and Development in Higher Education, University of California at Berkeley, and reported in the newsletter The Research Reporter, (Vol. IV, Number 1, 1969) reflects such feelings. Thirty percent of all administrators, and fifty percent of the academic vice-presidents disagreed with the statement, "Open flouting of the university rules is always wrong." Sixty-three percent of all administrators (in each of sixty-nine of the largest and most prestigious universities in the United States) agreed that "a show of 'student power' is sometimes necessary."

12. Anna Freud: *The Ego and the Mechanisms of Defence,* International Universities Press, New York, 1946, pp. 117–131.

13. The process is complicated by the presence of "projective identification." Students' perceptions of the administrators are exaggerated by the attribution to the administrators of unconscious hostility felt within the self. Thus, what is copied is not faithful to the original model. Once the process is initiated, however, the behavior of the students may instigate behavior by the administrators which brings out the very qualities students had assumed to be present, if concealed, from the beginning.

14. James Simon Kunen: *The Strawberry Statement: Notes of a College Revolutionary,* Random House, New York, 1969, p. 116.

15. Abrasive behavior between "hawks" and "doves" is not confined to the campus. It can break out anywhere and often disrupts cocktail and dinner parties. At the May 1969 annual meeting of the American Association of University Professors, in Minneapolis, a stormy session, punctuated by several angry shouting matches, followed a panel discussion of "confrontation tactics." In the general heat and din one professor accused a colleague of being a "cop-out" and "coward," and another asked in shocked tones, "Are you confronting me, sir?"

16. Here we meet the problem with labels again. The word "liberal" is beginning to lose its meaning. For example, in an article in the July 1969 *Atlantic Monthly,* entitled "The Campus Crucible," Nathan Glazer, traditionally a liberal, but "hawkish" on the subject of student rebellions, speaks about "the failure of the liberals." By this expression he means faculty members whose sympathy with the goals of the students prevents them from subjecting the tactics of the students to a sufficiently penetrating (and disapproving) critique. If we are forced to make a distinction between "hawkish" and "doveish" brands of liberalism, we might as well give up using the word altogether. Of course, the words "hawk" and "dove" are labels, too, but have the advantage of being issue oriented.

17. Some of the academic "hawks" are refugees from European communist or fascist regimes, or from left-wing parties in this country. Their experience, either in universities or in other contexts, has been so traumatic, their responses to political intransigence so conditioned and stigmatized, as to render them incapable of making any distinctions where goals of political activity are concerned. For them, any extreme position, whether of the right or the left, is devastating. Still, behind their fears lurks the authoritarianism and elitism of their country of origin, which the regime or party, whether communist or fascist, has exploited. Thus, there is something at once realistic and of fantasy origins in their responses. The sign of their inability to test reality on this score is their impatience. They cannot wait to find out how far or where student rebelliousness will go. It must be crushed, now, regardless of its emergent goals and of its constantly changing tactics.

18. John Dewey and Arthur F. Bentley: *Knowing and the Known* (Boston: Beacon Press, 1949).

19. Alfred North Whitehead: *Process and Reality: An Essay in Cosmology* (New York: Macmillan Co., 1929).

20. These views are quite similar to those labelled "general systems theory," though the two bodies of ideas developed independently. Transaction theory is more philosophical in orientation, general systems theory more empirical; but otherwise there is no fundamental inconsistency between the two.

21. Dewey and Bentley maintained that self-actional and interactional descriptions were always wrong—anachronistic and misleading. It can be argued, however, that though they are incomplete, they are not on that account necessarily wrong. All behaviorist theories of learning based on the stimulus-response model, for example, are self-actional. They are extremely incomplete. In most, only the unconditioned response repertoire of the organism is observed and worked with. The processes within the organism which are correlated with such responses are mainly ignored (the "little black box" approach). Nevertheless, the observed effects of the experimenter's conditioning procedures are valid within the highly restricted apea of his operations, and have useful applications.

22. John P. Spiegel: *Transactions: The Interplay between Individual, Family, and Society* (New York: Science House, 1971). See especially Part 1, "Transactional Theory."

23. The exclusion of economic systems from the previous discussion and from what follows, is a bias which, unfortunately, I am not in a position to control, though I hope to repair the omission in future studies.

24. For example, somatic factors such as fatigue and the effects of youth and such physical factors as weather (winter being unfavorable to, though not necessarily preventing, campus disorders) could obviously have been given extended consideration.

25. Florence R. Kluckhohn, and Fred L. Strodtbeck: *Variations in Value Orientations* (Evanston, Ill.: Row, Peterson and Co., 1961).

26. A cynic might say that they do not float to the top; they claw their way up! A cynic is a person who recognizes rather than denies a value conflict, but does not propose to do anything about it. However, many students, perhaps a majority, still want nothing more than the opportunity to fight their way up the ladder of achievement.

27. Each of the upsurges of student protest movements described by Lewis Feuer occurred at a time when the prospects for social change seemed excellent, given a push by a resolute minority. Despite its self-actional theory, Feuer's book contains many pertinent interactional descriptions, including precise accounts of the value conflict associated with each cycle of the movement.

28. I have discussed these techniques in detail in my paper, "The Resolution of Role Conflict Within The Family," in *A Modern Introduction to the Family,* ed. Norman W. Bell and Ezra F. Vogel (Glencoe, Ill.: Free Press, 1960).

29. I have discussed this problem in my paper "Toward a Theory of Collective Violence," in *The Dynamics of Violence,* ed. Jan Fawcett (Chicago: American Medical Association, 1971).

30. The greatest risk is that the intensity of the identification with the aggressor will result in a fixation on the use of force and violence so strong that the students must constantly seek new objects on which to discharge hostility. Under these circumstances, failure to find a suitable object may end in the turning of the hostility on the self, accompanied by depression or even by attempts at self-destruction.

7/Tactics and strategies adopted by university authorities to counter student opposition*

Cornelis J. Lammers

When new areas of sociological enquiry attract our professional attention, the floodlights of research are usually first focused on the lower participants in social institutions. Only later are they shifted to the holders of higher ranking positions. Thus, in the sociologies of industry, religion, and medicine, the factory workers, parishioners, and patients were "covered" at an earlier stage and more adequately than were the managers, clergymen, and doctors.

Leaving the reasons for this phenomenon to sociologists of knowledge we merely note the same development with respect to the sociological preoccupation with campus unrest and related phenomena. Starting in the mid-sixties there has been a tremendous proliferation of studies concerning student participation in and attitudes toward various forms of protest in institutions of higher learning (for a summary, see Lipset, 1972), but only in the last years have research reports concerning faculty response to student protest started to reach the journals (see, for example, Abramson and Wences, 1970; Barton, 1968; Bidwell, 1971; Cole and Adamsons, 1969; Cole and Adamsons, 1970; Lammers, 1974; Lipset, 1970; Lipset et al., 1970; Pugh et al., 1971; Wences and Abramson, 1970; Wilson and Gaff, 1969).

Most of these studies deal with attitudinal or reported behavioral responses of individual professors. In general, such responses are analyzed by aggregating them in terms of practically and/or theoretically more or less relevant categories such as age-groups, ranks, variations in socio-political outlook, and the like. This method provides sytematic insight into the "mood" of the faculty, but since it consists of the aggregate of their individual responses, the mood of the faculty is probably only one of the factors shaping the collective and more or less *organized* response of the decision-making administrative and faculty bodies to student opposition.

Therefore, an analysis of the ways in which university authorities actually react to student opposition appears to be in order. It seems likely that the tactics and strategies used by administrative and faculty power-holders in countering student actions are of major importance in determining the short-term course of events in campus conflicts and in influencing the long-term developments of the institutionalized interrelationships between students, faculty, and administration.

This area of study also deserves the attention of the social sciences, because in the Sixties most Western universities—in contrast to many industrial and military organizations—did not have ready-made strategies, prescribed ways of coping with extra-institutional opposition from the ranks. This state of affairs undoubtedly left ample scope for variations in tactics resulting from personality variables. On the other hand, certain more or less latent pecularities of the decision-making machinery of the organizational apparatus that was to adjudicate the conflicts, and in general various characteristics of the power structure of the institution in question, in all likelihood played a role in determining the course of events. This means that such crises supply the organizational theorist with rather unique opportunities to assess certain underlying properties of the institutional system not readily visible under normal circumstances.

In this paper an attempt will be made to design a typology of the tactics utilized by administration and faculty to cope with student opposition. Subsequently, the typology will be elaborated in the light of some of the available documentary evidence concerning the actions of university authorities in the face of student unrest. Then, the relationship between tactics and strategies will be discussed. Finally, some hypotheses will be offered concerning the conditions that could explain why one kind of strategy or tactics is adopted rather than another, and the consequences thereof.

The present analysis is not meant to be more than an exploratory study with a theoretical bent, intended to promote further and more systematic thinking and research on the problems involved.

A TYPOLOGY OF TACTICS

Taking a cue from Admiral Mahan's distinction between tactics and strategy (Brodie, 1968: 281), one can define tactics as: *ways of coping with adversaries when in contact with them.* Strategy can be taken to refer to: *a goal-directed general outline of ways of coping with adversaries.* Consequently, tactics emerge and vanish during the struggle, but a strategy can be said to exist before and after the struggle. Of course, to the extent that tactics form part of a strategy, *blueprints* of tactics or tactical *conceptions* also can be taken to exist before and after the actual conflict. Therefore, two different, albeit related, operationalizations of the concept of tactics can be put forward. In the first place, stress can be placed on the definition of the situation of the party in question. Then the investigator tries to assess what norms and expectations are held by a certain party regarding its own "battle behavior" and that of its adversaries. In the second place, the observer may try to infer from the interaction between the contending parties the regularities apparently characteristic of the ways in which one party tries to cope with its adversaries. In this article I will use the concept tactics primarily in this second sense, since there are precious few data about the ways in which university authorities define the situation. Moreover, it is even doubtful—as already pointed out in the first section of this article—that top functionaries in universities during the period covered actually had more or less clearcut tactical conceptions very often.

Examining various reports concerning the ways in which university authorities try to cope with student opposition, one gets the impression that two rather common ways to counter student opposition are the "fight off" and the "buy off." In the former case authorities try to repress the opposition; in the latter case they are willing to come to terms with their adversaries by making concessions. Light (1977) has drawn attention to a third and less prevalent form of tactics, the "stand off," a technique adopted primarily to wear out the protesters and to prevent escalation of the conflict.

According to Light, the "stand off" is a form of *duragraha* (nonviolent harassment), a type of resistance which Mahatma Gandhi considered inferior to *satyagraha* (truth-seeking), an approach which assumes that both parties are willing and able to recognize their own views on truth as partial and will seek together in good faith a "larger" truth. In a few instances in Europe, academic authorities have tried to cope with student protest by "joining in" with their opponents and trying to develop certain innovations in concert with them. It makes sense to view such efforts as forms of *satyagraha* and to include them in the present analysis as a fourth type of tactics.

In this way we arrive at an inductive typology consisting of tactics differing on a phenotypical level as to the nature of the interaction between authorities and opposition and on a more genotypical level as to the degree to which authorities strive to maintain the existing power

SCHEME A. TACTICS USED BY UNIVERSITY AUTHORITIES TO COUNTER STUDENT OPPOSITION

VARIABLES	"FIGHT OFF"	"BUY OFF"	"JOIN IN"	"STAND OFF"
Authorities' efforts with respect to power differential between them and the opposition.	Maintenance of the power differential	Giving up part of their power	Sharing (some of) their power	Maintenance of the power differential
Principal means used by authorities to cope with opposition.	Negative sanctions	Positive sanctions	Partial deinstitutionalization and participation in joint endeavours for innovation	Abstention from positive and negative sanctions, introduction of changes
Authorities' goals with respect to opposition.	Elimination	Appeasement	Copartnership	Dissolution
Nature of interaction between authorities and opposition.	Conflict	Negotiation	Cooperation	Competition
Authorities' image of opposition.	Subversive ringleaders + misguided bystanders	Spokesmen + sympathizing adherents	Innovators + sympathizing adherents	Ringleaders and idealists + authentically restive following
Authorities' definition of student role.	As customer	As client	As member	As client

174

differential between them and the opposition. When applying "fight off" or "stand off" tactics, the authorities defend their powers, be it by different means. "Fight off" tactics imply *conflict*, "stand off" tactics a form of *competition* between the parties involved.

In the case of "buy off" tactics, authorities are willing to give up part of their powers as a result of *negotiation*, whereas the "join in" means that authorities aim at *cooperation* with the opposition and are ready to share some of their powers with them.

In the following sections we will examine the applicability of this typology. In addition to the two variables mentioned already, i.e. the nature of the interaction between authorities and opposition and the authorities' efforts with respect to power differential between them and the opposition, attention will also be paid to the principal means used by the authorities, their goals with respect to their adversaries and the image they hold of the opposition, and the way in which they define the student role. The characteristics of these tactics are summarized in Scheme A.

"FIGHT OFF" TACTICS

A clearcut example of tactics with which authorities attempt vigorously and at times even relentlessly to fight off any encroachment of their dominant decision-making powers by student opposition, is to be found in the case of Berlin's Free University in the period from 1965 to 1968. A well-documented and detailed report by Ludwig von Friedeburg et al., (1968) provides us with information concerning the countertactics used by the Rector and Senate of the university and the Burgomaster of Berlin (who is *ex officio* president of the so-called *Kuratorium,* a body equivalent to a Board of Regents) and other functionaries.

On the whole, these authorities relied in this period mainly on threatened or applied *negative* sanctions, such as:

    a. Restriction of the use of university facilities by students wanting to invite guest speakers (of a supposedly rebellious or subversive inclination) or to hold meetings to air their views on and protest concerning political issues (which could prove embarrassing for the authorities or be conducive to further diffusion of protest, etc.); (see von Friedeburg et al., 1968: 247 ff., 289, 297 ff., 344, 409 ff.).

    b. Disciplinary action against student representatives, ringleaders, or ordinary participants, for engaging in or inciting to allegedly forbidden or improper activities (see von Friedeburg et al., 1968: 338, 360 ff., 371 ff.).

    c. Suspension of lectures and other forms of instruction, closing down of parts of the university (von Friedeburg et al., 1968: 448 ff.).

d. Invoking or condoning police action to remove or disperse forcibly students participating in demonstrations, occupations, etc. (von Friedeburg et al., 1968: 368).

By means of negative sanctions the authorities try to subdue recalcitrant students and "roll back" or at least "contain" the opposition, which is considered to be non-legitimate. Not only the efforts to suppress symptoms of dissent but also the conspicuous absence of any serious attempt to create opportunities to talk over the issues or explore student wishes and meet any reasonable demands, yield indications that *elimination* is the primary goal of the authorities with respect to student opposition.

The corresponding image of student opposition that circulates among the authorities is one of a bunch of (at worst malignant, at best irresponsible) *ringleaders,* a vanishing minority (von Friedeburg et al., 1968: 358, 371) which from time to time succeeds to some extent in seducing parts of the peace-loving, law-abiding majority of students into ill-conceived actions. Of course, this kind of perception of their adversaries enables the authorities to justify their application of negative sanctions. If the rebels are defined not as spokesmen for a much more comprehensive category of students but rather as troublemakers and a nuisance not only to faculty but also to the vast majority of their fellow students who just want the academic show to go on, there is every reason to make short work of them.

The dominant pattern of tactics adopted by the authorities of the Free University of Berlin—threats of and/or application of negative sanctions, in order to eliminate an opposition defined as a small and relatively isolated group of troublemakers—has been evident in many other cases of student revolt the world over. Of course, one seldom encounters a completely pure type. Nevertheless, in several other instances—e.g. at San Francisco State College in 1967/1968 (McEvoy and Miller, 1970); at Columbia in 1968 (The Cox Commission Report, 1968; Trimberger, 1970); at Kent State University in 1969 (Michener, 1971; 96–104); at Nanterre and the Sorbonne (Touraine, 1968: esp. Chapters III and IV; Fields, 1970)—the main characteristics of the "fight off" type of tactics come to the fore rather clearly.

"Buy off" tactics

The course of events at Cornell University in 1968/1969, reported by Friedland and Edwards (1970) provides an illustration of this type of tactics. Here, in sharp contrast to the way in which the Berlin dignitaries handled the situation, the president and other functionaries did not take recourse to negative but, at least during this period, rather to *positive sanctions,* such as:

a. Provision of special facilities for black students (housing, Friedland and Edwards, 1970: 81; a special program of Afro-American studies, Friedland and Edwards, 1970: 82).

b. Nullification of disciplinary measures (Friedland and Edwards, 1970: 90–95).

The latter kind of positive sanction consists of not applying a negative sanction and deserves special interest, for in the context of a predominantly concessive pattern of tactics, the threat of negative sanctions acquires a functional significance completely different from its significance in a "fight off" pattern. In the latter case, power-holders are determined to maintain their ascendancy over the opposition, and the threat of punitive measures then usually reinforces their commitment to negative sanctions. As a consequence of such threats or of their execution, namely, the rebels quite often either back down—which strengthens the authorities' belief in the effectiveness of negative sanctions—or an escalation of the conflict ensues, in the course of which the authorities feel compelled to use more negative sanctions.

However, if those in power primarily adopt a "buy off" line of action, the threat of negative sanctions often does not lead to further negative sanctions but instead reinforces the already prevailing pattern of trying to manipulate the opposition with positive sanctions. Public utterances of such threats in such cases create a new potential for positive sanctions, because of the possibility of not executing the threat. Therefore, regardless of their deliberate intentions, authorities who on the whole stick to a "buy off" policy, often tend to convert the threatening of opposition leaders with disciplinary measures into a series of fresh concessions.

In passing, it may be mentioned that the reverse holds true for the "fight off" type of tactics, since in the context of this pattern an occasional offer of positive sanctions often has the primary function of increasing the "fund" of possible negative sanctions (by indignant withdrawal of the offer). Naturally, such ostentatious threats of negative or offers of positive sanctions often are not seriously intended to compel or induce the opposition to a desired course of action, but are rather aimed at interested "third" parties (the public, the faculty, non-involved students).

The use of positive sanctions as concessions implies sustained contact with the adversary, either directly or through the services of intermediaries (Friedland and Edwards, 1970: 85). Sustained communication between authorities and opposition contains a *negotiation* process. In a way, negotiation itself can also be interpreted as a positive social sanction—the conferral of status (as "recognized" opposition leaders) by the local authorities on the self-appointed spokesmen of the rebels. Again, there is a striking similarity, in reverse, to the "fight off" type of tactics, where quite often the refusal to recognize informal leaders and the breaking off of deliberations with formal student representatives both function as negative sanctions.

The all-overriding objective of the administration in this situation appears to be *appeasement* and the maintenance of peace and order (Friedland and Edwards, 1970: e.g. 89-90). As Parsons (1960: 25) has remarked, the university belongs to a rather curious category of service organizations, where customers are "taken into" the organization as "operative members" with important implications for the nature of such an organization. The dualistic position of students in the university organization (customer *and* member) seems to enable the authorities in times of crisis to stress in their countertactics different conceptions of the student role: a customer role, a member role, or a "client" role, defining a "client" as a person with more rights than a customer but with fewer rights than a member. Consequently, repressive authorities define students primarily as customers entitled only to "take" the services offered or to "leave" the serving organization and try to obtain the demanded services elsewhere. Concessive authorities, on the other hand, define students primarily as "clients" who have a right to have their demands honored, whenever these demands can be called reasonable and legitimate in the perspective of the organization's official goals.

The aim of keeping the university community intact as a going concern and the related vision of students as an important category of "clients," also entails an image of the oppositional nucleus as representatives of legitimate student interests and viewpoints. Of course, the *de facto* recognition of opposition leaders as a result of negotiating with them, more or less means that the authorities must entertain an image of the opposition leader as a spokesman for part of the university community. Whereas the nature of the opposition is defined by the supporters of "fight off" tactics as troublemakers with a following of misguided bystanders, advocates of the "buy off" pattern are apt to see the opposition as a nucleus of serious defendants of causes with a following of students less dedicated to, but fundamentally in agreement with, these causes.

The concessive type of tactics as the dominant reaction pattern of authorities toward student opposition over a prolonged period has been conspicuous in The Netherlands and also at Columbia in 1966 and 1967 (Lammers, 1974; The Cox Commission Report, 1968; Trimberger, 1970).

The fact that one seldom encounters detailed reports of cases in which the authorities tried to "buy off" their adversaries does not mean that such cases seldom occur. On the contrary, as Light (1977) points out, many potential conflicts are prevented or resolved at an early stage by a settlement. Of course, such negotiations are rather routine, not very spectacular, and therefore receive little publicity, although they probably constitute one of the most important and successful tactics used to cope with student opposition.

"JOIN IN" TACTICS

An excellent case study of this approach can be found in Van Strien (1970: Part Two), which contains both a description and an analysis of developments in the Psychology Department of the University of Groningen (The Netherlands) in 1968–1969. The means used in this type of tactics consist of a mixture of *partial deinstitutionalization* and *participation in joint endeavors* for radical innovation up to the very limits of legality.

In response to the initiative of a small group consisting of two student activists and one staff member (Van Strien, 1970: 40), the decision was taken to reduce the functioning of the formal departmental organs to a bare minimum. Of crucial importance in this respect is the policy concerning the transfer of the planning, decision-making and execution of major innovations respecting both the departmental administration and the curriculum, from the official bodies to more or less spontaneously formed groups, committees, and mass meetings (Van Strien, 1970: 41, 53, 66–67).

Of course, organizational change is often brought about by assigning such tasks to special task forces, committees, project groups, etc. In such cases, however, the change agencies are appointed by the official bodies, which at a later stage reconsider the proposals and decide whether and if so to what extent and in what form these proposals shall be enacted. But "join in" tactics imply that the official decision-makers do not *appoint* but *recognize* the change agencies and only reserve some veto rights in case the proposals for change contain clearly illegal or professionally unacceptable elements. These change agencies are, moreover, not restricted to *advising* the regular "line" agencies but themselves *decide* to carry out the changes and even appoint new organs to realize their plans.

If the authorities in question merely abandoned the existing formal organizations, we would be concerned with an extreme case of wholesale "buy off" (or rather "sell out"), of the legalization of a revolution. This, however, is not the case, for the power-holders combine *partial* deinstitutionalization with participation in various ways in attempts to bring about major reforms. In the first place, they participate actively *à titre personnel* in the special committees, mass meetings, and other change agencies, and try to influence the course of events in accordance with their own convictions (Van Strien, 1970: 41, 52–53). In the second place, they specify the conditions under which they can endorse the decisions taken by these constituent assemblies and groups, ratify these decisions if they fall within the scope of those conditions, and, in general, guard the boundaries of the system (Van Strien, 1970: 53–56, 66–67).

Using Parsons' (1960: 60 ff.) well-known distinction between various levels in the hierarchical structure of organizations, one could say that the authorities dehierarchize decision-making procedures on the "technical" and on the "managerial" level as far as the administration of *internal* affairs is concerned, but *not*—at least not to the same extent—at the "managerial" level as regards *external* affairs (contacts with higher authorities) and certainly not at the "institutional" level, a level which, however, usually lies beyond the horizon of the authorities in question.

The formal decision-making bodies are kept intact expressly for these managerial-external functions and, of course, also to serve as a "safety net" (Van Strien, 1970: 88) in case some trapeze performances fail. Ensconced in this position, the officials are kept busy appeasing worried higher university and civil authorities and public opinion, and in general try to legitimize the current paralegal proceedings.

As will be evident from the means used, the goal aimed at here by the authorities is a form of *copartnership,* acceptance of the opposition on an equal footing. Consequently, the opposition is defined as *radical but sincere and constructive innovators, surrounded by sympathizers,* the majority of the students, silent or mumbling, remaining neutral or vaguely positive towards the changes (Van Strien, 1970: 53, 59–61).

Cooperation rather than negotiation with the opponents is characteristic of this approach. Van Strien (1970: 43–44) reports that initially some activists tried well-known confrontation tactics to "politicize" the mass of the student body. However, when these activists noticed that such militancy alienated rather than converted the more moderate students, they adopted—given the cooperative mood of the faculty—what they called the "non-dramatizing change ideology" and joined hands with the powers-that-be.

Copartnership and cooperation also entail a view of the student as a fullfledged member of the academic community. Evidence for an option of the student role as a *member role* can be found in the reports on "join-in" experiments in The Netherlands, where a marked deemphasis—and sometimes even a denial!—of differences in rights and duties between scientific staff and students occurred (Van Strien, 1970: 49, 69; Lammers, 1970: 194).

To the best of the present author's knowledge, this type of experimental approach has been adopted mainly at departmental levels in some European universities. In Berlin this was the case in the Otto Suhr Institute for Political Science of the Free University of Berlin (von Friedeburg et al., 1968: 437 ff.); at Nanterre (France) in the sociology department (at least, that is the impression one gets from the information in the report by Touraine, 1968: 107) and in several places in The Netherlands besides the Groningen psychology department (with one of which the present author is connected, i.e., the Institute of Sociology at the University of Leyden; see Lammers, 1970: Ch. 6). The only USA case in which authorities—at least at the critical stage—adopted a course of action resembling "join in" tactics in some respects is that of Brown University from 1966 to 1969 (Ladd, 1970: Ch. 9).

"STAND OFF" TACTICS

Events at the University of Chicago in 1966 (as reported by Light, 1977) reveal this type of approach. Light defines the "stand off" as a form of directed resistance, "when the authorities refuse to take action against those resisting but also refuse to yield to the demands made" (Light, 1977). So, on the one hand, authorities *do not take recourse to negative sanctions.* In this way they try not to embitter the opposition, to avoid arousing their fighting determination, and also to avoid providing the rebels with an opportunity to rally support for their cause. On the other hand, the officials *abstain from manipulating with positive sanctions* to avoid having the opposition appear in the eyes of its potential following as a more or less recognized and effective negotiation partner. The general objectives of "stand off" tactics appear to be the prevention of further spread and intensification of the conflict by not reinforcing the opposition by either repression or concession and thus achieving *dissolution* of the oppositional nucleus. Consequently, instead of establishing a cooperative relationship with the rebellious leaders, they try to outmaneuver them. The prevailing nature of the relations with the opposition is one of *competition.*

On the whole, such officials ignore—at least officially—the opposition leaders. This implies, among other things, that in these cases one finds few pronouncements by authorities concerning their perceptions of the "enemy." One may take it, however, that they consider the prominent rebels as a mixture of hot-tempered, irresponsible *idealists* and cold-blooded, subversive *conspirators.* Their following is probably regarded as authentically restive, as joiners of the wrong causes for the right reasons.

Sometimes—as happened in Chicago in 1966 (Light, 1977)—the officials' expressions of moral indignation about the "coercive nature" of the students' opposition and their steadfast refusal to negotiate with the protest leaders when under threat, are accompanied by informal communications between officials and faculty intermediaries on the one hand and the protesters on the other. Via such informal channels, a certain amount of agreement is suggested between authorities and protesters concerning the goals of the latters' protest, but severe disapproval of their means is conveyed and the impression is cultivated that once the students stop their offensive actions, the authorities will be glad to discuss the issues with them. Clearly, such a line of action on the part of officials can be interpreted as tactics to undermine the initiative of opposition leaders and insure that negotiations can only take place on the authorities' terms.

Finally, with respect to the authorities' definition of the student role, in all probability the *client* role conception prevails here. Therefore, in this context "buy off" and "stand off" tactics exhibit some resemblance to each other. Unlike "stand off" tactics however, "buy off" tactics imply willingness on the part of the authorities to utilize extra-institutional channels of communication for negotiations. This might mean that "concessive" authorities take a broader view of the student's client's role than do "stand offish" authorities.

In the former case a student's role also includes the right to codetermine—more or less on the spot—the framework of decision-making of the institution in question, whereas in the latter case the student has no such rights. In other words, when "buy off" tactics are applied, the role of the student as a client has a tinge of "membership," while in the case of "stand off" tactics, his client-role inclines toward a "customer" role.

As already pointed out, "stand off" tactics seldom occur. The only other cases encountered in the American literature are Brandeis in 1968–1969 (Light and Feldman, 1969) and Kent State in 1968 (Michener, 1971: 94–96). Perhaps, when student protests become more common at a university and when the authorities become more familiar with the costs of "fight off" tactics, they tend to resort more often to the "stand off" weapon. In The Netherlands, at least, after a "fight off" and "buy off" stage during 1969, most universities adopted a policy of "stand off" tactics whenever localized occupations of a university institute occurred during later years.

A TYPOLOGY OF STRATEGIES

A strategy was defined above as "a goal-directed general outline of ways of coping with adversaries." Therefore, in analogy with our typology of tactics, a typology of strategies can be constructed in which the long-range goals of the authorities in question with respect to present and future opposition can serve as the *principium divisionis*. As indicated in Scheme B, if *elimination* of oppositional movements is the goal, a "repressive" strategy can be said to exist, which will probably imply heavy reliance on "fight off" tactics to counter clear and present resistance. Likewise, a "concessive" strategy aiming at *appeasement* will frequently

SCHEME B. TACTICS AND STRATEGIES

TYPE OF STRATEGY	CORRESPONDING TACTICS	GOALS	INSTITUTIONAL MEASURES	COMMUNICATION POLICY
Repressive	"Fight off"	Elimination	Provisions and procedures to suppress opposition; application of "preventive" sanctions to demonstrate readiness to use these provisions and procedures	Efforts at disseminating official points of view
Concessive	"Buy off"	Appeasement	Provisions and procedures to canalize opposition	Using all means of communication to spot rise of opposition in time and starting to deal with it
Preventive	"Stand off"	Non-emergence; dissolution	Reconstruction of conditions furthering unrest or facilitating the organization of protest	Using all means of communication to spot in time grievances, interests, etc. and to do something about them one-sidedly
Experimental	"Join in"	Co-partnership	Keeping organization at maximum of flexibility	Using all means of communication to spot and encourage initiatives and working on them with initiators

183

include "buy off" tactics and an "experimental" strategy focusing on *copartnership* with oppositions will usually prescribe "join in" tactics to cope with actual opponents. A truly "preventive" strategy is oriented towards the goal of *nonemergence* of oppositions, but if this goal is not attained or is not quite attained and some sort of nonlegitimate opposition does emerge, authorities of a "preventive" bent will tend to adopt "stand off" tactics in an effort to prevent any further spread of the opposition and to bring about its dissolution.

TACTICS AND STRATEGIES

Although it is likely that in practice there will be a certain correlation between type of strategy and its corresponding type of tactics, due to the similarity of short and long run goals involved, usually one strategy will include a set of alternative tactics, to be adopted contingent on specified conditions. An elaborate strategy will take into account, for example, the (actual and potential) strength of the opposition movement, the nature of its demands and the chances of gaining support from interested parties, publics or (outside, higher) authorities.

Thus, in The Netherlands in 1969, top administrators of various universities on the whole stuck to a concessive strategy, but nevertheless allowed faculty responsible for the administration of some single institute or department to apply "join in" tactics. Probably, these higher university authorities saw such leniency as the most expedient way to appease the particular opposition in such instances, as a form of "protest absorption" (Leeds, 1964). Another example of the use of a "mix" of tactics within one kind of strategy is provided by Light (1977), who describes the use of the "stand off" as a way to demoralize the opposition and stigmatize it in the eyes of the academic community and public opinion during the height of the protest, so as to be able to retaliate ("fight off" tactics!) without much risk at a later stage.

Of course, a variety of tactics applied by authorities in the course of one conflict can also be due to a shift in strategic goals or to the coexistence of multiple, strategic goals. For instance, quite often during a conflict between authorities and students there is a certain alternation between "buy off" and "fight off" tactics (for example at Berkeley in 1964, Lipset and Wolin, 1965: 99–199; at the University of California, Santa Barbara in 1969/1970, Smith, 1970; the London School of Economics in 1967, Blackstone et al., 1970: Ch. 7; Waseda University in Japan in 1968, Shimbori, 1970: 284, and at Warwick University in 1970, Thompson, 1970: Ch. 2). Sometimes, authorities take to "fight off" tactics as a last resort when a dispute cannot be settled by negotiation. Sometimes, too, the costs of continuing the fight appear too high to policy makers, and they switch to a more conciliatory approach.

Such shifts in strategic goals often have to do with shifts in the balance of power among the authorities who have some say in the matter. In most universities "the" authorities that have to decide about tactics and strategy, consist of quite a few administrative officers and faculty members in various executive posts (exempli gratia as deans) and form a far from homogeneous group. The decentralization and diffuseness of powers of policy making in most university organizations—in addition to the number and heterogeneity of the decision-makers involved—often hinder the formulation and adoption of a clear and consistent strategy. This implies that in the short and in the long run in one conflict, various authorities may push for different goals. All depending on the amount of support mobilized from the inside and from the outside, at one time the advocates of one strategy or tactic may dominate the scene, at another time the proponents of quite a different policy may do so. Lipset (1970: 103–105), for example, has drawn attention to the fact that in several cases in response to student demonstrations, most of the active faculty members first tend to exert pressure on the administration to negotiate, while at later stages the majority calls for a hard line of action.

A "mixed" policy can also be pursued for quite some time as a compromise between two equally strong parties within a group of authorities. It should be emphasized in passing that in cases where authorities simultaneously pursue different strategic goals as to student opposition, the ensuing policy is not necessarily an inconsistent compromise. For example, a mixed repressive-concessive strategy can conceivably be consistent provided the authorities explicitly make a clearcut distinction between legitimate and illegitimate forms of opposition and between legitimate and illegitimate kinds of demands. Moreover, in such cases powerholders should have available sufficient provisions and procedures to permit negotiation with legitimate opposition regarding their legitimate demands, and sufficient ways and means to suppress or wear out illegitimate opposition. One gets the impression from the report on Chicago in 1969 (MINERVA, 1969) that perhaps this was the case at the University of Chicago at that time.

INSTITUTIONAL MEASURES IN VARIOUS STRATEGIES

A fullfledged strategy has other elements besides a conception of what kind of tactics to apply under what circumstances. There is reason to believe that an elaborate strategy concerning student opposition among other things, also contains a policy with respect to the *institutional conditions* favoring emergence of unrest and organization of protest, and/or a policy regarding the *institutional provisions and procedures* to canalize or suppress opposition. Repressive and concessive strategies will probably pay more attention to the latter category of measures, as a form of institutional "symptom-abatement," while experimental and preventive strategies are bound to focus on remedies for institutional "causes," i.e. the former category.

A *repressive* strategy will entail, for instance, a "deterrent" policy involving the use or threat of negative sanctions before the actual outbreak of a rebellion. Whereas the application of negative sanctions in tactics is a weapon to combat specific enemies here and now, the use or threat of negative sanctions in a strategy is a general warning signal for other—future—opponents rather than the victim who happens to receive the punishment. The "exemplary" dismissal by the Rector of Berlin's Free University of a staff member (who had publicly expressed his disapproval of the Rector's policy) and the decision of the Berlin city fathers to "warn" protest-prone students by a provisional withdrawal of subsidies for student facilities (von Friedeburg et al., 1968: 279 ff.; 350), illustrate the case in point. Such measures function as a reaffirmation by authorities that they are ready to make use of their institutional powers.

More or less by the same token, a repressive strategy can also include the policy of enlarging and strengthening the institutional powers at the disposal of the authorities to combat unlawful opposition. Thus, at a certain stage of the conflict (see Lipset and Wolin, 1965: 154–155), the Regents of the University of California at Berkeley approved recommendations to sharpen rules and regulations concerning violations and to provide the Office of the Dean of Students and the Police Department with sufficient staff to enforce these rules and regulations.

Another kind of provision one encounters in repressive strategies is aimed at curtailing or prohibiting public expression and organization of protest. In this vein, university authorities at Berlin first tried to introduce rules forbidding any kind of political meeting on university grounds, and, later on, the city government put a ban on demonstrations in the city (von Friedeburg et al., 1968: 300 ff., 344).

Institutional measures favored by authorities adopting a *concessive* strategy, often pertain to construction or reconstruction of organs and procedures for grievance handling and accommodation of conflicts of interests and viewpoints. Thus in The Netherlands after the disturbances in 1969 a new law was enacted that granted not only the students but also all other categories of members of the academic community at every level of decision-making, the "right to codecision"—one of the main issues at stake in 1969 (Lammers, 1974)—while at the same time all kinds of appeal procedures and representation rules were provided. In principle, Dutch universities now have a system of governance providing for legalized access to policy making for all potential opposition groups.

Another example of efforts to create institutional conditions that will ensure on the one hand timely detection of grievances, unrest, etc. and on the other hand timely settlement of disputes arising from them, is found in the Chicago case of 1969 (MINERVA, 1969; 833, 835, 838). Here in the framework of a repressive/concessive strategy the President and other officials urged the establishment of faculty/student committees in various areas as well as advocating student representation on disciplinary committees.

In a *preventive* strategy one expects efforts to eliminate "offensive" features of the institution as well as obvious opportunities for the organization of mass protests. Furthermore, such a policy should imply the intensive use of communication systems as a means of diffusing the official point of view and as a means of gathering intelligence as to what steps the authorities ought to take, at what time and in what form. Muller (1970: 170–173) reports about Cornell—which apparently switched from a concessive to a preventive policy—an emphasis on improving and effectively using all channels of communication with dissident groups and the introduction of an "ombudsman" on campus as precautionary measures to forestall student unrest and protest.

Muller also advocates (1970: 173–174) renewal of undergraduate teaching as a means of averting student disaffection. Although it is a moot point whether the quality or type of teaching does indeed have anything to do with campus unrest, this suggestion nevertheless offers an excellent example of the kind of institutional measures one would take in the context of a preventive strategy. Naturally, it is rather hard to find good examples of institutional measures that successfully prevent overt student protest, because such cases receive little or no publicity. However, one can surmise that a general innovative policy geared to timely taking into account shifts in interests among succesive student generations and changes in the societal functions of the university, could indeed achieve the prevention of serious unrest and protest. Some indications in this direction provided by a survey by Blau and Slaughter (1971) will be dealt with in the next section.

For the same reasons that make it hard to find data about preventive strategy, one encounters little evidence concerning experimental strategy. Presumably, such a strategy implies keeping one's organization at a low level of institutionalization so as to ensure maximum flexibility in responding quickly and positively to student initiatives.

In many ways the authorities will stress intensive communication with all personnel and students and be alert as to what is going on and should be done. However, this intelligence will not be used primarily—as in the preventive strategy—to take the wind out of the sails of an actual or potential opposition, but rather to start cooperating with those concerned on solutions to their problems. Perhaps experimental colleges like Antioch, Goddard, and the like provide a model of such a strategy.

CONDITIONS AND CONSEQUENCES

CONDITIONS FOR ADOPTING A GIVEN TYPE OF STRATEGY OR TACTICS

Both university officials and their adversaries act within a set of constraints imposed by processual, organizational, and societal conditions. Because research on this topic is badly needed, it may be of value to offer some hypotheses concerning the conditions that heighten or lessen the chance that particular types of strategy or tactics will be adopted. Attention could be paid to the following set of variables.

1. Nature of the Preexisting Relationship Between Oppositional Party (or Parties) and Authorities

One may surmise for example that authorities will be the more likely to adopt an experimental policy, the less pronounced the power differences between them and their opponents were at the outset. Some evidence supporting this hypothesis was found by Van den Ende et al. (1971) in a study in The Netherlands. The investigators compared four university departments where some kind of spontaneous democratization of the decision-making structure had occurred in May of 1969, with a control group of four similar departments where the usual hierarchical structure had remained intact. The results show that there had already been more participation in policy making by students and staff in the former four departments (where the responsible authorities had adopted "join in" tactics) than there had been in the non-democratized departments.

The counterpart of this supposition is of course the hypothesis that authorities will be the more likely to adopt a repressive line of action, the more the relations between them and their opponents were of a decidedly hierarchical nature initially. There also seems to be reason to suspect that a concessive strategy or "buy off" tactics are more likely to prevail if power differences between authorities and opposition are not too great and if there is a considerable social distance, cultural divergence, or conflict of interests between the parties involved.

2. Nature of the Opposition Movement

The nature of the countertactics and strategy used by the authorities in all probability often also depends to some extent on the nature of the protesters' tactics. At least in the Western culture area, the application of negative sanctions to crush student opposition requires legitimation. Therefore, if a protest action by students is carefully conducted within the scope of legality, as happened for example in the case of Brown University referred to above, authorities cannot find a real excuse to crack down on the protesters. Moreover, various escalation mechanisms are at play in any conflict, so that the use of negative sanctions by one party frequently evokes retaliation with negative sanctions by the other party. Thus, one could hypothesize that "fight off" tactics are the more likely to be adopted by authorities, the more violent and illegal the means used by the opposition.

The degree of illegality of its weapons is of course only the most obvious aspect of the nature of the opposition movement influencing the reactions of the officials. Other characteristics of the protest movement, such as its pertinacity, leadership, and "coverage" of potential following, probably limit the choice of alternatives—or at least the choice of promising alternatives—available to the authorities.

3. Type of Organizational Regime

Shils (1970a) has cogently argued that most American universities have become "a locus confederation of largely autonomous departments" (p. 4), leaving "a hole in the centre," a lack of "machinery for decisions on unversity-wide issues" (p. 1). In a similar vein, Ladd's diagnosis of the conspicuous failure of major efforts at change in educational policy in eleven American institutions of higher learning, points to the immobilizing effects of departmental powers (Ladd, 1970: Chs. 16, 17, and 18).

On the basis of these considerations one may suppose that the fewer the central authorities' actual powers of decision making on university policy, the greater the chance that they will adopt "loose" tactics in the event of student opposition, and not succeed in planning—let alone executing—a well-defined strategy. Perhaps the reason why the University of Chicago administration could adopt and execute a rather consistent strategy with respect to the student revolts in 1969 is that in this case we find a rather exceptional situation *without* a "hole in the center" (Shils, 1970b).

Circumstantial evidence in support of this hypothesis can also be inferred from a study made by Blau and Slaughter (1971). Their analysis of data from a sample of 115 American universities revealed correlations between the relative absence of student demonstrations and the presence of indications of a general innovative university policy (establishment of departments in new fields of learning; formal system of student ratings of teachers). As already hinted at, to a certain extent one may take the absence of student revolts as a result of a truly preventive strategy, of an official policy dealing with causes rather than with symptoms. For authorities to be willing and able to adopt such a policy, they must not only be responsive to scientific and societal trends but also dispose of a decision-making apparatus to enact this strategy.

4. Experience in the Past with Oppositions

As was noticed already, there are indications that authorities learn how to cope with student disturbances. In general one could suppose that a strategy is much more likely to be present when the need for it has been clearly demonstrated in the past due to the frequent occurrence of revolts. Futhermore, the results of the repressive strategy (which will be dealt with in the next section) are usually disastrous, while there are extreme difficulties in formulating and executing an experimental strategy. Consequently, one also can expect preventive and concessive strategies to become more popular relative to repressive and experimental strategies, as time moves on. Such a trend could be due not only to the accumulation of experience in individual institutions but also to the fact that administrators and faculties in the western world collectively acquire more first- or second-hand experience with the peculiarities of student uprisings and learn to live with them.

5. The State of the General Socio-cultural, Political, and Economic Conditions in the Environment

It goes without saying that all four of the variables mentioned thus far cannot be seen as being independent of conditions external to the university. It seems likely, however, that the encompassing societal environment influences, not only indirectly but also directly, the type of reaction by the authorities. For instance, in a totalitarian country organs of party and state will probably press the university administrators to adopt a repressive policy or will immediately intervene themselves (exempli gratia by using military or police forces) to subdue student revolts.

In non-totalitarian countries, too, public opinion and the stance taken on the issues in question by civic and professional authorities, can become major determinants of the strategy and tactics adopted, particularly when the university officials have no predetermined and firm strategy of their own or have one but not the means to realize it. Such specific intervention can in turn be conceived of as following from the power relationships in society at large, general political and educational traditions, etc. Careful comparative research could throw light on this problem.

CONSEQUENCES OF VARIOUS STRATEGIES AND TACTICS

Perhaps even more important than the reasons why authorities adopt a particular line of action, is the question of the implications of their policies. Given the present state of our knowledge, however, we can only speculate with some degree of confidence on the short-term effects of the tactics and strategies distinguished. Any statements concerning the long-run effects can only be pure conjecture, and therefore in this section the main emphasis will be placed on the short-run consequences.

In the first place, one wonders about the differential effects of these policies on the *educational process*. Given the fact that on the whole the majority of students condone the goals and, when not too violent, the tactics of protest demonstrations (see exampli gratia Somers, 1965: 540; Blackstone et al., 1970: 174–178; Barton, 1968: 336; Smith, 1970: 6–7; *Sociologisch Seminarium*, 1969), it comes as no surprise that many researchers and observers find indications of a mobilization of support for the opposition movement in response to "fight off" tactics on the part of the authorities. This process of a radicalization and widening of the opposition resulting from repressive efforts of administration and/or faculty was identified for Berkeley (Lyonns, 1965: 526; Lipset and Wolin, 1965: 108–118; Somers, 1965: 533), Nanterre and Paris (Touraine, 1968: 127–131), Columbia (Barton, 1968: 336; Trimberger, 1970: 36), Santa Barbara (Smith, 1970: 36–37), Berlin (von Friedeburg et al., 1968: 296; 340; 378; 444), and Kent State University (Michener, 1971: 104).

"Fight off" tactics are probably quite often also conducive to or promoted by a negative attitude of a large part of the faculty toward the opposition. Therefore, it probably must be concluded that "fight off" tactics tend to lead to a deterioration of relationships between rather large parts of the faculty and student body. This conclusion also follows from what Light (1977) calls the "law of passive advantage." For a (probably much smaller) group of students and faculty who have been on the same side in the battle, of course, interrelationships may have improved. But the net effect of "fight off" tactics is probably mutual embitterment and estrangement for many students and teachers. Since the educational process consists of an exchange of ideas, insights, and visions, of stimulating each other's intellectual and emotional growth, it is hardly conceivable that such mutual embitterment and estrangement would not seriously impair the educational process.

"Buy off" and "stand off" tactics are on the whole probably less harmful from an educational point of view, since they do not result in such a far-reaching polarization between large parts of the student body and faculty. "Buy off" tactics, however, if applied on a large scale, may kindle rather than extinguish the fires of protest and produce a climate of basic insecurity among students as to the question of what their educators really stand for. The drawback of "stand off" tactics from an educational point of view is under-utilization of the student potential for innovation, while its application in the context of a rather repressive strategy can sometimes produce more harmful effects on the relations between students and faculty than outright negative sanctions (see Light, 1977).

Only when authorities see fit to apply the "join in" approach is there a chance to try out educational innovations on the basis of a renewed solidarity between students and faculty who have jointly undertaken the experiment (Van Strien, 1970: 46–51; Lammers, 1970: 175–184). The de-hierarchization process provides opportunities for students and teachers not only to pursue new educational goals within the strictly academic fields of learning, but also with respect to learning how to cope with organizational change.

Nevertheless, as time goes on, the morning-after effect sets in, what one could also call the typical "experimental fatigue," and latent controversies about the course of educational innovation come to the fore. In particular, a fierce struggle usually develops between dedicated activists, who are interested in educational reform only as a means to reach drastic—and preferably immediate—societal revolution, and all those who advocate educational innovation for its own sake (for·instance, "self expression" as a basic human right), for the sake of certain professional improvements, or for the sake of gradual societal reform. When the usually Marxian-oriented activists are strong enough, a division of the educational estate may take place, as happened at the Berlin Otto Suhr Institute (see Der Spiegel, 1970). When these activists are too weak and/or too divided to accomplish that much, they may leave the academic scene, as has happened in most such cases in The Netherlands. From an educational point of view, this unquestionably implies a considerable loss, because these activists are often the most dedicated and sophisticated change agents and therefore carry the latent function of forming a crystallization focus for other, more reform- and liberal-minded students and faculty, who thanks to them become aware of their own goals and become motivated to do something about them.

Still, one gets the impression that for the educational process the net balance of "join in" tactics shows a positive gain. Some of the educational reforms persist, and in other respects a more realistic assessment of the value of conventional educational methods often prevails after the disadvantages of trying to do without them have been experienced.

On the whole, one gets the impression that the concessive and the preventive strategies are feasible and recommendable with an eye to the universities' educational goals. In this respect, both strategies are in all probability preferable to no strategy at all or to a repressive strategy. As has already been said, large-scale application of an experimental strategy in present-day society is hardly imaginable. Nevertheless, within preventive and concessive strategies room can be provided for experimentation.

In the second place it is interesting to speculate about the differential effects of these four tactics on the research process. It seems reasonable to assume that most factors that hamper the educational and administrative process also directly or indirectly interfere with the research process. Under repressive or concessive approaches, the time and energy that many faculty members have reserved for research are consumed by participation in disputes and decision making within the context of the campus crisis. Moreover, the prerequisites for creative output—for instance, the protective security flowing from a clearcut administrative policy and a rather stable structure as well as a relatively peaceful climate—are not fulfilled under the battle conditions often arising from these strategies.

Research is likewise bound to suffer from the exertions of academics engaged in "join in" tactics. Moreover, given the increase in student power, under these conditions the educational goals of the university are bound to become predominant. This means that in the short run, from the point of view of a flourishing research process, "join in" tactics are comparatively speaking the least desirable. In the long run, of course, the research process is highly dependent on the input of new research workers and therefore on the continuation and continuing development of the educational process that must deliver the new generation of science producers. This leads again to the conclusion that preventive and to some extent also concessive strategies are relatively well suited to secure the research process, but that some scope for experimentation is certainly also indicated.

In the third place, a few remarks concerning the *administrative* process. For two reasons, "fight off" tactics and *a fortiori* the repressive strategy probably have the effect of increased organizational slack. For one thing, so much energy must be expended by the authorities just to combat the opposition and to defend the *status quo,* that the amount of human resources available for designing and executing adaptive changes is smaller than otherwise would be the case. In addition, the authorities' engagement in defensive activities has the obvious sociopsychological effect of reinforcing commitments to the established university order and of lessening the susceptibilities of the powers-that-be to the need and possibilities for change.

Taken for granted that in most countries today a viable university requires an organization with built-in innovative capacities to cope with societal and scientific developments, it follows that "fight off" tactics often have a back-firing effect on the institution. The authorities may win the war, but they stand a good chance of losing the peace!

As already pointed out, "stand off" tactics, particularly when part of a truly preventive strategy, form no such impairment of the organization's capacity for adaptation. Not only are the pitfalls of increased rigidity inherent in the repressive approach avoided, but also the pitfalls of the concessive approach. "Buy off" tactics, namely, imply that whatever the innovations introduced, they come into being in a rather haphazard way, without much regard to their mutual compatability and long-term consequences.

With respect to "join in" tactics, one often encounters, as in the case of concessive tactics, a certain inconsistency of policy. Given a fair amount of disagreement about educational, research, and administrative goals among a considerable number of students and faculty anywhere, power equalization in the decision-making structure necessarily means greater difficulties in reaching the necessary consensus on policies. Therefore, whereas "buy off" tactics frequently entail inconsistency of policy due to too many incompatible decisions, "join in" tactics often lead to inconsistency of policy due to too few decisions or to decisions representing a provisional and fragile compromise.

CONCLUSIONS

In this final section, I wish to make just a few remarks on the problem of what kind of tactics and strategies university authorities can and should adopt under what conditions. This attempt is not meant to imply that I take social research—let alone an exploratory analysis like the present one—to be a sufficient basis for the drawing of unequivocal conclusions concerning such policy questions as how to cope with or, for that matter, how to conduct an opposition movement. It does not imply either that I consider personal tastes, prejudices, experiences, goals, and values to be the prime determinants of such policy views.

In my opinion, the sociological perspective and research results arrived at from this perspective should be at least as potent as are one's tastes, prejudices, experiences, goals, and values in influencing one's judgment and actions when confronted with—or being part of—a student protest movement. With the aid of such tools one can try to critically reexamine one's premises, to become aware of various implications relevant to a choice respecting a particular line of action.

Personally, I subscribe to the view that rather fundamental university reforms are overdue and should be brought about to change the conventional interpretation of academic freedom—defined in the past as freedom *from* outside interferences—in the direction of a new definition—as freedom *to* interfere with "the outside," where possible and suitable with the academic tools proper. From this point of view and taking into consideration the probable effects of various strategies and tactics, one necessarily arrives at the conclusion that a preventive strategy is in general the best policy and a concessive approach the second best choice, while a repressive strategy is just about the worst solution for the university's problems. Any strategy—with the exception of the repressive "solution"—is furthermore preferable to no strategy at all.

Adopting "loose" tactics as the occasion arises always means that the responsible authorities are on the defensive, *re*-act, and do not stand much of a chance to ensure consistency of over-all policy and the viability of their institution. As regards the repressive approach, the only thing that can be said on its behalf is that it is sometimes unavoidable. For example, when the opposition utilizes primarily illegal means and wants to do away with any kind of constitutional order or rule of law, authorities have no choice but to adopt a repressive strategy of "fight off" tactics.

A preventive strategy, as we have seen, has on the whole the least harmful effects on the processes of education, administration, and research. However, as we have shown, the conditions for adopting such a policy are rather exceptional. This implies that most of our efforts should be directed at equipping a university for preventive strategy as a general, pervasive capacity for innovation by the university organization. On the basis of the research results of Blau and Slaughter discussed above, we might presume that such preventive strategy is also the most suitable as a carrier to bring about the necessary university reform with an eye to the required shift in emphasis concerning the university's societal functions.

Given the conditions under which "join in" tactics flourish, it is highly unrealistic to suppose that such tactics stand much of a chance at the level of large, complex universities. Only in rather small institutions of higher learning or in rather autonomous parts of a larger university system are the conditions for such experiments met. But to try out fundamentally new solutions, such experiments are, it seems to me, crucial. Therefore, it would be highly recommendable for a preventive policy designed for a university system as a whole to include the necessary leeway for experimentation at lower levels. In this way, Mannheim's concept of "planning for freedom" (Mannheim, 1940: Part V) could acquire new meaning for the problems we are facing at present in the universities.

NOTES

* I want to express my gratitude to Wim J. Van den Ende for his assistance in interpreting and analysing the data, to Mrs. Seeger for editing the manuscript and to Peter M. Blau, Ernst L. Drukker, William M. Evan, Raymond Jurkovich, Dwight R. Ladd, Donald W. Light Jr., and Arie Muller for their helpful comments and criticisms of an earlier version of this paper.

REFERENCES

Abramson, H.J. and R. Wences. 1970. "Campus Dissent and Academic Punishment: The Response of College Professors to Local Political Activism." *Sociology of Education* 45 (Winter): 61–75.

Barton, Allen H. 1968. "The Columbia Crisis: Campus, Vietnam and the Ghetto." *Public Opinion Quarterly* 32 (Fall): 333–51

Bidwell, Charles E. 1971. "Faculty Responses to Student Activism: Some Preliminary Findings from a Survey of American Professors." Paper presented at the 7th World Congress of Sociology, Varna, Bulgaria.

Blackstone, Tessa; Kathleen Gales; Roger Hadley; and Wyn Lewis. 1970. *Students in Conflict: LSE, 1967.* London: Weiderfeld and Nicholson.

Blau, Peter M. and Ellen L. Slaughter. 1971. "Institutional Conditions and Student Demonstrations." *Social Problems* 18 (Spring): 475–87.

Brodie, Bernard. 1968. "Strategy." In *The International Encyclopedia of the Social Sciences,* Volume 15, edited by David L. Sills. New York: MacMillan.

Cole, Stephen and H. Adamsons. 1969. "Determinants of Faculty Support for Student Demonstrations." *Sociology of Education* 42 (Fall): 315–29.

Cole, Stephen and H. Adamsons. 1970. "Professional Status and Faculty Support of Student Demonstrations." *Public Opinion Quarterly* 34 (Fall): 389–94.

The Cox Commission Report. 1968. *Crisis at Columbia.* Report of the Fact Finding Commission Appointed to Investigate the Disturbances at Columbia University in April and May 1968. New York: Vintage Books.

Van den Ende, P.J., W.J. van den Ende, M.H.C. de Greef, G.C.W. Hooning van Duyvenbode and M.J. de Willigen. 1971. "Democratisering van universitaire instituten: een onderzoek naar organisatie-kenmerken. *Sociologische Gids* 18 (januari/februari): 30–41.

Fields, A. Belden. 1970. "The Revolution Betrayed: The French Student Revolt of May-June 1968." In *Students in Revolt,* edited by S.M. Lipset and Ph.G. Altbach. Boston: Beacon Press.

Von Friedeburg, Ludwig; Jürgen Hörlemann; Peter Hübner; Ulf Kadritzke, Jürgen Ritsert and Wilhelm Schumm. 1968. *Freie Universität und politisches Potential der Studenten.* Über die Entwicklung des Berliner Modells und den Anfang der Studentenbewegung in Deutschland. Neuwied und Berlin: Luchterhand.

Friedland, William H. and Harry Edwards. 1970. "Confrontation at Cornell." In *Campus Power Struggle,* edited by Howard S. Becker. New Brunswick, N.J.: Transaction Books.

Ladd, Dwight R. 1970. *Change in Education Policy. Self-studies in Selected Colleges and Universities.* A General Report Prepared for The Carnegie Commission on Higher Education. New York: McGraw Hill.

Lammers, Cornelis J. 1970. *Studenten, politiek en universitaire democratie.* Rotterdam: Universitaire Pers.

Lammers, Cornelis J. 1974. "Localism, Cosmopolitanism and Faculty Response." *Sociology of Education* 47 (Winter): 129–158.

Leeds, Ruth. 1964. "The Absorption of Protest: A Working Paper." In *New Perspectives in Organization Research,* edited by William W. Cooper, Harold J. Leavitt and Maynard W. Shelly. New York: Wiley.

Light, D.W. 1977. "Directed Resistance." Chapter 4 in this book.

Light, D.W. and David Feldman. 1969. "Black and White at Brandeis." *The North American Review* 254 (Fall).

Lipset, Seymour M. and Sheldon S. Wolin, eds. 1965. *The Berkeley Student Revolt. Facts and Interpretations.* Garden City, N.Y.: Anchor Books.

Lipset, Seymour M., Martin A. Trow, and Everett C. Ladd. 1970. *Survey of American Faculty Members* (as reported by Malcolm G. Scully in *The Chronicle of Higher Education* 4 (April)).

Lipset, Seymour M. 1970. "The Politics of Academia." In *Perspectives on Campus Tensions,* edited by David C. Nichols. Washington, D.C.: American Council on Education.

Lipset, Seymour M. 1972. *Rebellion in the University.* Boston: Little, Brown and Company.

Lyonns, G. 1965. "The Police Car Demonstration: A Survey of Participants." In *The Berkeley Student Revolt. Facts and Interpretations,* edited by S.M. Lipset and S.S. Wolin. Garden City, N.Y.: Anchor Books.

Mannheim, K. 1940. *Man and Society in an Age of Reconstruction. Studies in Modern Social Structure.* London: Routledge and Kegan Paul.

McEvoy, James and Abraham Miller. 1970. "The Crises at San Francisco State." In *Campus Power Struggle,* edited by Howard S. Becker. New Brunswick, N.J.: Transaction Books.

Michener, James A. 1971. *Kent State. What Happened and Why.* Greenwich, Conn.: Fawcett.

MINERVA. 1969. "Chronicle (VII) Illinois." *MINERVA. A Review of Science, Learning and Policy* VII (summer): 832–841.

Muller, Steven. 1970. "Preventing or Resolving Conflicts." In *Perspectives on Campus Tensions,* edited by David C. Nichols. Washington, D.C.: American Council on Education.

Parsons, Talcott. 1960. *Structure and Process in Modern Societies.* Glencoe, Ill.: Free Press.

Pugh, Meredith, Joseph Perry Jr. and Elmer Spreitzer. "Faculty Response to Student Dissent." Paper read at the Convention of the American Sociological Association, Denver, Colorado, September 1971.

Shils, Edward. 1970a. "The Hole in the Centre: University Government in the United States." *MINERVA. A Review of Science, Learning and Policy,* VIII (January): 1–7.

Shils, Edward. 1970b. "Presidents and Professors in American University Government." *MINERVA. A Review of Science, Learning and Policy,* VIII (July): 440 ff.

Shimbori, M. 1970. "The Sociology of a Student Movement—A Japanese Case Study." In *Students in Revolt,* edited by S.M. Lipset and Ph. G. Altbach. Boston: Beacon Press.

Smith, Robert B. 1970. "Campus Protests in the Vietnam War." Paper presented at the 65th Annual Meeting of the ASA, 1970. Washington, D.C.

Sociologisch Seminarium. 1969. "Voorlopige Uitkomsten van het Opinie-Onderzoek naar Aanleiding van de Gebeurtenissen Rondom het Maagdenhuis." *Sociologisch Semin-*

arium, afdeling Methoden en Technieken en Sociologisch Onderzoekscentrum, Universiteit van Amsterdam. Unpublished paper.

Somers, R.H. 1965. "The Main Springs of the Rebellion: A Survey of Berkeley Students in November, 1964." In *The Berkeley Student Revolt. Facts and Interpretations,* edited by S.M. Lipset and S.S. Wolin. Garden City, N.Y.: Anchor Books.

Der Spiegel. 1970. "'Nebenan ist Bibelstunde.' Spiegel-Report über den Wissenschaftsbetrieb im Otto-Suhr-Institut (OSI) der Freien Universität in Berlin." *Der Spiegel,* no. 29:66–73.

Van Strien, P.J. 1970. *Van Radenuniversiteit naar open arbeidersorganisatie.* Rotterdam: Universitaire Pers.

Thompson, E.P. ed. 1970. *Warwick University Ltd.* Harmondsworth, Middlesex, England: Penguin Books.

Touraine, A. 1968. *Le Mouvement de Mai ou le Communisme Utopique.* Paris: Editions de Seuil.

Trimberger, Ellen Kay. 1970. "Columbia: The Dynamics of a Student Revolution." In *Campus Power Struggle,* edited by Howard S. Becker. Brunswick, N.J.: Transaction Books.

Wences, Rosalie and Harold J. Abramson. 1970. "Faculty Opinion on the Issues of Job Placement and Dissent in the University." *Social Problems* 18 (Summer): 27–38.

Wilson, Robert C. and Gaff, Jerry G. 1969. "Student Voice—Faculty Response." *The Research Reporter* IV: 1–4.

ABOUT THE AUTHORS:

DONALD LIGHT, JR. is a senior research sociologist at the Center for Biomedical Education of the City College of New York.

He received a B.A. from Stanford University with honors and distinction in history, a master's degree in sociology from the University of Chicago and Ph.D. in sociology from Brandeis University. He taught sociology at Princeton from 1969 to 1975. Currently he teaches sociology of medicine and social aspects of medical care to medical students.

He is the author with Suzanne Keller of *Sociology*. He also has contributed numerous articles to professional periodicals.

JOHN P. SPIEGEL is a professor of social psychiatry at the Florence Heller Graduate School for Advance Students in Social Welfare at Brandeis University. He has taught and conducted research at Harvard University and Harvard Medical School and the University of Chicago. Dr. Spiegel has been chief of the psychiatric clinic at Michael Reese Hospital in Chicago.

He received a B.A. from Dartmouth College and his medical degree from Northwestern University School of Medicine.

Dr. Spiegel has contributed extensively to the literature in psychiatry, riots, war neuroses, violence and campus disorders in books, articles in professional journals, and the popular press.